‘Discoveries’, I
the Impe

The Imperial Archives

FROM DISCOVERY TO THE CIVILISATIONAL MISSION: ENGLISH WRITINGS ON INDIA

Volume 1

'Discoveries', Explorations and the Imperial Survey

Editor

Pramod K. Nayar

B L O O M S B U R Y
NEW DELHI • LONDON • OXFORD • NEW YORK • SYDNEY

BLOOMSBURY INDIA
Bloomsbury Publishing India Pvt. Ltd
Second Floor, LSC Building No. 4, DDA Complex, Pocket C – 6 & 7,
Vasant Kunj, New Delhi, 110070

BLOOMSBURY, BLOOMSBURY ACADEMIC INDIA and the Diana logo are trademarks of Bloomsbury Publishing Plc

First published in India 2022
This edition published 2022

Bloomsbury Academic
An imprint of Bloomsbury Publishing Plc

ISBN: HB: 978-93-54356-42-1; ePDF: 978-93-54356-50-6
2 4 6 8 10 9 7 5 3 1

Printed & bound in India by Replika Press Pvt. Ltd.

CONTENTS

PREFATORY NOTE

The archival texts have been retained in their original font, style and content in order to clearly show the environment of the time when these documents were produced. It is important to show in a book such as this the views held at that time and the profound effect they had on society. We acknowledge that several of the texts are derogatory about Indians, women and communities of different religious faiths like many hundreds of other colonial-era-based works. While these are clearly unacceptable to us today, we have not attempted to change any wording or redact the texts so that the contemporary reader may experience the rhetoric, attitude and ideologies that so clearly marked the Raj. In places, where the text had been smudged and rendered impossible to read, that specific segment has been deleted.

We would like to make clear that these are not the views held by the editor or Bloomsbury India and do not reflect our mission and values which are clearly stated on our website (https://www.bloomsbury.com/in/connect/about-us/missions-and-values/)

GENERAL INTRODUCTION: ARCHIVE AND EMPIRE

That the British writings on India occupy over several miles of shelf space in the British Library, London, is an apocryphal tale, but one which *may* have substance, given that there was no aspect of the subcontinent that did not pique the curiosity of the British or generate some document or the other.

In his *The Imperial Archive: Knowledge and the Fantasy of Empire* (1993), Thomas Richards demonstrated how the documentation (the subject of considerable work, notably in Bernard Cohn and others) and archivisation not only produced knowledge about the colonies but were also instrumental in generating the fantasy of absolute control. And yet, it is never easy to read these records produced by a diverse set of English, Irish and Scottish missionaries, administrators, men of leisure, nurses, teachers, wives and/or sisters of the men who occupied official posts in the colony, soldiers, mercenaries and others—many of whom, for many reasons, had their own dynamics and tensions with the *English*.

Several approaches to the imperial record exist, and this introductory chapter sets out some of them.[1] In the process, it also flags what the archive does in terms of the imperial structure and processes.[2]

The Power of the Archive

The archive is not a mere compilation of what John Malcolm (1823) advised his officers on the right approach to the native officers, or what Thomas Williamson (1808) described as the potential for the hunt in India. The archive is not a passive reflection of imperial power—it constitutes and constructs it. As diverse commentators—such as Cohn's work on the 'survey modality' (1997) and C.A. Bayly's *Empire and Information* (1999)—have pointed out, the Empire ran on information,

[1] I use the term 'imperial archive' throughout to refer to the corpus of published material across genres, as diverse as maps, geographical accounts, census reports, travelogues, administrative reports, ecclesiastical documents.

[2] These volumes work only with the print archive of British India, although a vast archive of visual material also exists, and has been the subject of significant studies. See, for example, Guégan (2011), Chaudhury (2012), Pinney (2014), Dohman (2017) on colonial photography, and Tobin (1999), De Silva (2011), Eaton (2013), among others, on colonial/imperial art and paintings.

and information-gathering constituted not just an act of power but was a *constituent* of the power structure. It classified, organised and legislated on the subject peoples, through the census, the geographies and anthropological studies. In the process, it defined who is counted as a subject/citizen. For instance, writing about the Todas or the Gonds, and then examining the numbers of Muslim students in schools, both the educationist and the statesman were constructing model imperial citizens who would benefit, resist or accept from 'modern' education. In other words, the imperial archive on education was not merely advocating 'modern' education: it was constructing *educate-able* citizens from among their colonial subjects while abandoning the others. Thus, archivisation and informatisation were ultimately about the power wielded over the identity-making and rights of the subjects.[3]

Relatedly, the archive and the documentation also made the subjects *visible to themselves*. With 'modern' education, for instance, the Indian colonial subject in school or college came to identify themselves in particular ways. They learnt what it means to be a good citizen, to be modern, to develop and demand certain skills, etc. They recognised their location on the civilisational scale in the books they read and assimilated (*primitive* and *non-modern* as opposed to the modern European). In an argument that resonates with my claims above, Antoinette Burton and Isabel Hofmeyr write about the power of the English book:

> The embodiment of English manly authority, the book was not simply 'a surrogate Englishman in his highest and most perfect state,' it was the very emblem of imperial sovereignty—with the rigorous spine a testimony to its singularity, its probity, its titular power ... books impressed themselves in the everyday lives of imperial subjects, manifesting the formal values of an elite or bourgeois self and modeling in their material form the coherence and commanding presence of British imperial power itself. (2014: 1–2)

The colonial subjects were told, through these English books, what kind of spiritual and moral training was required for them to 'improve'.

---

[3] It must be noted that it was not only the human subjects in the colony that became objects and subjects of the imperial archive. Fauna and flora, climate, landscape and topography—indeed the natural world in its entirety—were also archived. For studies, see Edney (1997) and Damodaran et al. (2015), among others.

As A.H. Benton of the Indian Civil Service wrote in *Indian Moral Instruction and Caste Problems*:

> [The Indian] People are on the whole kindly, docile, alert, keen-spirited, high and low, one of the best-mannered peoples in the world, and they would appear to offer a very promising field for right spiritual treatment. (1917: 92)

The education archive, and especially its insistence on moral training and moral apprenticeship of the subjects as a *preliminary* to training for political citizenship, was built on the

> founding assumption … that the native readership of English texts, and the recipients of English education, were amenable to their teachings, which led them to abandon their traditional manners and disciplines. This necessitated a solid moral training to make them good citizens. (Nayar 2020: 142)

The archive also, frequently, captures the rift and fracture within the colonial subject's responses to, say, Western/English education. See, for instance, Syed Mahmood's anguish about the Indian Muslim's refusal to accept this education:

> Such feelings of aversion towards English education entertained by the Mahomedans … stand in sharp contrast to the attitude of the Hindu community.… This difference in the sentiments of the two communities towards English education, is the real key to the reasons of the vast disparity of progress of English education which the two nationalities have respectively made. The effects of this disparity have been most baneful to the interests of British India in general, and to the Mahomedan community in particular. (1895: 23)

In time, the colonial subject, convinced of the 'truth' in the power of the Englishman's word or photographic record, not only accepted the arguments about their inferiority but also welcomed the interventions in the form of the civilisational mission of the Empire. The archive had, therefore, produced the *willing* colonial subject.

In particular cases, such as Thuggee, the archive enabled the colonial structures of law enforcement and the judiciary to enact legislation and, in the process, demonise specific cultural practices. Examining the Thuggee archive, Alexander Macfie writes:

> [W]hereas Sleeman and his colleagues tended to define the activities of the thugs in terms of wickedness, murder, deceit, cowardice and criminality, the thugs themselves tended to evaluate them in terms of courage, enterprise, bravery, daring, cunning, adventure and martial

> skill … in terms usually associated by both the British and the Indians with the heroic values of war. (2008: 396)

The Archive, the Coloniser, the Colonised and Cultural Exchanges

Shifting focus, Antoinette Burton has demonstrated how the imperial archive also fed into the coloniser's psyche, imagination and political imagination. A pithy summary of how the imperial corpus fuelled, inspired and controlled the social imaginary, policies, attitudes and responses of the Britons in the nineteenth century is available in Burton's *Empire in Question*. Victorian culture, writes Burton,

> as a racialized landscape shaped by decades, if not centuries, of colonial peoples, goods, and ideas coursing through its highways and byways … as always already imperial not just implicitly but as part of a pedagogical meta-narrative about the relationship of modernity to the world-historical phenomenon of colonialism in world history…. (2011: 2–3)

Burton proposes that English 'sensibility' was shaped by Britain's imperial role and character, and its concomitant racialised hierarchies—thus makes the production and consumption of texts (and commodities) about and from the colonised peripheries central to the making of Britain itself (also see Hall 2002).

The archive also instantiates, other than the racialised power binaries (white/black, coloniser/colonised), cross-cultural *influences* and *exchanges*. Contacts across races, ethnic groups and the coloniser–colonised divide were frequent through the colonial period.

The English language took into itself words from their colonial subjects. They also sought to document the grammars of the languages of the subcontinent for their own officers and staff. As a consequence, a vibrant field of cultural exchanges opened up in the languages, with Indian pandits and English philologists and grammarians collaborating. The imperial archive in this domain shows mutual influences of English on Indian languages and vice versa (including Sanskrit [Naregal 2001]) but also the *organisation* of knowledge around the latter (Lelyveld 1993; Rao 2004; Mir 2010; Auer 2014).[4] Scholars—the famous 'Orientalists'—translated texts from, say, Sanskrit into English. Organisations and societies, such as the Asiatic Society, the

---

[4] A detailed annotated bibliography on these and other aspects of English colonial discourse on India can be found in Nayar 2021.

Zoological Survey of India, the Archaeological Survey of India, were spaces through which the English statesman, *memsahib* and trader encountered Indian temples, art, food practices, superstitions, systems of healing, among others.

English literary texts, as numerous commentators have shown (Leask 1993; Teltscher 1997), began to introduce Indian 'themes' and motifs, whether the *sati* or the wealth of the country's landscape. This field of literary studies was one of contestation and adaptation (Vishwanathan 1990). Be that as it may, the circulation of the English novel in nineteenth-century India catered to the Indian audience attuned to the melodramatic and informed their own creative work (Joshi 2003). Other commentators like Harish Trivedi (1993) have noted how English literature was received in India and the transactional nature of this reception.

Local experts, *writers* and translators were an integral component of the East India Company and the British government. Even account and trade books were produced through a collaborative project (Ogborn 2007). In other domains, such as translations, Indian scholars like Kasinatha Bhattacharya enabled the work of Charles Wilkins (Davis 2015).

Manners, protocols of civic interaction and norms of social, interracial interaction were also sites where cultural exchange and mutual influence were visible. Even the idea of 'civility', as Anindyo Roy has argued, was treated by the native—and projected as such by *English* textbooks and teachers—as markers of 'modern progress and mobility' (Roy 2005: 11). Therefore, both English and Indian commentators (Webb 1915; El Edroos 1922) produced advice and courtesy books for Indians and Englishmen in India (Nayar 2016, 'Civil Modernity'). These contained suggestions like:

> Members of each class, without entering into political or official discussions and avoiding personal remarks, may have much pleasant intercourse by asking about and describing the manners and customs peculiar to each other's nationality, or about their art, music, poetry and literature.... Talk about sport is most suitable at club. (El Edroos: 89)

The Archive and the Global

Another approach to the imperial archive chooses to see the archive as instantiating not just the sensibilities, attitudes and modes of the British coloniser and the subcontinent's colonised, but as enabling *global and globalising imperial networks*. That is, the archive is seen as embodying not just the binary of an imperial 'centre' and 'periphery' (the colony), but a vast network of global connections. We see this interpretation in the work of John Darwin.

In *The Empire Project: The Rise and Fall of the British World-System, 1830–1970* (2009), Darwin shows how the 'interdependence' of various regions and colonies shaped the British Empire in four specific domains. First, there is the military interdependence of various geopolitical regions:

> the most obvious forms of such inter-dependence were naval and military.... British ability to provide naval protection or to send reinforcements to the scene of a conflict would have been very limited without the resources the imperial system supplied. It was strategic control of the Cape Colony (whose economic value was derisory before 1870) that secured the naval gateway to Asia from European waters. The prime function of Egypt, occupied by the British in 1882, was to preserve British use of the Suez Canal and protect the 'Clapham Junction' of imperial communications. Malta, Aden, Ceylon, Singapore, Hong Kong, Esquimalt (on Vancouver Island), the Falklands and Halifax, Nova Scotia, formed the network of bases from which the Royal Navy patrolled the world's sea-lanes. India played several roles in the British world-system, but perhaps its critical function was to be the main base from which British interests in Asia could be advanced and defended. Indian soldiers and a British garrison paid for by Indian revenues were the 'strategic reserve' of the British system in Asia. Because India played this role, other British possessions and spheres east and south of Suez were largely exempted from the costs of defence—a fact of crucial importance to their economic viability. (3–4)

Then there is the commercial interdependence and linkages:

> Both colonial territories and 'informal' colonies had to compete for investment and credits from London to expand their economies ... with the grand exception of the United States (which had received one-fifth of British foreign investment by 1913), British capital was shuttled by the City of London between the various sectors of its commercial empire (a vast global realm among whose key provinces were Canada, Argentina, India, Australia, Southern Africa, China and the Middle East), employing a calculus of prospective return and speculative gain. (4)

The third domain of such connections would be the demographic interdependence:

> Although two-thirds of British migrants went to the United States up until 1900, almost all the rest were distributed between the four main settlement zones of Canada, Australia, New Zealand and South Africa. Indeed, their economic development was usually seen as being closely dependent upon drawing labour and skills from the British supply.... Between 1834 and 1937, India exported some 30 million people to other British possessions as indentured labour, and perhaps one-fifth remained as permanent settlers. In the tropical empire (which British migrants avoided) they supplied much of the labour and business expertise to promote commercial expansion. (4–5)

Finally,

> the spheres of British expansion were progressively linked by a complex system of communication. From the 1840s onwards, this was provided by subsidised mail services, telegraph wires, undersea cables, an expanding rail network, fast passenger steamers and (in the twentieth century) imperial air routes. (5)

In consonance with the work of Darwin, other commentators have mapped these global connections and interdependencies of the British Empire. Thus, Tony Ballantyne, Jonathan Hyslop, among others, in their contributions to the *New Imperial Histories Reader*, map racial imaginings and knowledge formations, working-class presences across the Empire, from India to Australia and Southern Africa. The migration of people and goods in the 1850–1914 period, argue Gary Magee and Andrew Thompson in *Empire and Globalisation: Networks of People, Goods and Capital in the British World, c. 1850–1914* (2010), was instrumental in the making of an international economy. This, of course, put tremendous pressure on the colonised peoples but also made '"transnationalism"—living in and identifying with more than one country or place—a normal way of life for many British people in the half-century before 1914' (5); an argument that resonates with that of Antoinette Burton about Victorian England cited earlier.

Alan Lester's work in the field of imperial humanitarianism and the 'civilisational mission' has made similar connections to argue for a trans-imperial history. Through the late eighteenth and the nineteenth centuries, notes Alan Lester, we can discern the rise of a 'moral geography of the globe', where the Europeans felt responsible for 'distant strangers' (2000: 278). Thus, imperialism intersected with, fed into and drew from humanitarian ideologies and thought in *different* parts of the world/Empire. Subsequently, Lester et al.'s work focused on not 'national boundaries' (Britain's) but on 'transnational and trans-imperial connections' (2020: 2). They argue that 'the principles of freedom, civilisation and liberalism that motivated them were dissolved in a solution of violent racism through which British power was applied' in *various* colonies and geographical locations (2). Through a reading of three years—1838, 1857 and 1879—and the archive of Victorian imperialist statesmen and legal luminaries like James Stephen, Lester et al. demonstrate the linkage and common foundations (ideological, racism, etc.):

> [T]he ending of slavery and the rise of free trade doctrine, repeated Indian famines and the Uprising of 1857, the First and Second Afghan Wars, the First and Second Opium Wars, the Great Xhosa Cattle Killing and the Anglo-Zulu War, mass emigration from the British Isles, the self-governance of settler colonies in North America, Australasia and southern Africa and the devastation of Indigenous societies. (11)[5]

The Archive in 'New Imperial Histories'

The modes through which the archive has been read and employed have come in for criticism in the *new imperial history* turn. Nicholas Dirks summarises the problem with the slide between the production of the imperial archive and the production of the historical events within imperialism. Dirks writes:

> Begins the histories behind and beneath the production of the kinds of primary sources that have represented colonial knowledge even as they have been used to determine and justify colonial policy. The archive has enshrined, in [Michel] Foucault's sense, this raw material

[5] Philippa Levine and John Marriott in their Introduction to the massive *The Ashgate Research Companion to Modern Imperial Histories* (2012) argue that for many commentators, such as C.A. Bayly, 'modernity' in Europe itself is a consequence of its imperial actions—'The putative simultaneity of Europe's imperial ascent, globalisation and the birth of the modern world has led many to see an intimate interconnectedness.' (2)

However the trouble with this reading is, they note, 'that not only did Europe (or the west if we include the Americas) continue to display significant characteristics that might be regarded as pre-modern, but many of the features identified as modern were to be found equally in societies beyond and often unconnected to Europe.' (2)

> for subsequent historical representation. In the Indian case, the archive is both the precipitate of the history of conquest and rule and the basis on which that history has been written by colonial administrators. (2010: 95)

This 'colonial history' most notably in the 'Cambridge School' of historians, argues Dirks reading the archive of John Seeley and others, was in fact 'colonial fiction', which forwarded the idea that 'Indian politics emerged as a direct reflex of administrative initiatives set in motion by colonial rule' (95). Dirks continues:

> [such colonial histories argued] that local elites, the very groups that had been the collaborators for British rule, turned nationalist—in the context of participation in the progressively enlarged electoral arenas of provincial and municipal politics—when they realized that more of the pie could be obtained through autonomous political institutions than through colonial ones.... (95)

This meant

> [The Cambridge School] proved its arguments by using colonial sources—frequently police records and confidential files—that documented the spurious activities of nationalist figures in what was a large-scale colonial effort to track, contain, and debunk the very politics that sought to overthrow colonial rule. (96)

More recent readings have shown how colonial and imperial legacies and their discursive remains, even in the postcolonial era, turn to and retain its ideologies and representational modes. Nadine Attewell writes in *Better Britons*:

> [in] the afterlife of empire insofar as the projects of nation building with which it is concerned ... sexual reproduction [is the] key to, and a potent figure for, the (re)constitution of the national body after the 'end' of empire. (2014: 6)

This implies that the archive and the historical record—even as we debate what counts as the historical record—is very much an active constituent of the present postcolonial thought and actions as well.

*

The volumes here are only a small sample of the imperial archive. The range and depth of the archive are impossible to encapsulate in a few volumes. While I have made attempts elsewhere to capture some of this variety (Nayar 2007; 2009; 2013; 2016 [*Siege and Prison Writings*]; 2017; 2019), much more is required and possible. For example, the visual archive of the Empire, with its modalities and aesthetic grammars of 'composing' the subcontinent, whether in photography or painting (some of which may be found in Archer 1972), requires much more presence in the form of collections.

The present volumes focus on select aspects of the imperial archive: the accounts of 'discovery' and exploration—flora and fauna, geography, climate—the people of the subcontinent, English domesticity and social life in the subcontinent, the wars and skirmishes—including the *Mutiny* of 1857–1858—and the *civilisational mission*. It excludes legal documents and the many Acts and laws enacted by the British government.

Volume I consists of documents that deal with England's *discovery* of India, its exploration and mapping of the Indian land. This volume includes material as diverse as the letter from India of Thomas Stephens, often called 'the first Englishman in India', chorographic and cartographic accounts from geographical, meteorological, archaeological surveys that the various organisations and societies established for the purpose produced.

Volume II includes English studies of Indian languages and the social order. Ethnographic surveys of the subcontinent's people and cultural practices were published from the late eighteenth century. Practices like female infanticide, sati and thugee, seen as emblematic of the 'barbarous' Oriental, received special attention in the documentation. The characteristics of various tribes and ethnic group were also mapped in considerable detail.

Volume III shifts the focus entirely to the English home and social life. The documents include advice on gardening—an integral part of the English home—and on housekeeping. In the latter, the English were given instructions on how to monitor the domestic economy and manage the servants. Advice manuals on hunting and field sports were also published. Given the interracial dynamics at work, officers were issued manuals on etiquette and behaviour. Accounts of hill-stations and camps, and the social life in the Presidencies make up the rest of the volume.

Volume IV is a collection of accounts of a very different British life in India: as prisoners, under siege and in conditions of war. Starting with the notorious *Black Hole* of Calcutta to the 1857 *Mutiny*, the English wrote about being assailed, besieged and tormented in their war journals and prison accounts. These documented physical and emotional suffering, the losses of families and lives, even as they strove to depict British grit and determination.

Volume V documents England's *civilisational mission*. These documents offer a glimpse into British opinions and strategies on diverse subjects. It includes Macaulay's (in)famous Minute of 1835, accounts of medical missionary activities, views on establishing missionary activities and the British views on women's education.

Works Cited

Archer, Mildred. *Company Drawings in the India Office Library*. London: HMSO, 1972.

Attewell, Nadine. *Better Britons: Reproduction, National Identity, and the Afterlife of Empire*. Toronto: University of Toronto Press, 2014.

Auer, Blain. 'Early Modern Persian, Urdu, and English Historiography and the Imagination of Islamic India under British Rule', *Études de Lettres* 2–3 (2014): 199–206.

Bayly, C.A. *Empire and Information: Intelligence-Gathering and Social Communication in India*. Cambridge: Cambridge University Press, 1999.

Benton, A.H. *Indian Moral Instruction and Caste Problems: Solutions*. London: Longmans, Green and Co., 1917.

Burton, Antoinette and Isabel Hofmeyr. 'Introduction. The Spine of Empire? Books and the Making of an Imperial Commons'. In *Ten Books that Shaped the British Empire: Creating an Imperial Commons*, edited by Antoinette Burton and Isabel Hofmeyr. Durham and London: Duke University Press, 2014.

Burton, Antoinette. *Empire in Question: Reading, Writing, and Teaching British Imperialism*. Durham and London: Duke University Press, 2011.

Chaudhury, Zahid R. *Afterimage of Empire: Photography in Nineteenth-Century India*. Minneapolis: University of Minnesota Press, 2012.

Cohn, Bernard S. *Colonialism and Its Forms of Knowledge: The British in India*. New Delhi: Oxford University Press, 1997.

Damodaran, Vinita, Anna Winterbottom and Alan Lester, eds. *The East India Company and the Natural World*. London: Palgrave Macmillan, 2015.

Darwin, John. *The Empire Project: The Rise and Fall of the British World-System, 1830–1970*. Cambridge: Cambridge University Press, 2009.

Davis, Richard. 'Wilkins, Kasinatha, Hastings, and the First English *Bhagavad Gītā*', *International Journal of Hindu Studies* 19, no. 1–2 (2015): 39–57.

De Silva, Prasannajit. 'Representing Home Life Abroad: British Domestic Life in Early Nineteenth-Century India', *Visual Culture in Britain* 12, no. 3 (2011): 313–331.

Dirks, Nicholas B. 'Coda: The Burden of the Past.' In *The New Imperial Histories Reader*, edited by Stephen Howe, 92–105. Oxford: Routledge, 2010.

Dohman, Renata, ed. *Empire and Art: British India*. Manchester, UK: Manchester University Press, 2017.

Eaton, Natasha. *Colour, Art and Empire: Visual Culture and the Nomadism of Representation*. London: I.B. Tauris, 2013.

Edney, Matthew. *Mapping an Empire: The Geographical Construction of British India, 1753–1843*. Chicago: University of Chicago Press, 1997.

El Edroos, Aboobaker. *Modern Indian Etiquette: Of Mixed Society, Describing Ancient Social Usages and Important Indian Manners and Customs, Aiming at Social Amity Between Indians and Non-Indians*. Surat: H.R. Scott at the Mission Press, 1922.

Guégan, Xavier. 'Visualizing Alienation: Symbolism and Duality in Samuel Bourne's Photographs of British India', *Visual Culture in Britain* 12 no. 3 (2011): 349–365.

Hall, Catherine. *Civilising Subjects: Colony and Metropole in the English Imagination, 1830–1867*. Chicago: University of Chicago Press, 2002.

Joshi, Priya. *In Another Country: Colonialism, Culture, and the English Novel in India*. Oxford: Oxford University Press, 2003.

Leask, Nigel. *British Romantic Writers and the East: Anxieties of Empire*. Cambridge: Cambridge University Press, 1993.

Lelyveld, David. 'The Fate of Hindustani: Colonial Knowledge and the Project of a National Language'. In *Orientalism and the Postcolonial Predicament: Perspectives on South Asia*, edited by Carol Breckenridge and Peter van der Veer, 189–214. Philadelphia: University of Pennsylvania Press, 1993.

Lester, Alan, Kate Boehme and Peter Mitchell. *Ruling the World: Freedom, Civilisation and Liberalism in the Nineteenth-Century British Empire*. Cambridge: Cambridge University Press, 2021.

Lester, Alan. 'Obtaining the "due observance of justice": The geographies of colonial humanitarianism', *Environment and Planning D Society and Space* 20, no. 3 (2000): 277–293.

Levine, Philippa and John Marriott, eds. *The Ashgate Research Companion to Modern Imperial Histories*. London: Ashgate, 2016.

Macfie, Alexander Lyon. 'Thuggee: An Orientalist Construction?' *Rethinking History* 12, no. 3 (2008): 383–397.

Magee, Gary and Andrew Thompson. *Empire and Globalisation: Networks of People, Goods and Capital in the British World, c. 1850–1914*. Cambridge: Cambridge University Press, 2010.

Mahmood, Syed. *History of English Education in India, Its Rise, Development, Progress, Present Condition and Prospects. Being a Narrative of the Various Phases of Educational Policy and Measures Adopted under the British Rule from Its Beginning to the Present Period (1781 to 1893)*. Aligarh: M.A-O. College, 1895.

Malcolm, John. 'Notes of Instructions to Assistants and Officers Acting under the Orders of Major-General Sir John Malcolm, GCB.' In *A Memoir of*

Central India: Including Malwa, and Adjoining Provinces, Vol. 2, edited by John Malcolm. London: Kingsbury, Parbury and Allen, 1823.

Mir, Farina. *The Social Space of Language: Vernacular Culture in British Colonial Punjab*. Berkeley: University of California Press, 2010.

Naregal, Veena. *Language Politics, Elites, and the Public Sphere: Western India under Colonialism*. New Delhi: Permanent Black, 2001.

Nayar, Pramod K. 'English Discourse and India'. *Oxford Bibliographies Online*. New York: Oxford University Press, 2021, https://www.oxfordbibliographies.com/view/document/obo-9780190221911/obo-9780190221911-0114.xml.

______. 'Civil Modernity: The Management of Manners and Polite Imperial Relations in India, 1880–1930', *South Asia: Journal of South Asian Studies* 39, no. 4 (2016): 740–757.

______. 'Moral Readership and Political Apprenticeship: Commentaries on English Education in India, 1875–1930'. In *The Edinburgh History of Reading. Vol. IV. Subversive Readers*, edited by Jonathan Rose, 138–161. UK: Edinburgh University Press, 2020.

______. *Colonial Education and India*, 5 vols. London: Routledge, 2019.

______. *Days of the Raj: Life and Leisure in British India*. New Delhi: Penguin, 2009.

______. *English Siege and Prison Writings: From the 'Black Hole' to the 'Mutiny'*. London: Routledge, 2016.

______. *Indian Travel Writing, 1830–1947*. 1830–1947, 5 vols.

______. *The Penguin 1857 Reader*. New Delhi: Penguin, 2007.

______. *Women in Colonial India: Historical Documents and Sources*, 5 vols. London: Routledge, 2013.

Ogborn, Miles. *Indian Ink: Script and Print in the Making of the English East India Company*. Chicago and London: Chicago University Press, 2007.

Orsini, Francesca. *The Hindi Public Sphere: Language and Literature in the Age of Nationalism*. Oxford: Oxford University Press, 2010.

Pinney, Christopher. 'Sepia Mutiny: Colonial Photography and Its Others in India.' In *Feeling Photography*, edited by Elspeth Brown and Thy Phu, 71–92. Durham, NC: Duke University Press, 2014.

Rao, Velcheru Narayana. 'Print and Prose: Pundits, *Karanams*, and the East India Company in the Making of Modern Telugu'. In *India's Literary History: Essays on the Nineteenth Century*, edited by Stuart Blackburn and Vasudha Dalmia, 146–166. New Delhi: Permanent Black, 2004.

Richards, Thomas. *The Imperial Archive: Knowledge and the Fantasy of Empire*. London: Verso, 1993.

Roy, Anindyo. *Civility and Empire: Literature and Culture in British India, 1822–1922*. London: Routledge, 2005.

Teltscher, Kate. *India Inscribed: European and English Writing on India, 1600–1800*. Delhi: Oxford University Press, 1997.

Tobin, Beth Fowkes. *Picturing Imperial Power: Colonial Subjects in Eighteenth-Century British Painting*. Durham, NC: Duke University Press, 1999, 110–138.

Trivedi, Harish. *Colonial Transactions: English Literature and India*. Calcutta: Papyrus, 1993.

Viswanathan, Gauri. *Masks of Conquest: English Literary Studies and India*. London: Faber & Faber, 1990.

Webb, William Trego. *English Etiquette for Indian Gentlemen*. 5th ed. 1895. Calcutta: S.K. Lahiri, 1915.

Williamson, Thomas. *Oriental Field Sports*. London: W. Bulmer, 1808.

INTRODUCTION

The texts collected here are accounts of how the British 'discovered' the subcontinent. The narrative of discovery, with the freshness of the 'new', was couched very often in the rhetoric of wonder. But this sense of wonder, even astonishment in some cases at the variety, magnitude and sheer difference of the land and its people, was tempered over time with a narrative of exploration. If the 'discovery' moment had a surprise, awe and a sense of uncertainty at facing something totally new—which, in many ways, the subcontinent was—in the early writings of the seventeenth century, the tone, emphasis and attitude shifts later on. The 'enumerative' modality that Bernard Cohn (1997) identified in colonial discourse is very visible in these texts as the British sought to map every aspect of the landscape they occupied and governed.

The narrative of exploration, whether dealing with weather patterns, cultural practices and/or the people in all their variety, was an attempt to describe, classify and document. The imperial survey was an extraordinary method of knowledge production about the space and people the British would set out to rule. Alexander Cunningham described the various archaeological sites he explored. He used the 'evidence' he collected from the surveys to produce not only the rhetoric of ruin but also a rhetoric of conservation of the Indian past. Henry Piddington documented the weather patterns over the Bay of Bengal so as to prepare updated maps of sea routes and conditions of navigation.

The survey is an indispensable tool of colonial documentation and discovery, and the various organisations set up in the late nineteenth century remain to this day, albeit serving the postcolonial state.

Thomas Stevens's letter describes his journey, the tensions and excitement of the voyage and his first 'sighting' of India.

Geographical explorations provide a fascinating archive. Robert Barker's meticulous record-keeping of weather conditions, over several months, is an exercise in meteorological documentation which he (and others) would engage upon in various parts of India. In close parallel is Henry Piddington—famous for coining the term 'cyclone'—who studied the storms in the Bay of Bengal and other places, and wrote extensively on these. James Rennell who wrote extensive atlases and geographical accounts of the subcontinent (and other places, including Africa) also mapped the major river systems in India, of which a sample is included here. John Goldingham's account of the Trigonometrical Survey of

India, one of the largest mapping projects in the British Empire, is also excerpted. The fauna and flora mapped in various regions produced works like John Royle's.

From an entirely different field is Alexander Cunningham, who would set up the Archaeological Survey of India in 1861, whose accounts of various historical sites provided the foundation for an archaeological history of the subcontinent. Resonating with Cunningham's text is William Chambers's, with all its orientalist emphases on ruins and demons, about Mahabalipuram. The ruin trope in Chambers and Cunningham's but also in numerous others (such as the artist William Hodges) enabled the British administrator to justify colonial presence as necessary to 'save' and 'preserve' the subcontinent from further ruin. An excerpt from *The Imperial Gazetteer of India*, describing the Chilka Lake, shows the mix of the language of aesthetics ('the scenery is ... picturesque') and the language of chorography. From a completely different field, excerpted from the records of the Geological Survey of India, is an account of the Kangra earthquake of 1905.

ACKNOWLEDGEMENTS

The Raj has been a perennial favourite when it comes to research and writing, and I cannot remember a year when I did *not* do some 'Raj work'.

Chandra Sekhar of Bloomsbury was very receptive to the project idea, and has been incisive and encouraging when it came to subjects like the volumes' organisation, content and final form—to him, this project owes much.

I express my thanks to journals and anthologies, and their editors and reviewers whose comments have enabled me to sharpen my thoughts on the Raj-topic-of-the-moment. Among journals, I acknowledge: *South Asia, South Asian Review, Anglo-Saxonica* and *Asiatic*. Among the anthologies, I acknowledge *Ireland's Imperial Connections*; *The Edinburgh History of Reading*; *The English Renaissance, Orientalism, and the Idea of Asia*; *Cultural Histories of India*. To Debra Johanyak and Walter S. Lim, Rita Banerjee, Daniel Roberts and Jonathan Wright, Mary Hammond and Jonathan Rose, editors of these fabulous anthologies, many thanks for your invitation to contribute and the work you put into the volumes of which I am now a part.

To Kate Teltscher, whose work *India Inscribed* showed me where to go way back in the mid-1990s, I owe an intellectual debt of enormous proportions.

I am also grateful to publishers and editors at Penguin, Bloomsbury, Palgrave-Macmillan, Edinburgh University Press, Orient BlackSwan, Wiley-Blackwell and Routledge for their comments, suggestions and, above all, interest in this area and my contributions to it.

To Soma Ghosh, Librarian (English) at the Salar Jung Museum, Hyderabad, and her constant efforts, all undertaken with cheer and grace, to obtain materials when I have worked there, immeasurable gratitude.

Many books germinate in conversations with Anna Kurian, who is always enthusiastic about any Raj-work I do, especially if they are multivolume projects. For the constant-traveller role that you assay with such commitment, solidarity and affection, it is my privilege, Anna, to acknowledge you.

Thank you, Molly ('Chechu'), for enquiring lovingly about her 'little one'.

Nandana Dutta has been unceasing in her interest in my work, and her always gentle and loving urging to think in certain ways, even as she tries to catch up with her reading of what I publish. To your attention, insights and perspicacity, Nandana—much, much gratitude.

Professor K. Narayana Chandran established, for some of us willing ones, the standards in academic scholarship and publishing—that he sustains these standards even now, after four decades, is nothing short of the marvellous. To KNC's indomitable spirit of inquiry and work ethic, and showing us the way to do things, I am very grateful.

Friends who drop in 'WhatsAppingly', regularly, to check on me—Neelu, Bhalla, Ajeet, Kulsoom, Om, Archana, Ashish, Krishna Ram, Sai Jawahar, Savita, Vaishali, Soma and Zahid—thank you.

To Nandini, Pranav, my parents and parents-in-law, I owe unquantifiable gratitude, for never complaining at the volume of work I take on, my frequently distracted state of being and, more importantly, for creating an extraordinarily supportive environment.

And thank you, Shubha, for obtaining, wizard-like, essays and journal articles in minutes, and for your enthusiasm for my work.

To the works of P.G. Wodehouse, Agatha Christie, Stephen King, the comics around Batman—my regular reading—many of which unwittingly capture the horror, the abyss and the comedy of academia, I can never express enough gratitude.

It is a pleasure to thank Atul Nair who compiled many of the materials meticulously.

I am grateful to the Institution of Eminence (IoE) project's Professional Development Fund.

Thomas Stephens's. 'Letter'. 1579.

In *The First Englishmen in India: Letters and Narratives by Sundry Elizabethans written by Themselves*, edited by J. Courtney Locke. London: George Routledge & Sons, 1930

The First Englishmen in India

A letter written from Goa, the principal City of all the East Indies, by one Thomas Stevens[1]*, an Englishman, and sent to his father Master Thomas Stevens, Anno* 1579.

After most humble commendations these shall be to crave your daily blessing, with like commendations unto my mother, and withal to certify[2] you of my being[3]; according to your will and my duty.

I wrote unto you taking my journey from Italy to Portugal, which letters I think are come to your hands; so that, presuming thereupon, I think I have the less need at this time to tell you the cause of my departing, which nevertheless in one word I may conclude[4], if I do but name Obedience[5].

I came to Lisbon toward the end of March, eight days before the departure of the ships; so late, that if they had not been stayed about some weighty matters they had been long gone before our coming; insomuch that there were others ordained[6] to go in our places, that the King's provision and ours also might not be in vain. Nevertheless our sudden coming took place, and the 4th of April five ships departed for Goa; wherein, besides shipmen and soldiers, there were a great number of children, which in the seas bear out better than men ; and no marvel, when that many women also pass very well.

The setting forth from the port, I need not to tell how solemn it is, with trumpets and shooting of ordnance. You may easily imagine it, considering that they go in the manner of war.

The 10th of the foresaid month we came to the sight of Porto Santo, near unto Madera[1], where an English ship set upon ours (which was then also alone) with a few shots which did no harm. But after that our ship had laid out her greatest ordnance they straight departed as they came.

The English ship was very fair and great, which I was sorry to see so ill-occupied, for she went roving about, so that we saw her again at the Canarian Isles, unto the which we came the 13th of the said month. And good leisure we had to wonder at the high mountain of the Island Tenerif, for we wandered between that and Great Canaria four days by reason of contrary winds. And, briefly, such evil weather we had until the 14th of May that they despaired to compass the Cape of Good Hope that year.

Nevertheless, taking our voyage between Guinea and the Islands of Capo Verde, without seeing of any land at all, we arrived at length unto the coast of Guinea which the Portugals so call chiefly that part

VIEW OF LISBON ABOUT 1570

of the Burning Zone which is from the sixth degree unto the Equinoctial[1].

In which parts they suffered so many inconveniences of heats and lack of winds that they think themselves happy when they have passed it. For sometimes the ship standeth there, almost, by the space of many days ; sometime she goeth, but in such order that it were almost as good to stand still. And the greatest part of this coast not clear, but thick and cloudy ; full of thunder and lightning, and rain so unwholesome that if the water stand a little while all is full of worms, and falling on the meat which is hanged up it maketh it straight full of worms[2].

Along all that coast we oftentimes saw a thing swimming upon the water like a cock's comb, which they call a Ship of Guinea, but the colour much fairer. Which comb standeth upon a thing almost like the swimmer of a fish in colour and bigness, and beareth underneath in the water strings which save it from turning over. This thing is so poisonous that a man cannot touch it without great peril[3].

In this coast—that is to say, from the sixth degree unto the Equinoctial—we spent no less than thirty days ; partly with contrary winds, partly with calm.

The 30th of May we passed the Equinoctial with contentation, directing our course as well as we could to pass the Promontory[4]. But in all that gulf, and in all the way beside, we found so often calms that the expertest mariners wondered at it. And in places where are always wont to be most horrible tempests we found most quiet calms ; which was very troublesome to those ships which be the greatest of all other and cannot go without good winds. Insomuch that when it is tempest almost intolerable for other ships and maketh them maine all their sails, these hoise[1] up and sail excellent well, unless the waters be too, too furious, which seldom happened in our navigation.

You shall understand that being passed the Line they cannot straightway go the next[2] way to the Promontory, but according to the wind they draw always as near South as they can, to put themselves in the latitude of the Point[3]—which is 35 degrees and an half—and then they take their course towards the East and so compass the Point. But the wind served us so, that at 33 degrees we did direct our course toward the Point or Promontory of Good Hope.

You know that it is hard to sail from East to West or contrary, because there is no fixed point in all the sky whereby they may direct their course ; wherefore I shall tell you what helps God provided for these men. There is not a fowl that appeareth, or sign in the air or in the sea, which they have not written which have made the voyages heretofore. Wherefore, partly by their own experience, and pondering, withal, what space the ship was able to make with such a wind and such direction, and partly by the experience of others, whose books and navigations they have, they guess whereabouts they be, touching degrees of longitude, for of latitude they be always sure[1].

But the greatest and best industry of all is to mark the variation of the needle, or compass ; which in the meridian of the Island of St. Michael (which is one of the Azores in the latitude of Lisbon) is just North[2], and thence swarveth[3] towards the East so much that betwixt the Meridian aforesaid and the Point of Africa[4] it carrieth three or four quarters of thirty-two[5]. And again, in the Point of Africa, a little beyond the point that is called Cape das Agulias (in English, The Needles), it returneth again unto the North ; and that place passed, it swarveth again toward the West, as it did before proportionally[6].

As touching our first signs, the nearer we came to the people[7] of Africa the more strange kinds of fowls appeared ; insomuch that when we came within no less than thirty leagues (almost an hundred miles), and six hundred miles, as we thought, from any Island, as good as three thousand fowls of sundry kinds followed our ship, some of them so great that their wings, being opened, from one point to the other contained seven spans[8], as the Mariners said.

A marvellous thing to see how God provided ; so that in so wide a sea these fowls are all fat and nothing wanteth them[1].

The Portugals have named them all according to some propriety[2] which they have. Some they call Rushtails, because their tails be not proportionable to their bodies but long and small like a rush ; some Forked Tails, because they be very broad and forked ; some Velvet Sleeves, because they have wings of the colour of velvet and bow them as a man boweth his elbow[3]. This bird is always welcome, for he appeareth nearest the Cape.

I should never make an end if I should tell all particulars, but it shall suffice briefly to touch a few ; which yet shall be sufficient, if you mark them, to give occasion to glorify Almighty God in His wonderful works and such variety in His creatures.

And to speak somewhat of fishes : in all places of calm, especially in the Burning Zone near the Line (for without we never saw any), there waited on our ship fishes as long as a man, which they call Tuberones[4]. They come to eat such things as from the ship fall into the sea, not refusing men themselves if they light upon them ; and if they find any meat tied in the sea they take it for theirs. These have waiting on them six or seven small fishes (which never depart) with gardes[5] blue and green round about their bodies, like comely serving-men ; and they go two or three before him and some on every side[1]. Moreover they have other fishes which cleave always unto their body and seem to take such superfluities as grow about them ; and they are said to enter into their bodies also to purge them if they need[2]. The Mariners in time past have eaten of them[3], but since they have seen them eat men their stomachs abhor them. Nevertheless, they draw them up with great hooks, and kill of them as many as they can, thinking that they have made a great revenge.

There is another kind of fish as big, almost, as a herring, which hath wings and flieth, and they are together in great number. These have two enemies, the one in the sea, the other in the air. In the sea the fish which is called Albocore[4], as big as a Salmon, followeth them with great swiftness to take them. This poor fish, not being able to swim fast (for he hath no fins but swimmeth with moving of his tail), shutting his wings, lifteth himself above the water and flieth not very high. The Albocore seeing that, although he have no wings yet he giveth a great leap out of the water, and sometimes catcheth him ; or else he keepeth himself under the water, going that way on as fast as he flieth, and when the fish—being weary of the air or thinking himself out of danger—returneth into the water the Albocore meeteth with him, but sometimes his other enemy, the Sea-Crow, catcheth him before he falleth[1].

With these and like sights, but always making our supplications to God for good weather and salvation of the ship, we came at length unto the Point, so famous and feared of all men[2] (but we found there no tempest, only great waves), where our Pilot was a little overseen[3]. For whereas commonly all other never come within sight of land, but seeing signs ordinary and finding bottom go their way sure and safe, he—thinking himself to have wind at will—shot so nigh the land that the wind turning into the South and the waves being exceeding great rolled us so near the land that the ship stood in less than fourteen fathoms of water, no more than six miles from the Cape which is called Das Agulias. And there we stood as utterly cast away ; for under us were rocks of main[4] stone so sharp and cutting that no anchor could hold the ship, the shore so evil that nothing could take land, and the land itself so full of Tigers[5] and people that are savage and killers of all strangers that we had no hope of life nor comfort, but only in God and a good conscience. Notwithstanding, after we had lost anchors, hoising up the sails for to get the ship a coast in some safer place or when it should please God, it pleased His mercy suddenly, where no man looked for help, to fill our sails with wind from the land. And so we escaped, thanks be to God.

And the day following, being in the place where they are always wont to catch fish, we also fell a-fishing; and so many they took that they served all the ship for that day and part of the next. And one of them pulled up a coral of great bigness and price; for there they say (as we saw by experience) that the corals do grow in the manner of stalks upon the rocks in the bottom and wax hard and red. The day of peril was the 29th of July.

And you shall understand that, the Cape passed, there be two ways to India; one within the Isle of St. Laurence[1], which they take willingly because they refresh themselves at Mosambique a fortnight or a month, not without great need, and thence in a month more land in Goa.

The other is without the Isle of St. Laurence, which they take when they set forth so late and come so late to the Point that they have no time to take the foresaid Mosambique; and then they go heavily[2], because in this way they take no port. And by reason of the long navigation and want of food and water they fall into sundry diseases; their gums wax great and swell and they are fain to cut them away, their legs swell and all the body becometh sore, and so benumbed that they cannot stir hand nor foot, and so they die for weakness. Others fall into fluxes and agues and die thereby[1].

And this way it was our chance to make, yet though we had more than one hundred and fifty sick there died not past seven and twenty ; which loss they esteemed not much in respect of other times[2]. Though some of ours[3] were diseased in this sort, yet, thanks be to God, I had my health all the way, contrary to the expectation of many. God send me my health so well in the land, if it may be to His honour and service.

This way is full of privy[4] rocks and quicksands, so that sometimes we durst not sail by night ; but by the providence of God we saw nothing nor never found bottom until we came to the coast of India.

When we had passed again the Line and were come to the third degree or somewhat more we saw crabs swimming on the water that were red as though they had been sodden[5] ; but this was no sign of land. After, about the eleventh degree, the space of many days more than ten thousand fishes, by estimation, followed round about our ship ; whereof we caught so many that for fifteen days we did eat nothing else, and they served our turn very well. For at this time we had neither meat nor almost anything else to eat, our navigation growing so long that it drew near to seven months, whereas commonly they go it in five. I mean when they sail the inner way. But these fishes were not sign of land, but rather of deep sea.

At length we took a couple of birds, which were a kind of Hawks, whereof they joyed much, thinking that they had been of India, but indeed they were of Arabia, as we found afterward. And we that thought we had been near India were in the same latitude near Zocotoro[1], an Isle in the mouth of the Red Sea. But there God sent us great winds from the North-east or North-north-east, whereupon unwillingly they bare up toward the East ; and thus we went ten days without seeing sign of land, whereby they perceived their error.

For they had directed their course before always North-east, coveting to multiply degrees of latitude[2] ; but partly the difference of the Needle, and, most of all, the running seas (which at that time ran North-west), had drawn us to this other danger[3] had not God sent us this wind, which at length waxed larger and restored us to our right course.

These running seas be so perilous that they deceive the most part of the governors[4]; and some be so little curious, contenting themselves with ordinary experience, that they care not to seek out any means to know when they swarve, neither by the compass nor by any other trial.

The first sign of land were certain fowls which they knew to be of India ; the second, boughs of palms and sedges ; the third, snakes swimming on the water, and a substance which they call by the name of a coin of money, as broad and as round as a groat, wonderfully printed and stamped of nature ; like unto some coin[1]. And these two last signs be so certain that the next day after, if the wind serve, they see land. Which we did, to our great joy, when all our water (for you know they make no beer in those parts[2]) and victuals began to fail us.

And to Goa we came the 24th day of October, there being received with passing great charity.

The people be tawny, but not disfigured in their lips and noses, as the Moors and Cafres[3] of Ethiopia. They that be not of reputation—or, at least, the most part—go naked, saving an apron of a span long and as much in breadth before them, and a lace[4] two fingers broad before them girded about with a string, and no more. And thus they think themselves as well as we with all our trimming.

Of the fruits and trees that be here I cannot now speak, for I should make another letter as long as this. For hitherto I have not seen a tree here whose like I have seen in Europe, the vine excepted, which, nevertheless, here is to no purpose, so that all the wines are brought out of Portugal.

The drink of this country is good water, or wine of the Palm tree[5] or of a fruit called Cocos[6].

And this shall suffice for this time. If God send me my health I shall have opportunity to write to you once again. Now the length of my letter compelleth me to take my leave; and thus I wish your most prosperous health.

From Goa, the 10th of November 1579.

Your loving son Thomas Stevens.

Here is set a Letter[1] *written by the Queen's Majesty to Zelabdim Echebar,*[2] *King of Cambaia,*[3] *and sent by John Newbery. In February, Anno* 1583.

Elizabeth by the grace of God etc. To the most invincible and most mighty Prince, Lord Zelabdim Echebar, King of Cambaia; Invincible Emperor, etc.

The great affection[4] which our Subjects have to visit the most distant places of the world (not without good will and intention to introduce the trade of merchandise of all nations whatsoever they can; by which means the mutual and friendly traffic of merchandise on both sides may come), is the cause that the bearer of this letter, John Newbery, jointly with those that be in his company, with a courteous and honest boldness do repair to the borders and countries of your Empire. We doubt not but that your Imperial Majesty, through your royal grace, will favourably and friendly accept him. And that you would do it the rather for our sake, to make us greatly beholding[1] to your Majesty, we should more earnestly and with more words require it if we did think it needful. But by the singular report that is of your Imperial Majesty's humanity in these uttermost parts of the world we are greatly eased of that burden, and therefore we use the fewer and less words. Only we request that because they are our subjects they may be honestly entreated and received, and that in respect of the hard journey which they have undertaken to places so far distant it would please your Majesty with some liberty and security of voyage to gratify it[2], with such privileges as to you shall seem good. Which courtesy if your Imperial Majesty shall to our subjects at our requests perform, We, according to our Royal Honour, will recompense the same with as many deserts as we can.

And herewith we bid your Imperial Majesty to farewell.

And here a Letter written by her Majesty to the King of China, in February, 1583.

Elizabeth, by the grace of God, Queen of England, etc. Most Imperial and invincible Prince.

Our honest subject, John Newbery, the bringer hereof, who, with our favour, hath taken in hand the voyage which now he pursueth to the parts and countries of your Empire, not trusting upon any other ground than upon the favour of your Imperial clemency and humanity, is moved to undertake a thing of so much difficulty, being persuaded that, he having entered into so many perils, your Majesty will not dislike the same, especially if it may appear that it be not damageable unto your Royal Majesty, and that to your people it will bring some profit. Of both which things he not doubting, with more willing mind hath prepared himself for his predestinated voyage—unto us well liked of.

For by this means we perceive that the profit which, by the mutual trade on both sides, all the princes our neighbours in the West do receive, your Imperial Majesty and those that be subject under your dominion to their great joy and benefit, shall have the same ; which consisteth in the transporting outward of such things whereof we have plenty and in bringing in such things as we stand in need of. It cannot otherwise be (but that), seeing we are born and made to have need one of another, and that we are bound to aid one another, but that[1] your Imperial Majesty will well like of it, and by your subjects with like endeavour will be accepted.

Robert Barker

'An Account of Some Thermometrical Observations, Made by Sir Robert Barker, F. R. S. at Allahabad in the East Indies, in Lat. 25° 30' N. during the Year 1767'.

Philosophical Transactions (1683–1775)
65 (1775)

XIX. *An Account of some Thermometrical Observations, made by Sir* Robert Barker, *F. R. S. at* Allahabad *in the* East Indies, *in Lat.* 25° 30′ *N. during the Year* 1767, *and also during a Voyage from* Madras *to* England, *in the Year* 1774. *Extracted from the original Journal by the Hon.* Henry Cavendish, *F. R. S.*

Redde, April 6, 1775.

THE greatest part of the observations at Allahabad were made within doors; several were made within a tent placed under the shade of trees, some in the open air in the Sun, and some in the open air in the shade; but there is no regular series of observations in any one place; nor were they made at stated times of the day. Though a thermometer kept within doors is but a very indifferent measure of the heat of any climate; yet as I have not seen any thermometrical observations made in that country, except a few during the heats of the summer, and printed in the Philosophical Transactions, vol. LVII. page 218. I have set down the great and least heights I meet with in each month.

January

	Leaſt.	Greateſt.		Leaſt.	Greateſt.
January	58	72	July	81	90
February	60	84	Auguſt	80	86
March	62	94	September	78	83
April	79	96	October	72	87
May	72	101	November	52	86
June	81	99	December	51	64

From the 3d of May to the 4th of June incluſive, a thermometer placed within a tent, under the ſhade of trees, was almoſt every day above 100°, and ſeveral times above 109°, once at 112°. The trees under which the tent was placed formed, as I have been informed, a very thick ſhade; ſo that I think theſe heights are more likely to fall ſhort of the true heat of the open air at that time, than to exceed it. The leaſt height I meet with of the thermometer in the open air in the ſhade, is 42°; which it was at twice in the month of January, at 7 A.M. The greateſt heat is on June 9th, at noon, when it was at 114°, the ſky cloudy; the thermometer within doors at the ſame time 95°, which is leſs than it had frequently been in the month of May; ſo that it ſeems likely, that the heat in the open air in May had frequently been above 114°. During the voyage to England, the thermometer was placed in the round-houſe, and was obſerved regularly at eight in the morning, at noon, and at three in the afternoon; the winds and weather are alſo ſet down. The round-houſe,

I have been informed, is one of the uppermoſt row of cabbins, and is reckoned the cooleſt and moſt airy part of the ſhip. From February 13. to April 7. between Madras and the Southern tropic, the thermometer was conſtantly between 77° and 86°, and very ſeldom lower than 80°. From thence to April 23, lat. 34° 12′, about 15° E. of the Cape of Good Hope, between 70° and 80°. From thence to May 20, at St. Helena, between 62° and 72°. Thence to Auguſt 2. in lat. 43° 14′ N. between 71° and 80°; and from thence to Auguſt 15, in the Britiſh Channel, between 62° and 70°. At land it is well known, that the heat is uſually conſiderably greater in the middle of the day than in the morning or night; but it appears from theſe obſervations, that in the open ſea, there is ſcarce any ſenſible difference; for in ſettled weather, the difference between the different times of the day was rarely more than 1°, oftener none at all. In unſettled weather there was frequently a difference of 2°, ſometimes 4°, ſcarce ever more; but then there ſeems no connexion between this difference and the time of the day, it being as often colder in the middle of the day than in the morning or evening, as warmer. There is added a regiſter of the thermometer, in the ſoldiers barracks at Allahabad, on June 8, 1769, when from 10 in the morning to 8 in the afternoon it ſtood conſtantly above 100°, in the hotteſt part of the day at 107°, and during the whole night between 99° and 98°.

Sir Robert Barker, at my requeſt, has been ſo good as to add the following account of the general ſtate of the weather in Bengal.

THE rains at Bengal generally ſet in between the 1ſt and 15th of June, and continue till the middle of October, when it remains fair till February, the wind blowing moſtly from the N.E. quarter, in which month and March it is interrupted by the N.W. ſqualls, attended with violent guſts of wind, thunder, and lightning, with ſhort, but exceſſive hard, ſhowers of rain or hail, commonly one, but rarely two, in each day. From the middle of March to the middle of June the weather is very hot. At Allahabad and the upper country the rains are not expected till the 20th of June, and ſeldom exceed the 30th, excepting in extraordinary ſeaſons, when it has been known to keep off till the 5th of July; but ſuch an event is uſually attended with a great mortality both of men and beaſts. They break up about the middle of September, and from this time to the beginning of January it continues fair cold weather. In January there are, almoſt always, a few days rain, ſeldom more than a week, and that gentle and pleaſant, which is productive of a ſecond crop, which they uſually reap. The winds at Allahabad ſet in Eaſterly from the beginning of the rains, and blow almoſt conſtantly from that quarter until the concluſion of the cold weather in March, when it changes more Northerly, and is attended by violent North-weſt ſqualls of thunder, lightning, rain, and hail, at which time it changes to the Weſt, blowing with violence, and a heat which frequently deſtroys the birds and beaſts in the fields, till the rains afford a relief.

lief. The river Ganges begins to ſwell before the commencement of the rains, reported by the natives to proceed from the melting of the ſnow on the Northern mountains during the heats of May and June. But the ſudden riſe of the waters in the Ganges, a few days after the ſetting in of the rains, is almoſt incredible; ſince it has been known to riſe twenty feet in forty-eight hours; and its ſudden fall is as extraordinary. In Bengal the rivers are of courſe affected by the riſe and fall of the Ganges. Floods continue the whole time of the rains, more or leſs; but the greateſt overflowings are generally at the beginning and the end or the breaking up of the rains, at which period it rains with the greateſt violence. The waters at Allahabad and in all the upper countries run off into the rivers as ſoon as the rain has ceaſed, the ſoil being for the moſt part of ſand, and the country interſected with ſmall rivulets; but in Bengal, and particularly ſo low down as Calcutta, being of a clay ſoil and an extenſive flat, the whole country is overflowed, forming lakes of great extent, ſome of them being ſix miles over. The water, therefore, generally remains till the Sun has exhaled it, by which it becomes putrid, and renders thoſe parts extremely unwholeſome, occaſioning thoſe deadly putrid fevers, which carries off the patient in a few hours, known by the name of *pucker fevers*.

James Rennell

'An Account of the Ganges and Burrampooter Rivers', communicated by Joseph Banks. *Philosophical Transactions of the Royal Society* (1781)'

IX. *An Account of the* Ganges *and* Burrampooter *Rivers.* *By* James Rennell, *Esq. F. R. S.*; *communicated by* Joseph Banks, *Esq. P. R. S.*

Read January 25, 1781.

THE * Ganges and † Burrampooter Rivers, together with their numerous branches and adjuncts, interfect the country of Bengal in fuch a variety of directions, as to form the moft compleat and eafy inland navigation that can be conceived. So equally and admirably diffufed are thofe natural canals, over a country that approaches nearly to a perfect plane, that, after excepting the lands contiguous to Burdwan, Birboom, &c. (which altogether do not conftitute a fixth part of Bengal) we may fairly pronounce, that every other part of the country has, even in the dry feafon, fome navigable ftream within 25 miles at fartheft, and more commonly within a third part of that diftance.

It is fuppofed, that this inland navigation gives conftant employment to 30,000 boatmen. Nor will it be wondered at, when it is known, that all the falt, and a large proportion of the

* The proper name of this river in the language of Hindooftan (or Indoftan) is Pudda or Padda. It is alfo named Burra-Gonga, or the Great River; and Gonga, the River, by way of eminence; and from this, doubtlefs, the European names of the river are derived.

† The orthography of this word, as given here, is according to the common pronunciation in Bengal; but it is faid to be written in the Sanfcrit language, Brahma-pootar, which fignifies the Son f Brahma.

food conſumed by ten millions of people are conveyed by water within the kingdom of Bengal and its dependencies. To theſe muſt be added, the tranſport of the commercial exports and imports, probably to the amount of two millions ſterling *per annum*; the interchange of manufactures and products throughout the whole country; the fiſheries; and the article of travelling *.

Theſe rivers, which a late ingenious gentleman aptly termed ſiſters and rivals (he might have ſaid *twin* ſiſters, from the contiguity of their ſprings), exactly reſemble each other in length of courſe; in bulk, until they approach the ſea; in the ſmoothneſs and colour of their waters; in the appearance of their borders and iſlands; and, finally, in the height to which their floods riſe with the periodical rains. Of the two, the Burrampooter is the largeſt; but the difference is not obvious to the eye. They are now well known to derive their ſources from the vaſt mountains of Thibet †; from whence they proceed in oppoſite directions; the Ganges ſeeking the plains of Hindooſtan (or Indoſtan) by the weſt; and the Burrampooter by the eaſt; both purſuing the early part of their courſe through rugged vallies and defiles, and ſeldom viſiting the habitations of men. The Ganges, after wandering about 750 miles through theſe mountainous regions, iſſues forth a deity to the ſuperſti-

* The embarkations made uſe of vary in bulk from 180 tons down to the ſize of a wherry. Thoſe from 30 to 50 tons are reckoned the moſt eligible for tranſporting merchandize.

† Theſe are amongſt the higheſt of the mountains of the old hemiſphere. I was not able to determine their height; but it may in ſome meaſure be gueſſed, by the circumſtance of their riſing conſiderably above the horizon, when viewed from the plains of Bengal, at the diſtance of 150 miles.

tious, yet gladdened, inhabitant of Hindooſtan *. From Hurdwar (or Hurdoar) in latitude 30°, where it guſhes through an opening in the mountains, it flows with a ſmooth navigable ſtream through delightful plains during the remainder of its courſe to the ſea (which is about 1350 miles) diffuſing plenty immediately by means of its living productions; and ſecondarily by enriching the adjacent lands, and affording an eaſy means of tranſport for the productions of its borders. In a military view, it opens a communication between the different poſts, and ſerves in the capacity of a *military way* through the country; renders unneceſſary the forming of magazines; and infinitely ſurpaſſes the celebrated inland navigation of North America, where the *carrying places* not only obſtruct the progreſs of an army, but enable the adverſary to determine his place and mode of attack with certainty.

In its courſe through the plains, it receives eleven rivers, ſome of which are equal to the Rhine, and none ſmaller than the

* The fabulous account of the origin of the Ganges (as communicated by my learned and ingenious friend C. W. BOUGHTON ROUSE, Eſq.) is, that it flows out of the foot of Beſchan * (from whence, ſay the Bramins, it has its name Padda; that word ſignifying foot in the Sanſcrit language); and that in its courſe to the plains of Hindooſtan it paſſes through an immenſe rock ſhaped like a Cow's-head.

The allegory is highly expreſſive of the veneration which the Hindoos have for this famous ſtream; and no leſs ſo of their gratitude to the Author of Nature for beſtowing it: for it deſcribes the bleſſing as flowing purely from his bounty and goodneſs.

The rock before mentioned has, I believe, never been viſited by any European; and is even allowed by moſt of the natives to bear no reſemblance to the object from whence it is denominated. However, as the effects of ſuperſtition do often long ſurvive the illuſions that gave it birth, the rock or cavern ſtill preſerves the name of *Gowmooky*, or Cow's-head.

* Beſchan is the ſame with Viſtnou, the PRESERVING DEITY.

Thames, besides as many others of lesser note. It is owing to this vast influx of streams, that the Ganges exceeds the Nile so greatly in point of magnitude, whilst the latter exceeds it in length of course by one-third. Indeed, the Ganges is inferior in this last respect, to many of the northern rivers of Asia; though I am inclined to think that it discharges as much or more water than any of them, because those rivers do not lie within the limits of the periodical rains *.

The bed of the Ganges is, as may be supposed, very unequal in point of width. From its first arrival in the plains at Hurd-

* The proportional lengths of course of some of the most noted rivers in the world are shewn nearly by the following numbers:

European Rivers.	
Thames, - -	1
Rhine, - -	$5\frac{1}{4}$
Danube, - -	7
Wolga, - -	$9\frac{1}{2}$
Asiatic rivers.	
Indus, - - -	$5\frac{1}{2}$
Euphrates, - -	$8\frac{1}{2}$
Ganges, - -	$9\frac{1}{2}$
Burrampooter, - -	$9\frac{1}{2}$
Nou Kian, or Ava River, -	$9\frac{1}{2}$
Jennisea, - -	10
Oby, - -	$10\frac{1}{2}$
Amoor, - -	11
Lena, - -	$11\frac{1}{2}$
Hoanho (of China), -	$13\frac{1}{2}$
Kian Keu (of ditto), -	$15\frac{1}{2}$
African river.	
Nile, - -	$12\frac{1}{2}$
American rivers.	
Missisipi, -	8
Amazons, -	$15\frac{3}{4}$

war, to the conflux of the Jumnah (the firſt river of note that joins it) its bed is generally from a mile to a mile and a quarter wide; and, compared with the latter part of its courſe, tolerably ſtraight. From hence, downward, its courſe becomes more winding, and its bed conſequently wider *, till, having alternately received the waters of the Gogra, Soane, and Gunduck, beſides many ſmaller ſtreams, its bed has attained its full width; although, during the remaining 600 miles of its courſe it receives many other principal ſtreams. Within this ſpace it is, in the narroweſt parts of its bed, half a mile wide, and in the wideſt, three miles; and that, in places where no iſlands intervene. The ſtream within this bed is always either increaſing or decreaſing, according to the ſeaſon. When at its loweſt (which happens in April) the principal channel varies from 400 yards to a mile and a quarter; but is commonly about three quarters of a mile.

The Ganges is fordable in ſome places above the conflux of the Jumnah, but the navigation is never interrupted. Below that, the channel is of conſiderable depth, for the additional ſtreams bring a greater acceſſion of depth than width. At 500 miles from the ſea, the channel is thirty feet deep when the river is at its loweſt; and it continues at leaſt this depth to the ſea, where the ſudden expanſion of the ſtream deprives it of the force neceſſary to ſweep away the bars of ſand and mud thrown acroſs it by the ſtrong ſoutherly winds; ſo that the principal branch of the Ganges cannot be entered by large veſſels.

About 220 miles from the ſea (but 300 reckoning the windings of the river) commences the head of the Delta of the Ganges, which is conſiderably more than twice the area of that of the Nile. The two weſternmoſt branches, named the

* This will be explained when the windings of the river are treated of.

Coſſimbuzar and Jellinghy Rivers, unite and form what is afterwards named the Hoogly River, which is the port of Calcutta, and the only branch of the Ganges that is commonly navigated by ſhips *. The Coſſimbuzar River is almoſt dry from October to May; and the Jellinghy River (although a ſtream runs in it the whole year) is in ſome years unnavigable during two or three of the dryeſt months; ſo that the only ſubordinate branch of the Ganges, that is at all times navigable, is the Chundnah River, which ſeparates at Moddapour, and terminates in the Hooringotta.

That part of the Delta bordering on the ſea, is compoſed of a labyrinth of rivers and creeks, all of which are ſalt, except thoſe that immediately communicate with the principal arm of the Ganges. This tract, known by the name of the Woods, or Sunderbunds, is in extent equal to the principality of Wales; and is ſo completely enveloped in woods, and infeſted with Tygers, that if any attempts have ever been made to clear it (as is reported) they have hitherto miſcarried. Its numerous canals are ſo diſpoſed as to form a compleat inland navigation throughout and acroſs the lower part of the Delta, without either the delay of going round the head of it, or the hazard of putting to ſea. Here ſalt, in quantities equal to the whole conſumption of Bengal and its dependencies, is made

* The Hoogly River, or weſternmoſt branch of the Ganges, has a much deeper outlet to the ſea than the principal branch. Probably this may be owing to its precipitating a leſs quantity of mud than the other; the quantity of the Ganges water diſcharged here being leſs than in the other in the proportion of one to ſix. From the difficulties that occur in navigating the entrance of the Hoogly River, many are led to ſuppoſe, that the channels are ſhallow. The difficulties, however, ariſe from bringing the ſhips acroſs ſome of the ſand-banks, which project ſo far into the ſea, that the channels between them cannot eaſily be traced from without.

and tranſported with equal facility: and here alſo is found an inexhauſtible ſtore of timber for boat-building. The breadth of the lower part of this Delta is upwards of 180 miles; to which, if we add that of the two branches of the river that bound it, we ſhall have about 200 miles for the diſtance to which the Ganges expands its branches at its junction with the ſea.

It has been obſerved before, that the courſe of this river, from Hurdwar to the ſea, is through an uniform plain, or, at leaſt, what appears ſuch to the eye: for, the declivity is much too ſmall to be perceptible. A ſection of the ground, parallel to one of its branches, in length 60 miles, was taken by order of Mr. HASTINGS; and it was found to have about nine inches deſcent in each mile, reckoning in a ſtraight line, and allowance being made for the curvature of the earth. But the windings of the river were ſo great, as to reduce the declivity on which the water ran, to leſs than four inches *per* mile: and by a compariſon of the velocity of the ſtream at the place of experiment with that in other places, I have no reaſon to ſuppoſe, that its general deſcent exceeds it *.

The medium rate of motion of the Ganges is leſs than three miles an hour in the dry months. In the wet ſeaſon, and during the draining off of the waters from the inundated lands, the current runs from five to ſix miles an hour; but there are inſtances of its running ſeven, and even eight miles, in particular ſituations, and under certain circumſtances. I have an

* M. DE CONDAMINE found the deſcent of the river Amazons, in a ſtraight courſe of about 1860 miles, to be about 1020 Engliſh feet, or $6\frac{1}{3}$ inches in a mile. If we allow for the windings, it comes out nearly the ſame as the Ganges (which winds about $1\frac{1}{3}$ mile in three, taking its whole courſe through the plains), namely, about 4 inches in a mile.

experiment of my own on record, in which my boat was carried 56 miles in eight hours; and that againſt ſo ſtrong a wind, that the boat had evidently no progreſſive motion through the water.

When we conſider, that the velocity of the ſtream is three miles in one ſeaſon, and five or more in the other, on the ſame deſcent of four inches *per* mile; and, that the motion of the inundation is only half a mile *per* hour, on a much greater deſcent; no further proof is required how ſmall the proportion of velocity is, that the deſcent communicates. It is then, to the impetus originating at the ſpring head, or at the place where adventitious waters are poured in, and ſucceſſively communicated to every part of the ſtream, that we are principally to attribute the velocity, which is greater or leſſer, according to the quantity of water poured in.

In common, there is found on one ſide of the river an almoſt perpendicular bank, more or leſs elevated above the ſtream, according to the ſeaſon, and with deep water near it: and on the oppoſite ſide a bank, ſhelving away ſo gradually as to occaſion ſhallow water at ſome diſtance from the margin. This is more particularly the caſe in the moſt winding parts of the river, becauſe the very operation of winding produces the ſteep and ſhelving banks *: for the current is always ſtrongeſt on the external ſide of the curve formed by the ſerpentine courſe of the river; and its continual action on the banks

* Hence it is, that the ſection of a river, that winds through a looſe ſoil, approaches nearly to an obtuſe angled-triangle, one of whoſe ſides is exceedingly ſhort and diſproportioned to the other two . But when a river perſeveres in a ſtraight courſe, the ſection becomes nearly the half of an ellipſis divided longitudinally .

either undermines them *, or washes them down. In places where the current is remarkably rapid, or the soil uncommonly loose, such tracts of land are swept away in the course of one season, as would astonish those who have not been eye-witnesses to the magnitude and force of the mighty streams occasioned by the periodical rains of the tropical regions. This necessarily produces a gradual change in the course of the river; what is lost on one side being gained on the other, by the mere operation of the stream: for the fallen pieces of the bank dissolve quickly into muddy sand, which is hurried away by the current along the border of the channel to the point from whence the river turns off to form the next reach, where the stream growing weak, it finds a resting place, and helps to form a shelving bank, which commences at the point, and extends downwards, along the side of the succeeding reach.

To account for the slackness of the current at the point, it is necessary to observe, that the strongest part of it, instead of turning short round the point, preserves for some time the direction given it by the last steep bank, and is accordingly thrown obliquely across the bed of the river to the bay on the opposite side, and pursues its course along it, till the intervention of another point again obliges it to change sides.

In those few parts of the river that are straight, the banks undergo the least alteration †, as the current runs parallel to

* In the dry season some of these banks are more than 30 feet high, and often fall down in pieces of many tons weight, and occasion so sudden and violent an agitation of the water, as sometimes to sink large boats that happen to be near the shore.

† It is more than probable, that the straight parts owe their existence to the tenacity of the soil of which their banks are composed. Whatever the cause may be, the effect very clearly points out such situations as the properest for placing towns in.

them; but the leaſt inflection of courſe has the effect of throwing the current againſt the bank; and if this happens in a part where the ſoil is compoſed of looſe ſand, it produces in time a ſerpentine winding.

It is evident, that the repeated additions made to the ſhelving bank before mentioned, become in time an encroachment on the channel of the river; and this is again counter-balanced by the depredations made on the oppoſite ſteep bank, the fragments of which, either bring about a repetition of the circumſtances above recited, or form a bank or ſhallow in the midſt of the channel. Thus a ſteep and a ſhelving bank are alternately formed in the crooked parts of the river (the ſteep one being the *indented* ſide, and the ſhelving one the *projecting*); and thus, a continual fluctuation of courſe is induced in all the winding parts of the river; each meander having a perpetual tendency to deviate more and more from the line of the general courſe of the river, by eating deeper into the bays, and at the ſame time adding to the points, till either the oppoſite bays meet, or the ſtream breaks through the narrow iſthmus, and reſtores a temporary ſtraightneſs to the channel.

Several of the windings of the Ganges and its branches are faſt approaching to this ſtate; and in others, it actually exiſts at preſent. The experience of theſe changes ſhould operate againſt attempting canals of any length, in the higher parts of the country; and I much doubt, if any in the lower parts would long continue navigable. During eleven years of my reſidence in Bengal, the outlet or head of the Jellinghy River was gradually removed three quarters of a mile farther down: and by two ſurveys of a part of the adjacent bank of the Ganges, taken about the diſtance of nine years from each other, it appeared that the breadth of an Engliſh mile and a half had been taken away. This is, however, the moſt rapid change that I have noticed; a mile in ten or twelve years being the uſual rate of incroachment, in places where the current ſtrikes with the greateſt force, namely, where two adjoining reaches approach neareſt to a right angle. In ſuch ſituations it not unfrequently excavates gulfs * of conſiderable length within the bank. Theſe gulfs are in the direction of the ſtrongeſt parts of the ſtream; and are, in fact, the *young ſhoots* (if I may ſo expreſs myſelf) which in time ſtrike out and become branches of the river; for we generally find them at thoſe turnings that have the ſmalleſt angles †.

Two cauſes, widely different from each other, occaſion the meandering courſes of rivers; the one, the irregularity of the ground through which they run, which obliges them to wander in queſt of a declivity; the other, the looſeneſs of the ſoil, which yields to the friction of the border of the ſtream. The meanders in the firſt caſe, are, of courſe, as digreſſive and irregular as the ſurface they are projected on: but, in the latter, they are ſo far reducible to rule, that rivers of unequal bulk will, under ſimilar circumſtances, take a circuit to wind in, whoſe extent is in proportion to their reſpective breadths: for I have obſerved, that

* The Count DE BUFFON adviſes the digging of ſuch gulfs in the banks of ordinary rivers, with a view to divert the current, when bridges or other buildings are endangered by it.

† The courſes of theſe branches at the efflux, generally, if not always, become retrograde to the courſe of the river: for, a ſand bank accumulating at the upper point of ſeparation, gives an oblique direction upwards, to the ſtream, which would otherwiſe run out at right angles. This ſand bank being always on the increaſe, occaſions a corroſion of the oppoſite bank; and by this means all, or moſt of the outlets have a progreſſive motion downwards; as I have before remarked of the Jellinghy River, in the foregoing page.

when a branch of the Ganges is fallen ſo low as to occupy only a part of its bed, it no longer continues in the line of its old courſe; but works itſelf a new channel, which winds from ſide to ſide acroſs the former one. I have obſerved too, that in two ſtreams, of equal ſize, that which has the ſloweſt current has alſo the ſmalleſt windings: for as theſe (in the preſent caſe) are ſolely owing to the depredations made on the banks by the force of the current; ſo the extent of theſe depredations, or, in other words, the dimenſions of the windings, will be determined by the degree of force acting on the banks.

The windings of the Ganges in the plains, are, doubtleſs, owing to the looſeneſs of the ſoil: and (I think) the proof of it is, that they are perpetually changing; which thoſe, originally induced by an inequality of ſurface, can ſeldom, or never do*.

I can eaſily ſuppoſe, that if the Ganges was turned into a ſtraight canal, cut through the ground it now traverſes in the moſt winding parts of its courſe, its ſtraightneſs would be of ſhort duration. Some yielding part of the bank, or that which happened to be the moſt ſtrongly acted on, would firſt be corroded or diſſolved: thus a bay or cavity would be formed in the ſide of the bank. This begets an inflection of the current, which, falling obliquely on the ſide of the bay, corrodes it inceſſantly. When the current has paſſed the innermoſt part of the bay, it receives a new direction, and is thrown

* It has been remarked, that the courſes of rivers become more winding as they approach the ſea. This, I believe, will only hold good in ſuch as take the latter part of their courſe through a ſandy ſoil. In the Ganges, and other rivers ſubject to conſiderable variations in the bulk of their ſtreams, the beſt marks of the vicinity of the ſea are, the lowneſs of the river banks, and the increaſing muddineſs of the ſhallows in its bed.

obliquely towards the oppofite fide of the canal, depofiting in its way the matter excavated from the bay, and which begins to form a fhallow or bank contiguous to the border of the canal. Here then is the origin of fuch windings as owe their exiftence to the nature of the foil. The bay, fo corroded, in time becomes large enough to give a new direction to the body of the canal: and the matter excavated from the bay is fo difpofed as to affift in throwing the current againft the oppofite bank, where a procefs, fimilar to that I have been defcribing, will be begun.

The action of the current on the bank will alfo have the effect of deepening the border of the channel near it; and this again increafes the velocity of the current in that part. Thus would the canal gradually take a new form, till it became what the river now is. Even when the windings have leffened the defcent one half, we ftill find the current too powerful for the banks to withftand it.

There are not wanting inftances of a total change of courfe in fome of the Bengal rivers*. The Cofa River (equal to the Rhine) once ran by Purneah, and joined the Ganges oppofite Rajemal. Its junction is now 45 miles higher up. Gour, the ancient capital of Bengal, ftood on the banks of the Ganges.

Appearances favour very ftrongly the opinion, that the Ganges had its former bed in the tract now occupied by the lakes and moraffes between Nattore and Jaffiergunge, ftriking out of its prefent courfe at Bauleah, and paffing by Pootyah. With an equal degree of probability (favoured by tradition) we may trace its fuppofed courfe by Dacca, to a junction with the Burrampooter or Megna near Fringybazar; where the accumu-

* The Mootyjyl lake is one of the windings of a former channel of the Cof-fimbuzar River.

lation of two ſuch mighty ſtreams probably ſcooped out the preſent amazing bed of the Megna *.

In tracing the ſea coaſt of the Delta, we find no leſs than eight openings; each of which, without heſitation, one pronounces to have been in its time the principal mouth of the Ganges. Nor is the occaſional deviation of the principal branch, probably, the only cauſe of fluctuation in the dimenſions of the Delta. One obſerves, that the Deltas of capital rivers (the tropical ones particularly) encroach upon the ſea. Now, is not this owing to the mud and ſand brought down by the rivers, and gradually depoſited, from the remoteſt ages down to the preſent time? The rivers, we know, are loaded with mud and ſand at their entrance into the ſea; and we alſo know, that the ſea recovers its tranſparency at the diſtance of twenty leagues from the coaſt; which can only ariſe from the waters having precipitated their earthy particles within that ſpace. The ſand and mud banks at this time, extend twenty miles off ſome of the iſlands in the mouths of the Ganges and Burrampooter; and in many places riſe within a few feet of the ſurface. Some future generation will probably ſee theſe banks riſe above water, and ſucceeding ones poſſeſs and cultivate them! Next to earthquakes, perhaps the floods of the tropical rivers produce the quickeſt alterations in the face of our globe. Extenſive iſlands are formed in the channel of the Ganges, during a period far ſhort of that of a man's life; ſo that the whole proceſs lies

* Megna and Burrampooter are names belonging to the ſame river in different parts of its courſe. The Megna falls into the Burrampooter; and, though a much ſmaller river, communicates its name to the other during the reſt of its courſe.

within the compaſs of his obſervation *. Some of theſe iſlands, four or five miles in extent, are formed at the angular turnings of the river, and were originally large ſand banks thrown up round the points (in the manner before deſcribed) but afterwards inſulated by breaches of the river. Others are formed in the ſtraight parts of the river, and in the middle of the ſtream; and owe their origin to ſome obſtruction lurking at the bottom. Whether this be the fragments of the river bank; a large tree ſwept down from it; or a ſunken boat; it is ſufficient for a foundation: and a heap of ſand is quickly collected below it. This accumulates amazingly faſt: in the courſe of a few years it peeps above water, and having now uſurped a conſiderable portion of the channel, the river borrows on each ſide to ſupply the deficiency in its bed; and in ſuch parts of the river we always find ſteep banks on both ſides †. Each periodical flood brings an addition of matter to this growing iſland; increaſing it in height as well as extenſion, until its top is perfectly on a level with the banks that include it: and at that period of its growth it has mould enough on it for the purpoſes of cultivation, which is owing to the mud left on it when the waters ſubſide, and is indeed a part of the œconomy which nature obſerves in fertilizing the lands in general.

Whilſt the river is forming new iſlands in one part, it is ſweeping away old ones in other parts. In the progreſs of this deſtructive operation, we have opportunities of obſerving, by means of the ſections of the falling bank, the regular diſtri-

* Accordingly, the laws reſpecting alluvion are aſcertained with great preciſion.

† This evidently points out the means for preventing encroachments on a river bank in the ſtraight parts of its courſe, *viz.* to remove the ſhallows in the middle of its channel.

bution of the ſeveral ſtrata of ſand and earths, lying above one another in the order in which they decreaſe in gravity. As they can only owe this diſpoſition to the agency of the ſtream that depoſited them, it would appear, that theſe ſubſtances are ſuſpended at different heights in the ſtream, according to their reſpective gravities. We never find a ſtratum of earth under one of ſand; for the muddy particles float neareſt the ſurface *. I have counted ſeven diſtinct ſtrata in a ſection of one of theſe iſlands. Indeed, not only the iſlands, but moſt of the river banks wear the ſame appearance: for as the river is always changing its preſent bed, and verging towards the ſite of ſome former one now obliterated, this muſt neceſſarily be the caſe.

As a ſtrong preſumptive proof of the wandering of the Ganges from the one ſide of the Delta to the other, I muſt obſerve, that there is no appearance of *virgin* earth between the Tiperah Hills on the eaſt, and the province of Burdwan on the weſt; nor on the north till we arrive at Dacca and Bauleah. In all the ſections of the numerous creeks and rivers in the Delta, nothing appears but ſand and black mould in regular ſtrata, till we arrive at the clay that forms the lower part of their beds. There is not any ſubſtance ſo coarſe as gravel either in the Delta or nearer the ſea than 400 miles †, where a rocky point, a part of the baſe of the neighbouring hills, projects into the river: but out of the vicinity of the great rivers the ſoil is either red, yellow, or of a deep brown.

* A glaſs of water taken out of the Ganges, when at its height, yields about one part in four of mud. No wonder then that the ſubſiding waters ſhould quickly form a ſtratum of earth; or that the Delta ſhould encroach upon the ſea!

† At Oudanulla.

I come now to the particulars of the annual ſwelling and overflowing of the Ganges *.

It appears to owe its increaſe as much to the rain water that falls in the mountains contiguous to its ſource, and to the ſources of the great northern rivers that fall into it, as to that which falls in the plains of Hindooſtan; for it riſes fifteen feet and a half out of thirty-two (the ſum total of its riſing) by the latter end of June: and it is well known, that the rainy ſeaſon does not begin in moſt of the flat countries till about that time. In the mountains it begins early in † April; and by the latter end of that month, when the rain-water has reached Bengal, the rivers begin to riſe, but by very ſlow degrees; for the increaſe is only about an inch *per* day for the firſt fortnight. It then gradually augments to two and three inches before any

* An opinion has long prevailed, that the ſwelling of the Ganges, previous to the commencement of the rainy ſeaſon in the flat countries, is in a great meaſure owing to the melting of the ſnow in the mountains. I will not go ſo far as totally to diſallow the fact; but can by no means ſuppoſe, that the quantity of ſnow water bears any proportion to the increaſe of the river.

† The vaſt collection of vapours, wafted from the ſea by the ſoutherly or ſouth-weſt monſoon, are ſuddenly ſtopped by the lofty ridge of mountains that runs from eaſt to weſt through Thibet. It is obvious, that the accumulation and condenſation of theſe vapours, muſt firſt happen in the neighbourhood of the obſtacle; and ſucceſſively in places more remote, as freſh ſupplies arrive to fill the atmoſphere. Hence the priority of commencement of the rainy ſeaſon in places that lie neareſt the mountains.

All the rivers that are ſituated within the limits of the monſoons, or ſhifting trade winds, are ſubject to overflowings at annually ſtated periods, like the Ganges: and theſe periods return during the ſeaſon of the ſoutherly wind, that being the only wind which brings vapours from the ſea; and this being periodical, the falls of rain muſt neceſſarily be ſo too.

The northerly wind, which blows only over the land, is dry; for no rain (except caſual ſhowers) falls during the continuance of that monſoon.

quantity of rain falls in the flat countries; and when the rain becomes general, the increaſe on a medium is five inches *per* day. By the latter end of July all the lower parts of Bengal, contiguous to the Ganges and Burrampooter, are overflowed, and form an inundation of more than a hundred miles in width; nothing appearing but villages and trees, excepting very rarely the top of an elevated ſpot (the artificial mound of ſome deſerted village) appearing like an iſland.

The inundations in Bengal differ from thoſe in Egypt in this particular, that the Nile owes its floods *entirely* to the rain-water that falls in the mountains near its ſource; but the inundations in Bengal are as much occaſioned by the rain that falls there, as by the waters of the Ganges; and as a proof of it, the lands in general are overflowed to a conſiderable height long before the bed of the river is filled. It muſt be remarked, that the ground adjacent to the river bank, to the extent of ſome miles, is conſiderably higher than the reſt of the country*, and ſerves to ſeparate the waters of the inundation from thoſe of the river until it overflows. This high ground is in ſome ſeaſons covered a foot or more; but the height of the inundation within, varies, of courſe, according to the irregularities of the ground, and is in ſome places twelve feet.

Even when the inundation becomes general, the river ſtill ſhews itſelf, as well by the graſs and reeds on its banks, as by its rapid and muddy ſtream; for the water of the inundation acquires a blackiſh hue, by having been ſo long ſtagnant

* This property of the bank is well accounted for by Count BUFFON, who imputes it to the precipitation of mud made by the waters of the river, when it overflows. The inundation, ſays he, purifies itſelf as it flows over the plain; ſo that the precipitation muſt be greateſt on the parts neareſt to the margin of the river.

amongſt graſs and other vegetables: nor does it ever loſe this tinge, which is a proof of the predominancy of the rain water over that of the river; as the ſlow rate of motion of the inundation (which does not exceed half a mile *per* hour) is of the remarkable flatneſs of the country.

There are particular tracts of land, which, from the nature of their culture, and ſpecies of productions, require leſs moiſture than others; and yet, by the lowneſs of their ſituation, would remain too long inundated, were they not guarded by dikes or dams, from ſo copious an inundation as would otherwiſe happen from the great elevation of the ſurface of the river above them. Theſe dikes are kept up at an enormous expence; and yet do not always ſucceed, for want of tenacity in the ſoil of which they are compoſed.

During the ſwoln ſtate of the river, the tide totally loſes its effect of counteracting the ſtream; and in a great meaſure that of ebbing and flowing, except very near the ſea. It is not uncommon for a ſtrong wind, that blows up the river for any continuance, to ſwell the waters two feet above the ordinary level at that ſeaſon: and ſuch accidents have occaſioned the loſs of whole crops of rice*. A very tragical event happened at Luckipour † in 1763, by a ſtrong gale of wind conſpiring with a high ſpring tide, at a ſeaſon when the periodical flood was within a foot and half of its higheſt pitch. It is ſaid that the waters roſe ſix feet above the ordinary level. Certain it is, that

* The rice I ſpeak of is of a particular kind; for the growth of its ſtalk keeps pace with the increaſe of the flood at ordinary times, but is deſtroyed by a too ſudden riſe of the water. The harveſt is often reaped in boats. There is alſo a kind of graſs which overtops the flood in the ſame manner, and at a ſmall diſtance has the appearance of a field of the richeſt verdure.

† This place is ſituated about fifty miles from the ſea.

the inhabitants of a confiderable diftrict, with their houfes and cattle, were totally fwept away; and, to aggravate their diftrefs, it happened in a part of the country which fcarce produces a fingle tree for a drowning man to efcape to.

Embarkations of every kind traverfe the inundation: thofe bound upwards, availing themfelves of a direct courfe and ftill water, at a feafon when every ftream rufhes like a torrent. The wind too, which at this feafon blows regularly from the fouth-eaft *, favours their progrefs; infomuch, that a voyage, which takes up nine or ten days by the courfe of the river when confined within its banks, is now effected in fix. Hufbandry and grazing are both fufpended; and the peafant traverfes in his boat, thofe fields which in another feafon he was wont to plow; happy that the elevated fite of the river banks place the herbage they contain, within his reach, otherwife his cattle muft perifh.

The following is a table of the gradual increafe of the Ganges and its branches, according to obfervations made at Jellinghy and Dacca.

	At Jellinghy.		At Dacca.	
	Ft.	In.	Ft.	In.
In May it rofe -	6	0	2	4
June - - -	9	6	4	6
July - - -	12	6	5	6
In the firft half of Auguft	4	0	1	11
	32	0	14	3

* Although in the gulf or bay of Bengal the monfoon blows from the S.S.W, and S.W. yet in the eaftern and northern parts of Bengal it blows from the S.E, or E.S.E.

These obſervations were made in a ſeaſon, when the waters roſe rather higher than uſual; ſo that we may take 31 feet for the medium of the increaſe.

The inundation is nearly at a ſtand for ſome days preceding the middle of Auguſt, when it begins to run off; for although great quantities of rain fall in the flat countries, during Auguſt and September, yet, by a partial ceſſation of the rains in the mountains, there happens a deficiency in the ſupplies neceſſary to keep up the inundation *. The quantity of the daily decreaſe of the river is nearly in the following proportion: during the latter half of Auguſt, and all September, from three to four inches; from September to the end of November, it gradually leſſens from three inches to an inch and a half; and from November to the latter end of April, it is only half an inch *per* day at a medium. Theſe proportions muſt be underſtood to relate to ſuch parts of the river as are removed from the influence of the tides; of which more will be ſaid by and by. The decreaſe of the inundation does not always keep pace with that of the river, by reaſon of the height of the banks; but after the beginning of October, when the rain has nearly ceaſed, the remainder of the inundation goes off quickly by evaporation, leaving the lands highly manured, and in a ſtate fit to receive the ſeed, after the ſimple operation of plowing.

There is a circumſtance attending the increaſe of the Ganges, and which, I believe, is little known or attended to; becauſe few people have made experiments on the heights to which the

* I have ſtated the middle of Auguſt for the period when the waters begin to run off; and in general it happens with more regularity than the viciſſitudes of the ſeaſons do. But there are exceptions to it; for in the year 1774 the rivers kept up for near a month after the uſual time.

periodical flood rifes in different places. The circumftance I allude to, is, the difference of the quantity of the increafe (as expreffed in the foregoing table) in places more or lefs remote from the fea. It is a fact, confirmed by repeated experiments, that from about the place where the tide commences, to the fea, the height of the periodical increafe diminifhes gradually, until it totally difappears at the point of confluence. Indeed, this is perfectly conformable to the known laws of fluids: the Ocean preferves the fame level at all feafons (under fimilar circumftances of tide) and neceffarily influences the level of all the waters that communicate with it, unlefs precipitated in the form of a cataract. Could we fuppofe, for a moment, that the increafed column of water, of 31 feet perpendicular, was continued all the way to the fea, by fome preternatural agency: whenever that agency was removed, the head of the column would diffufe itfelf over the Ocean, and the remaining parts would follow, from as far back as the influence of the Ocean extended; forming a flope, whofe perpendicular height would be 31 feet. This is the precife ftate in which we find it. At the point of junction with the fea, the height is the fame in both feafons at equal times of the tide. At Luckipour there is a difference of about fix feet between the heights in the different feafons; at Dacca, and places adjacent, 14; and near Cuftee, 31 feet. Here then is a regular flope; for the diftances between the places bear a proportion to the refpective heights. This flope muft add to the rapidity of the ftream; for, fuppofing the defcent to have been originally four inches *per* mile, this will increafe it to about five and an half. Cuftee is about 240 miles from the fea, by the courfe of the river; and the furface of the river there, during the dry feafon, is about 80 feet above the level of the ſea at high water *. Thus far does the Ocean manifeſt its dominion in both ſeaſons: in the one by the ebbing and flowing of its tides; and in the other by depreſſing the periodical flood, till the ſurface of it coincides as nearly with its own, as the deſcent of the channel of the river will admit †.

Similar circumſtances take place in the Jellinghy, Hoogly, and Burrampooter Rivers; and, I ſuppoſe, in all others that are ſubject either to periodical or occaſional ſwellings.

Not only does the flood diminiſh near the ſea, but the river banks diminiſh in the ſame proportion; ſo that in the dry ſeaſon the height of the periodical flood may be known by that of the bank.

I am aware of an objection that may be made to the above ſolution; which is, that the lowneſs of the banks in places near the ſea, is the true reaſon why the floods do not attain ſo conſiderable a height, as in places farther removed from it, and where the banks are high; for that the river, wanting a bank to confine it, diffuſes itſelf over the ſurface of the country. In

* The tides in the River Amazons are perceptible at 600 miles above its mouth; but at an elevation of only 90 feet, according to M. DE CONDAMINE. It e mains to be told what the ſtate of the river was at the time of making the experiment; becauſe the land-floods have the effect of ſhortening the limits of the tide's way.

† The Count DE BUFFON has ſlightly mentioned this circumſtance attending the ſwelling of rivers; but imputes it to the increaſed velocity of the current, as the river approaches the ſea: which, ſays he, carries off the inundation ſo quick, as to abate its height. Now (with the utmoſt deference to ſo great an authority) I could never perceive, that the current, either in the Ganges, or any other river, was ſtronger near the ſea than at a diſtance from it. Even if we admit an acceleration of the current during the ebb tide, the flux retards it in ſo conſiderable a degree, as at leaſt to counter-balance the effects produced by the temporary increaſe of velocity.

anſwer to this, I ſhall obſerve, that it is proved by experiment, that at any given time, the quantity of the increaſe in different places, bears a juſt proportion to the ſum total of the increaſe in each place reſpectively: or, in other words, that when the river has riſen three feet at Dacca, where the whole riſing is about 14 feet; it will have roſe upwards of ſix feet and a half at Cuſtee, where it riſes 31 feet in all.

The quantity of water diſcharged by the Ganges, in one ſecond of time, during the dry ſeaſon, is 80,000 cubic feet; but in the place where the experiment was made, the river, when full, has thrice the volume of water in it; and its motion is alſo accelerated in the proportion of 5 to 3: ſo that the quantity diſcharged in a ſecond at that ſeaſon is 405,000 cubic feet. If we take the medium the whole year through, it will be nearly 180,000 cubic feet in a ſecond.

THE Burrampooter, which has its ſource from the oppoſite ſide of the ſame mountains that give riſe to the Ganges, firſt takes its courſe eaſtward (or directly oppoſite to that of the Ganges) through the country of Thibet, where it is named Sanpoo or Zanciu, which bears the ſame interpretation as the Gonga of Hindooſtan: namely, the River. The courſe of it through Thibet, as given by Father DU HALDE, and formed into a map by Mr. D'ANVILLE, though ſufficiently exact for the purpoſes of general geography, is not particular enough to aſcertain the preciſe length of its courſe. After winding with a rapid current through Thibet, it waſhes the border of the territory of Laſſa (in which is the reſidence of the grand Lama) and then deviating from an eaſt to a ſouth-eaſt courſe, it approaches within 220 miles of Yunan, the weſternmoſt province of China. Here it appears, as if undetermined whether to attempt a paſſage to the ſea by the Gulf of Siam, or by that of Bengal; but ſeemingly determining on the latter, it turns ſuddenly to the weſt through Aſſam, and enters Bengal on the north-eaſt. I have not been able to learn the exact place where it changes its name; but as the people of Aſſam call it Burrampoot, it would appear, that it takes this name on its entering Aſſam. After its entry into Bengal, it makes a circuit round the weſtern point of the Garrow Mountains; and then, altering its courſe to ſouth, it meets the Ganges about 40 miles from the ſea.

Father DU HALDE expreſſes his doubts concerning the courſe that the Sanpoo takes after leaving Thibet, and only ſuppoſes generally that it falls into the gulf of Bengal. M. D'ANVILLE, his geographer, with great reaſon ſuppoſed the Sanpoo and Ava River to be the ſame: and in this he was juſtified by the information which his materials afforded him: for the Burrampooter was repreſented to him, as one of the inferior ſtreams that contributed its waters the Ganges, and not as its equal or ſuperior; and this was ſufficient to direct his reſearches, after the mouth of the Sanpoo River, to ſome other quarter. The Ava River, as well from its bulk, as the bent of its courſe for ſome hundred miles above its mouth, appeared to him to be a continuation of the river in queſtion: and it was accordingly deſcribed as ſuch in his maps, the authority of which was juſtly eſteemed as deciſive; and, till the year 1765, the Burrampooter, as a capital river, was unknown in Europe.

On tracing this river in 1765, I was no leſs ſurprized, at finding it rather larger than the Ganges, than at its courſe previous to its entering Bengal. This I found to be from the eaſt; although all the former accounts repreſented it as from the north: and this unexpected discovery soon led to enquiries, which furnished me with an account of its general course to within 100 miles of the place where DU HALDE left the Sanpoo. I could no longer doubt, that the Burrampooter and Sanpoo were one and the same river: and to this was added the positive assurances of the Assamers, "That *their* river came "from the north-west, through the Bootan mountains." And to place it beyond a doubt, that the Sanpoo River is not the same with the river of Ava, but that this last is the great Nou Kian of Yunan; I have in my possession a manuscript draught of the Ava River, to within 150 miles of the place where DU HALDE leaves the Nou Kian, in its course towards Ava; together with very authentic information that this river (named Irabattey by the people of Ava) is navigable from the city of Ava into the province of Yunan in China*.

The Burrampooter, during a course of 400 miles through Bengal, bears so intimate a resemblance to the Ganges, except in one particular, that one description may serve for both. The exception I mean is, that, during the last 60 miles before its junction with the Ganges, it forms a stream which is regularly from four to five miles wide, and but for its freshness might pass for an arm of the sea. Common description fails in an attempt to convey an adequate idea of the grandeur of this magnificent object; for,

—— Scarce the muse
Dares stretch her wing o'er this enormous mass
Of rushing water; to whose dread expanse,
Continuous depth, and wond'rous length of course,

* The courses of the Burrampooter and Ganges, as well as that of the Ava River from Yunan to the sea, will shortly be described in a large sheet map of Hindoostan.

Our floods are rills ———
Thus pouring on, it proudly ſeeks the deep,
Whoſe vanquiſh'd tide, recoiling from the ſhock,
Yields to this liquid weight ———

THOMSON'S Seaſons.

I have already endeavoured to account for the ſingular breadth of the Megna, by ſuppoſing that the Ganges once joined it where the Iſſamutty now does; and that their joint waters ſcooped out its preſent bed. The preſent junction of theſe two mighty rivers below Luckipour, produces a body of running freſh water, hardly to be equalled in the old hemiſphere, and, perhaps, not exceeded in the new. It now forms a gulf interſperſed with iſlands, ſome of which rival, in ſize and fertility, our Iſle of Wight. The water at ordinary times is hardly brackiſh at the extremities of theſe iſlands; and, in the rainy ſeaſon, the ſea (or at leaſt the ſurface of it) is perfectly freſh to the diſtance of many leagues out.

The *Bore* (which is known to be a ſudden and abrupt influx of the tide into a river or narrow ſtrait) prevails in the principal branches of the Ganges, and in the Megna; but the Hoogly River, and the paſſages between the iſlands and ſands ſituated in the gulf, formed by the confluence of the Ganges and Megna, are more ſubject to it than the other rivers. This may be owing partly, to their having greater embouchures in proportion to their channels, than the others have, by which means a larger proportion of tide is forced through a paſſage comparatively ſmaller; and partly, to there being no capital openings near them, to draw off any conſiderable portion of the accumulating tide. In the Hoogly or Calcutta River, the *Bore* commences at Hoogly Point (the place where the river firſt contracts itſelf)

PLAN of part of the Course of the **GANGES**, *to e*

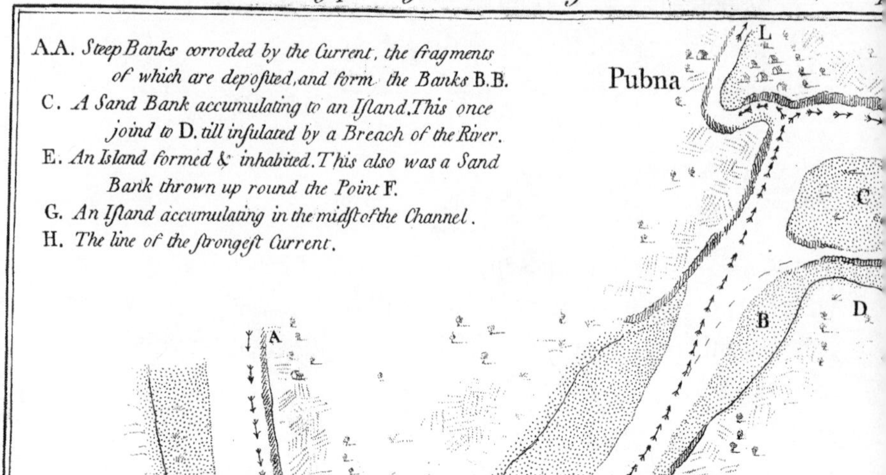

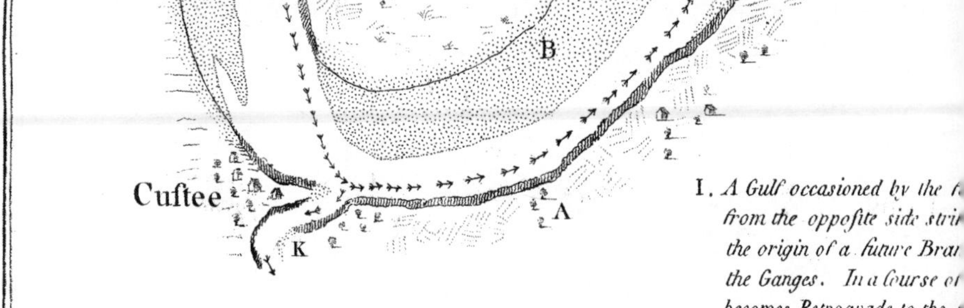

…nature of the steep and shelving Banks, &c.

Philos. Trans. Vol. LXXI. Tab. IV. p. 114.

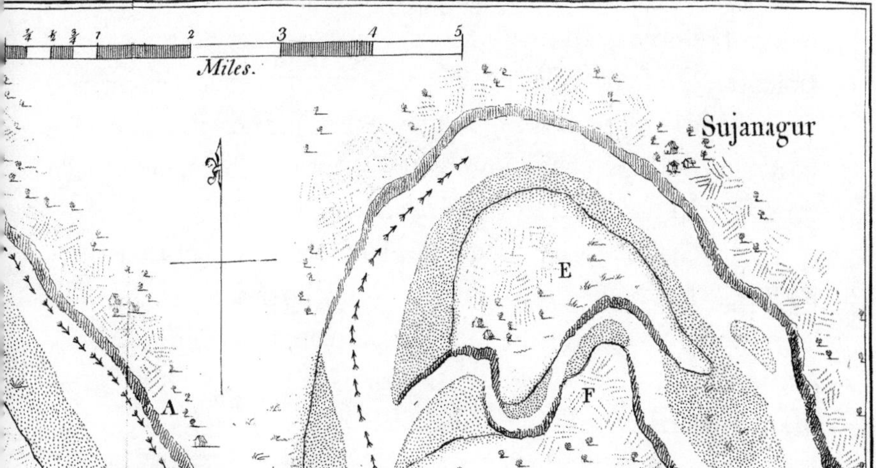

…planation of the steep and shelving Banks.

…except in the article of width.

and is perceptible above Hoogly Town; and ſo quick is its motion, that it hardly employs four hours in travelling from one to the other, although the diſtance is near 70 miles. At Calcutta, it ſometimes occaſions an inſtantaneous riſe of five feet: and both here, and in every other part of its track, the boats, on its approach, immediately quit the ſhore, and make for ſafety to the middle of the river.

In the channels, between the iſlands in the mouth of the Megna, &c. the height of the *Bore* is ſaid to exceed twelve feet; and is ſo terrific in its appearance, and dangerous in its conſequences, that no boat will venture to paſs at ſpring tide. After the tide is fairly paſt the iſlands, no veſtige of a *Bore* is ſeen, which may be owing to the great width of the Megna, in compariſon with the paſſages between the iſlands; but the effects of it are viſible, enough by the ſudden riſing of the tides.

William Jones

‘The Plants of India’.

Asiatic Researches 2 (1807 [1787])

XXII.

THE DESIGN OF A TREATISE ON THE PLANTS OF INDIA.

BY THE PRESIDENT.

THE greatest, if not the only, obstacle to the progress of knowledge in these provinces, except in those branches of it which belong immediately to our several professions, is our want of leisure for general researches; and, as *Archimedes*, who was happily master of his time, had not *space* enough to move the greatest weight with the smallest force, thus we, who have ample space for our inquiries, really want *time* for the pursuit of them. "Give me a place to "stand on, said the great mathematician, and I will "move the whole earth:" *Give us time*, we may say, *for our investigations, and we will transfer to* Europe *all the sciences, arts, and literature of* Asia. "Not to have despaired," however, was thought a degree of merit in the *Roman* General, even though he was defeated; and, having some hope that others may occasionally find more leisure than it will ever, at least in this country, be my lot to enjoy, I take the liberty to propose a work, from which very curious information, and possibly very solid advantage, may be derived.

Some hundreds of plants, which are yet imperfectly known to *European* botanists, and with the virtues of which they are wholly unacquainted, grow wild on the plains and in the forests of *India*. The *Amarcosh*, an excellent vocabulary of the *Sanscrit* language, contains in one chapter the names of about three hundred medicinal vegetables; the *Medini* may comprize many more; and the *Dravyabidana*, or *Dictionary of Natural Productions*, includes, I believe, a far greater number; the properties of which are distinctly related in medical tracts of approved authority. Now the first step, in compiling a treatise on the plants of *India*, should be to write their true names in *Roman* letters, according to the most accurate orthography, and in *Sanscrit* preferably to any vulgar dialect; because a learned language is fixed in books, while popular idioms are in constant fluctuation, and will not perhaps, be understood a century hence by the inhabitants of these *Indian* territories, whom future botanists may consult on the common appellations of trees and flowers. The childish denominations of plants from the persons who first described them, ought wholly to be rejected; for *Champaca* and *Hinna* seem to me not only more elegant, but far properer, designations of an *Indian* and an *Arabian* plant, than *Michelia* and *Lawsonia;* nor can I see without pain, that the great *Swedish* botanist considered it as *the supreme and only reward of labour* in this part of natural history, to preserve a name by hanging it on a blossom, and that he declared this mode of promoting and adorning botany, worthy of being *continued with holy reverence*, though so high an honour, he says, *ought to be conferred with chaste reserve, and not prostituted for the purpose of conciliating the good-will, or eternizing the memory, of any but his chosen followers; no, not even of saints.* His list of *an hundred and fifty* such names, clearly shows that his excellent works are the true basis of his just celebrity, which would have been feebly supported by the stalk of the *Linnæa.* From what proper name the *Plantain* is called *Musa,* I do not know; but it seems to be the *Dutch* pronunciation of the *Arabic* word for that vegetable, and ought not, therefore, to have appeared in his list; though, in my opinion, it is the only rational name in the muster-roll. As to the system of *Linnæus,* it is the system of Nature, subordinate indeed to the beautiful arrangement of *natural orders*, of which he hath given a rough sketch, and which may hereafter, perhaps, be completed: but the distribution of vegetables into *classes*, according to the number, length, and position of the stamens and pistils, and of those *classes* into *kinds* and *species*, according to certain marks of discrimination, will ever be found the clearest and most convenient of methods, and should therefore be studiously observed in the work which I now suggest; but I must be forgiven, if I propose to reject the *Linnæan* appellations of the twenty-four *classes*, because, although they appear to be *Greek* (and, if they really were so, that alone might be thought a sufficient objection) yet in truth they are not *Greek*, nor even formed by analogy to the language of *Grecians;* for *Polygamos*, *Monandros*, and the rest of that form, are both masculine and feminine; *Polyandra*, in the abstract, never occurs, and *Polyandrion* means a public cemitery; *diæcia* and *hiæcus* are not found in books of authority; nor, if they were, would they be derived from *dis*, but from *dia*, which would include the *triæcia;* let me add that the *twelfth* and *thirteenth* classes are ill distinguished by their appellations, independently of other exceptions to them, since the real distinction between them consists not so much in the *number* of their stamens, as in the *place* where they are inserted; and that the *fourteenth* and *fifteenth* are not more accurately discriminated by two words formed in defiance of grammatical analogy, since there are but *two* powers, or two *diversities of length* in each of those classes. *Calycopolyandros* might, perhaps, not inaccurately denote a flower of the *twelfth* class; but such a compound would still savour of barbarism or pedantry; and the best way to amend such a system of words is to efface it, and supply its place by a more simple nomenclator, which may easily be found. Numerals may be used for the *eleven* first classes, the former of two numbers being always appropriated to the *stamens*, and the latter to the *pistils*. Short phrases, as *on the calyx* or *calice*, *in the receptacle*, *two long*, *four long from one base*, *from two* or *many bases*, *with anthers connected*, *on the pistils*, *in two flowers*, *in two distinct plants*, *mixed*, *concealed*, or the like, will answer every purpose of discrimination; but I do not offer this as a perfect substitute for the words, which I condemn. The allegory of *sexes* and *nuptials*, even if it were complete, ought, I think, to be discarded, as unbecoming the gravity of men, who, while they search for truth, can have no business to inflame their imaginations; and, while they profess to give descriptions, have nothing to do with metaphors. Few passages in *Aloisia*, the most impudent book ever composed by man, are more wantonly indecent than the hundred forty-sixth number of the *Botanical Philosophy*, and the broad comment of its grave author, who *dares*, like *Octavius* in his epigram, *to speak with* Roman *simplicity*; nor can the *Linnæan* description of the *Arum*, and many other plants, be read in *English* without exciting ideas which the occasion does not require. Hence it is that no well-born and well educated woman can be advised to amuse herself with botany as it is now explained, though a more elegant and delightful study, or one more likely to assist and embellish other female accomplishments, could not possibly be recommended.

When the *Sanscrit* names of the *Indian* plants have been correctly written in a large paper-book, one page being appropriated to each, the fresh plants themselves, procured in their respective seasons, must be concisely, but accurately, *classed* and *described*; after which their several *uses* in medicine, diet, or manufactures, may be collected with the assistance of *Hindu* physicians, from the medical books in *Sanscrit*, and their accounts either disapproved or established by repeated experiments, as fast as they can be made with exactness.

By way of example, I annex the descriptions of five *Indian* plants; but am unable, at this season, to re-examine them, and wholly despair of leisure to exhibit others, of which I have collected the names, and most of which I have seen in blossom.

I. MUCHUCUNDA.

Twenty, from One Base.

Cal. Five-parted, thick; leaflets oblong.
Cor. Five petals, oblong.
Stam. From twelve to fifteen, rather long, fertile; five shorter, sterile. In some flowers, the *unprolific* stamens longer.
Pist. *Style* cylindric.
Peric. A capsule, with five cells, many-seeded.
Seeds. Roundish, compressed, winged.
Leaves. Of many different shapes.
Uses. The quality refrigerant.

One flower, steeped a whole night in a glass of water, forms a cooling mucilage, of use in virulent gonorrhœas. The *Muchucunda*, called also *Pichuca*, is exquisitely fragrant: its calyx is covered with an odoriferous dust; and the dried flowers in fine powder, taken as snuff, are said, in a *Sanscrit* book, almost instantaneously to remove a nervous head-ach.

Note. This plant differs a little from the *Pentapetes* of *Linnæus*.

II. BILVA, OR MALURA.

Many on the Receptacle, and One.

Cal. Four or five cleft beneath.

Cor. Four or five petals; mostly reflex.

Stam. Forty to forty-eight filaments; anthers mostly erect.

Pist. *Germ*, roundish; *Style* smooth, short; *Stigma* clubbed.

Peric. A spheroidal berry, very large; many-seeded.

Seeds. Toward the surface ovate, in a pellucid mucus.

Leaves. Ternate; common petiole long; leaflets subovate; obtusely notched with short petioles; some almost lanced.

Stem. Armed with sharp thorns.

Uses. The fruit nutritious, warm, cathartic; in taste delicious, in fragrance exquisite: its aperient and detersive quality, and its efficacy in removing habitual costiveness, having been proved by constant experience. The mucus of the seed is, for some purposes, a very good cement.

Note. This fruit is called *Srip'hala*, because it sprang, say the *Indian* poets, from the milk of *Sri*, the Goddess of Abundance, who bestowed it on mankind at the request of *Iswara*. whence he alone wears a chaplet of *Bilva* flowers: to him only the *Hindus* offer them; and, when they see any of them fallen on the ground, they take them up with reverence, and carry them to his temple. From the first blossom of this plant, that I could inspect, I had imagined that it belonged to the same class with the *Durio*, because the filaments appeared to be distributed in five sets; but in all that I have since examined, they are perfectly distinct.

III. SRINGATACA.

Four and One.

Cal. Four cleft, with a long peduncle above.

Cor. Four petals.

Stam. Anthers kidney-shaped.

Pist. *Germ* roundish; *Style* long, as the filaments; *Stigma* clubbed.

Seed. A *Nut* with four opposite angles (two of them *sharp* thorns) formed by the *Calyx*.

Leaves. Those which float on the water are rhomboidal; the two upper sides unequally notched, the two lower, right lines. Their petioles buoyed up by spindle-shaped spongy substances, not bladders.

Root. Knotty, like coral.

Uses. The fresh kernel, in sweetness and delicacy, equals that of the filbert. A mucus, secreted by minute glands, covers the wet leaves, which are considered as cooling.

Note. It seems to be the floating *Trapa* of *Linnæus*.

IV. PUTICARAJA.

Ten and One.

Cal. Five-cleft.

Cor. Five equal petals.

Peric. A thorny legumen; two seeds.

Leaves. Oval, pinnated.

Stem. Armed.

Uses. The seeds are very bitter, and, perhaps, tonic; since one of them, bruised and given in two doses, will, as the *Hindus* assert, cure an intermittent fever.

V. MADHUCA. *(See Vol. 1. page 300.)*

Many, *not* on the Receptacle, and One.

Cal. *Perianth* four or five-leaved.

Cor. One-petaled. *Tube* inflated, fleshy. *Border* nine, or ten, parted.

Stam. *Anthers* from twelve to twenty-eight, erect, acute, subvillous.

Pist. *Germ* roundish; *Style* long, awl-shaped.

Peric. A *Drupe*, with two or three *Nuts*.

Leaves. Oval, somewhat pointed.

Uses. The *tubes* esculent, nutritious; yielding, by distillation, an inebriating spirit, which, if the sale of it were duly restrained by law, might be applied to good purposes. A useful oil is expressed from the seed.

Note. It resembles the *Bassia* of *Koenig*.

Such would be the method of the work which I recommend; but even the specimen which I exhibit, might, in skilful hands, have been more accurate. Engravings of the plants may be annexed; but I have more than once experienced, that the best anatomical and botanical prints give a very inadequate, and sometimes a very false notion of the objects which they were intended to represent. As we learn a new language by reading approved compositions in it with the aid of a Grammar and Dictionary, so we can only study with effect the natural history of vegetables by analysing the plants themselves with the *Philosophia Botanica*, which is the *Grammar*, and the *Genera et Species Plantarum*, which may be considered as the *Dictionary* of that beautiful language, in which Nature would teach us what plants we must avoid as noxious, and what we must cultivate as salutary; for that the qualities of plants are *in some degree* connected with the *natural orders* and *classes* of them, a number of instances would abundantly prove.

William Chambers

‘Some account of the Sculptures and Ruins at Mavalipuram’. *Asiatic Researches* 1 (1788)

V.

SOME ACCOUNT OF THE

SCULPTURES AND RUINS AT MAVALIPURAM.

A PLACE A FEW MILES NORTH OF SADRAS, AND KNOWN TO SEAMEN BY THE NAME OF THE SEVEN PAGODAS.

BY WILLIAM CHAMBERS, ESQ.

AS amidst inquiries after the histories and antiquities of *Asia* at large, those of that division of it in which this society resides, may seem on many accounts to lay claim to a particular share of its attention, a few hints put down from recollection, concerning some monuments of *Hindoo* antiquity, which, though situated in the neighbourhood of *European* settlements on the *Choromandel* coast, have hitherto been little observed, may it is conceived, be acceptable, at least as they may possibly give rise hereafter to more accurate observations, and more complete discoveries on the same subject. The writer of this account went first to view them in the year 1772, and curiosity led him thither again in 1776; but as he neither measured the distances nor size of the objects, nor committed to writing at the time the observations he made on them, he hopes to be excused if, after the lapse of so many years, his recollection should fail him in some respects, and his account fall far short of that precision and exactness, which might have been expected, had there then existed in *India* so powerful an incentive to diligent inquiry, and accurate communication, as the establishment of this society must now prove.

The monuments he means to describe, appear to be the remains of some great city, that has been ruined many centuries ago; they are situated close to the sea, between *Covelong* and *Sadras*, somewhat remote from the high road, that leads to the different *European* settlements. And when he visited them in 1776, there was still a native village adjoining to them, which retained the ancient name, and in which a number of *Brahmins* resided, that seemed perfectly well acquainted with the subjects of most of the sculptures to be seen there.

The rock, or rather hill of stone, on which great part of these works are executed, is one of the principal marks for mariners as they approach the coast, and to them the place is known by the name of the *Seven Pagados*, possibly because the summits of the rock have presented them with that idea as they passed: but it must be confessed, that no aspect which the hill assumes, as viewed on the shore, seems at all to authorize this notion; and there are circumstances, which will be mentioned in the sequel, that would lead one to suspect, that this name has arisen from some such number of Pagados that formerly stood here, and in time have been buried in the waves. But, be that as it may, the appellation by which the natives distinguish it, is of a quite different origin: in their language, which is the *Tamulic*, (improperly termed *Malabar*,) the place is called *Mávalipuram*, which, in *Shanscrit*, and the languages of the more northern *Hindoos*, would be *Mahábalipúr*, or the *City of the great Bali*. For the *Tamulians*, (or *Malabars*,) having no *h* in their alphabet, are under a necessity of shortening the *Shanscrit* word *mahá*, *great*, and write it *má**. They are obliged also, for a similar reason, to substitute a *v* for a *b*, in words of *Shanscrit*, or other foreign original that begin with that letter; and the syllable *am*, at the end, is merely a termination, which, like *um* in *Latin*, is generally annexed to neuter substances†. To this etymology of the name of this place it may be proper to add, that *Bálí* is the name of a hero very famous in *Hindoo* romance; and that the river *Mávaligonga*, which waters the eastern side of *Ceylone*, where the *Tamulic* language also prevails, has probably taken its name from him, as, according to that orthography, it apparently signifies the *Ganges* of the great *Bálí*.

The rock, or hill of stone, above mentioned, is that which first engrosses the attention on approaching the place; for, as it rises abruptly out of a level plain of great extent, consists chiefly of one single stone, and is situated very near to the sea beach, it is such a kind of object as an inquisitive traveller would naturally turn aside to examine. Its shape is also singular and romantic, and, from a dis-

* They do indeed admit a substitute, but the abbreviation is most used.

† This explains also, why the *Shanscrit* word *Véd*, by which the *Hindoos* denominate the books of the law of their religion, is written by the *Tamulians Védam*, which is according to the true orthography of their language, and no mistake of *European* travellers, as some have supposed; while the same word is called *Béd* by the *Bengalies*, who have in effect no *V* in their alphabet.—See Dow, Vol. I. Dissert. P.41.

tant view, has an appearance like some antique and lofty edifice. On coming near to the foot of the rock from the north, works of imagery* and sculpture croud so thick upon the eye, as might seem to favour the idea of a petrified town, like those that have been fabled in different parts of the the world by too credulous travellers†. Proceeding on by the foot of the hill, on the side facing the sea, there is a pagoda rising out of the ground, of one solid stone, about sixteen or eighteen feet high, which seems to have been cut upon the spot out of a detached rock, that has been found of a proper size for that purpose. The top is arched, and the style of architecture, according to which it is formed, different from any now used in those parts. A little further on, there appears upon an huge surface of stone, that juts out a little from the side of the hill, a numerous group of human figures in bass relief, considerably larger than life, representing the most remarkable persons, whose actions are celebrated in the *Mahâbharit*, each of them in an attitude, or with weapons or other insignia, expressive of his character, or of some one of his most famous exploits. All these figures are, doubtless, much less distinct than they were at first; for, upon comparing these and the rest of the sculptures that are exposed to the sea air, with others at the same place, whose situation has afforded them protection from that element, the difference is striking; the former being every where much defaced, while the others are fresh as recently finished. This defacement is no where more observable, than in the piece of sculpture which occurs next in the order of description. This is an excavation in another part of the east side of the great rock, which appears to have been made on the same plan, and for the same purpose that Chowltries are usually built in that country; that is to say, for the accommodation of travellers. The rock is hollowed out to the size of a spacious room, and two or three rows of pillars are left, as a seeming support to the mountainous mass of stone which forms the roof. Of what pattern these pillars have originally been, it is not easy now to conjecture; for the air of the sea has greatly corroded them, as well as all the other parts of the

* Among these, one object, though a mean one, attracts the attention, on account of the grotesque and ridiculous nature of the design; it consists of two monkies cut out of one stone, one of them in a stooping posture, while the other is taking the insects out of his head.

† See SHAW's Travels, P. 155, et seq.

cave. And this circumstance renders it difficult to discover, at first sight, that there is a scene of sculpture on the side fronting the entrance. The natives, however, point it out, and the subject of it is manifestly that of *Krishen* attending the herds of *Nund Ghose*, the *Admetus* of the *Hindoos*; from which circumstance, *Krishen* is also called *Gopaul*, or the cowherd, as *Apollo* was entitled *Nomius*.

The objects which seem next to claim regard, are those upon the hill itself, the ascent of which, on the north, is, from its natural shape, gradual and easy at first, and is in other parts rendered more so, by very excellent steps cut out in several places, where the communication would be difficult or impracticable without them. A winding stair of this sort leads to a kind of temple cut out of the solid rock, with some figures of idols in high relief upon its walls, very well finished, and perfectly fresh, as it faces the west, and is therefore sheltered from the sea air. From this temple again there are flights of steps, that seem to have led to some edifice, formerly standing upon the hill; nor does it seem absurd to suppose, that this may have been a palace, to which this temple, as a place of worship, may have appertained. For, besides the small detached ranges of stairs that are here and there cut in the rock, and seem as if they had once led to different parts of one great building, there appear in many places, small water channels cut also in the rock, as if for drains to an house; and the whole top of the hill is strewed with small round pieces of brick, which may be supposed, from their appearance, to have been worn down to their present form, during the lapse of many ages. On ascending the hill by its slope on the north, a very singular piece of sculpture presents itself to view. On a plain surface of the rock, which may once have served as the floor of some apartment, there is a platform of stone, about eight or nine feet long, by three or four wide, in a situation rather elevated, with two or three steps leading up to it, perfectly resembling a couch or bed, and a lion very well executed at the upper end of it by way of pillow, the whole of one piece, being part of the hill itself. This the *Brahmins*, inhabitants of the place, call *the bed of Dhermarâjah*, or *Judishter*, the eldest of the five brothers, whose fortunes and exploits are the leading subject in the *Mahabhârit*. And at a considerable distance from this, at such a distance, indeed, as the apartment of the women might be supposed to be from that of the men, is a bath excavated also from the solid rock, with steps in the inside, which the *Brahmins* call the bath of *Dropedy*, the wife of *Judishter* and his brothers. How much credit is due to this tradition, and whether this stone couch may not have been anciently used as a kind of throne rather than a bed, is matter for future inquiry. A circumstance, however, which may, seem to favour this idea is, that a throne in the *Shanscrit*, and other *Hindoo* languages, is called *Singhâsen*, which is composed of the words *Singh*, a lion ; and *âsen*, a seat.

These are all that appear on that part of the upper surface of the hill, the ascent to which is on the north ; but, on descending from thence, you are led round the hill to the opposite side, in which there are steps cut from the bottom to a place near the summit, where is an excavation that seems to have been intended for a place of worship, and contains various sculptures of *Hindoo* Deities. The most remarkable of these, is a gigantic figure of *Vishnoo*, asleep on a kind of bed, with a huge snake wound about in many coils by way of pillow for his head ; and these figures, according to the manner of this place, are all of one piece, hewn from the body of the rock.

But though these works may be deemed stupendous, they are surpassed by others that are to be seen at the distance of about a mile, or a mile and an half, to the southward of the hill. They consist of two Pagodas, of about thirty feet long by twenty feet wide, and about as many in heighth, cut out of the solid rock, and each consisting originally of one single stone. Near these also stand an elephant full as big as life, and a lion much larger than the natural size, but very well executed, each hewn also out of one stone. None of the pieces that have fallen off in cutting these extraordinary sculptures, are now to be found near or any where in the neighbourhood of them, so that there is no means of ascertaining the degree of labour and time that has been spent upon them, nor the size of the rock or rocks from which they have been hewn, a circumstance which renders their appearance the more striking and singular. And though their situation is very near the sea-beach, they have not suffered at all by the corrosive air of that element, which has provided them with a defence against itself, by throwing up before them a high bank, that completely shelters them. There is also great symmetry in their form ; though that of the Pagodas is different from the style of architecture, according to which idol temples are now built in that country. The latter resembles the *Egyptian ;* for the towers are always pyramidical, and the gates and roofs flat, and without arches ; but these sculptures approach nearer to the *Gothic* taste, being surmounted by arched roofs or domes, that are not semicircular, but composed of two segments of circles meeting in a point at top. It is also observable that the lion in this group of sculptures, as well as that upon the stone couch above mentioned, are perfectly just representations of the true lion ; and the natives there give them the name, which is always understood to mean a lion in the *Hindoo* language, to wit, *Singh* ; but the figure, which they have made to represent that animal in their idol temples for centuries past, though it bears the same appellation, is a distorted monster, totally unlike the original ; insomuch that it has from hence been supposed that the lion was not anciently known in this country, and that *Singh* was a name given to a monster that existed only in *Hindoo* romance. But it is plain that that animal was well known to the authors of these works, who, in manners as well as arts, seem to have differed much from the modern *Hindoos.*

There are two circumstances attending these monuments, which cannot but excite great curiosity, and on which future inquiries may possibly throw some light. One is, that, on one of the Pagodas last mentioned, there is an inscription of a single line, in a character at present unkown to the *Hindoos.* It resembles neither the *Deyva-nágre,* nor any of the various characters connected with or derived from it, which have come to the writer's knowledge from any part of *Hindostan.* Nor did it, at the time he viewed it, appear to correspond with any character, *Asiatic* or *European,* that is commonly known. He had not then, however, seen the alphabet of the *Balic,* the learned language of the *Siamese,* a sight of which has since raised in his mind a suspicion, that there is a near affinity between them, if the character be not identically the same. But as these conjectures, after such a lapse of time, are somewhat vague, and the subject of them is perhaps yet within the reach of our researches, it is to be hoped that some method may be fallen upon of procuring an exact copy of this inscription.

The other circumstance is, that though the outward form of the Pagodas is complete, the ultimate design of them has manifestly not been accomplished, but seems to have been defeated by some extraordinary convulsion of nature. For the western side of the most northerly one, is excavated to the depth of four or five feet, and a row of pillars left on the outside to support the roof; but here the work has been stopped, and an uniform rent of about four inches breadth has been made throughout the solid rock, and appears to extend to its foundations, which are probably at a prodigious depth below the surface of the ground. That this rent has happened since the work begun, or while it was carrying on, cannot be doubted; for the marks of the mason's tools are perfectly visible in the excavated part on both sides of the rent, in such a manner as to show plainly that they have been divided by it. Nor is it reasonable to suppose that such a work would ever have been designed, or begun, upon a rock that had previously been rent in two.

Nothing less than an earthquake, and that a violent one, could apparently have produced such a fissure in the solid rock: and that this has been the case in point of fact, may be gathered from other circumstances, which it is necessary to mention in an account of this curious place.

The great rock above described is at some small distance from the sea, perhaps fifty or an hundred yards, and in that space the *Hindoo* village before mentioned stood in 1776. But close to the sea are the remains of a Pagoda, built of brick, and dedicated to *Sib*, the greatest part of which has evidently been swallowed up by that element; for the door of the innermost apartment, in which the idol is placed, and before which there are always two or three spacious courts surrounded with walls, is now washed by the waves; and the pillar used to discover the meridian at the time of founding the Pagoda* is seen standing at some distance in the sea. In the neighbourhood of this building there are some detached rocks,

* See Voyage du M. Gentil, Vol. I. Page 158.

washed also by the waves, on which there appear sculptures, though now much worn and defaced. And the natives of the place declared to the writer of this account, that the more aged people among them remembered to have seen the tops of several Pagodas far out in the sea, which being covered with copper (probably gilt) were particularly visible at sun rise, as their shining surface used then to reflect the sun's rays, but that now that effect was no longer produced, as the copper had since become incrusted with mould and verdegrease.

These circumstances look much like the effects of a sudden inundation ; and the rent in the rock above described makes it reasonable to conjecture, that an earthquake may have caused the sea to overflow its boundaries, and that these two formidable enemies may have joined, to destroy this once magnificent city. The account which the *Brahmins*, natives of the place, gave of its origin and downfal, partly, it should seem, on the authority of the *Mahabhârit*, and partly on that of later records, at the same time that it countenances this idea, contains some other curious particulars, which may seem to render it worthy of attention. Nor ought it to be rejected on account of that fabulous garb, in which all nations, but especially those of the east, have always clad the events of early ages.

" *Hirinâcheren* (said they) was a gigantic prince, that rolled " up the earth into a shapeless mass, and carried it down to the " abyss, whither *Vishnoo* followed him in the shape of an hog, " killed him with his tusks, and replaced the earth in its original " situation. The younger brother of *Hirinâcheren* was *Hirinakas-* " *sap*, who succeeded him in his kingdom, and refused to do homage " to *Vishnoo*. He had a son named *Pralhaud*, who at an early " age openly disapproved this part of his father's conduct, being " under the tuition of *Sokerâchârj*. His father persecuted him on " this account, banished him, and even sought to kill him, but was " prevented by the interposition of heaven, which appeared on " the side of *Pralhaud*. At length *Hirinakassap* was softened, " and recalled his son to his court, where, as he sat in full assembly, " he began again to argue with him against the supremacy of " *Vishnoo*, boasted that he himself was lord of all the visible world,

"and asked what *Vishnoo* could pretend to more. *Pralhaud* re-
"plied, that *Vishnoo* had no fixed abode, but was present every
"where. Is he, said his father, in that pillar? Yes, returned *Pral-*
"*haud.* Then let him come forth, said *Hirinakassap;* and, rising
"from his seat, struck the pillar with his foot; upon which *Vishnoo,*
"in the *Narasinghah Awtâr,* that is to say, with a body like a man,
"but an head like a lion, came out of the pillar, and tore *Hirina-*
"*kassap* in pieces. *Vishnoo* then fixed *Pralhaud* on his father's
"throne; and his reign was a mild and virtuous one, and as such
"was a contrast to that of his father. He left a son named *Nama-*
"*chee,* who inherited his power and his virtues, and was the father
"of *Balee,* the founder of the once magnificent city of *Mahâbali-*
"*poor,* the situation of which is said to be described in the following
"verse, taken from the *Mahabhârit.*

গঙ্গায়াঃ দক্ষিণেভাগে যোজনানাং শতদ্বয়ং
পঞ্চযোজন মাত্রো পূর্ব্বাব্ধিস্তু পশ্চিমে ।

The sense of which is literally this:

"South of the *Ganges* two hundred Yojen
"Five Yojen* westward from the eastern sea.

Such is the *Brahmin* account of the *origin* of this place. The *sequel* of its history, according to them, is as follows:

"The son of *Balee* was *Banâcheren,* who is represented as a
"giant with a thousand hands. *Anuredh,* the son of *Krishen,* came
"to his court in disguise, and seduced his daughter; which pro-
"duced a war, in the course of which *Anuredh* was taken prisoner,
"and brought to *Mahâbalipoor;* upon which *Krishen* came in
"person from his capital *Duârikah,* and laid siege to the place.
"*Sîb* guarded the gates, and fought for *Banâcheren,* who worship-

* The *Yojen* is a measure often mentioned in the *Shanscrit* books, and, according to some accounts, is equal to nine, according to others twelve *English* miles. But at that rate the distance here mentioned, between this place and the *Ganges,* is prodigiously exaggerated, and will carry us far south of *Ceylone.* This, however, is not surprising in an *Hindoo* poem; but, from the second line it seems pretty clear, that this city, at the time this verse was composed, must have stood at a great distance from the sea.

"ped him with his thousand hands; but *Krishen* found means to "overthrow *Sib*, and having taken the city, cut off all *Banâcheren's* "hands, except two, with which he obliged him to do him homage. "He continued in subjection to *Krishen* till his death; after which "a long period ensued, in which no mention is any where made "of this place, till a prince arose, whose name was *Malĕcheren*, who "restored the kingdom to great splendour, and enlarged and beau- "tified the capital. But in his time the calamity is said to have "happened by which the city was entirely destroyed; and the "cause and manner of it have been wrapt up by the *Brahmins* in "the following fabulous narration. *Malĕcheren*, (say they,) in an "excursion which he made one day alone, and in disguise, came to "a garden in the environs of the city, where was a fountain so "inviting, that two celestial nymphs had come down to bathe there. "The *Rajah* became enamoured of one of them, who condescended "to allow of his attachment to her; and she and her sister nymph "used thenceforward to have frequent interviews with him in that "garden. On one of those occasions, they brought with them a "male inhabitant of the heavenly regions, to whom they intro- "duced the *Rajah*; and between him and *Malĕcheren* a strict "friendship ensued; in consequence of which he agreed, at the "*Rajah's* earnest request, to carry him in disguise to see the court "of the divine *Inder*, a favour never before granted to any mortal. "The *Rajah* returned from thence with new ideas of splendour and "magnificence, which he immediately adopted in regulating his "court, and his retinue, and in beautifying his seat of government. "By this means *Mahâbalipoor* became soon celebrated beyond all "the cities of the earth; and an account of its magnificence "having been brought to the gods assembled at the court of *Inder*, "their jealousy was so much excited at it, that they sent orders to "the God of the Sea to let loose his billows, and overflow a place "which impiously pretended to vie in splendour with their celestial "mansions. This command he obeyed, and the city was at once "overflowed by that furious element, nor has it ever since been able "to rear its head."

Such is the mode in which the *Brahmins* choose to account for the signal overthrow of a place devoted to their wretched superstitions.

It is not, however, improbable, that the rest of this history may contain, like the mythology of *Greece* and *Rome*, a great deal of real matter of fact, though enveloped in dark and figurative representations. Through the disguise of these we may discern some imperfect records of great events, and of revolutions that have happened in remote times; and they perhaps merit our attention the more, as it is not likely that any records of ancient *Hindoo* history exist but in this obscure and fantastic dress. Their poets seem to have been their only historians, as well as divines; and whatever they relate, is wrapped up in this burlesque garb, set off, by way of ornament, with circumstances hugely incredible and absurd, and all this without any date, and in no other order or method, than such as the poet's fancy suggested, and found most convenient. Nevertheless, by comparing names and grand events, recorded by them, with those interspersed in the histories of other nations, and by calling in the assistance of ancient monuments, coins, and inscriptions, as occasion shall offer, some probable conjectures, at least, if not important discoveries, may, it is hoped, be made on these interesting subjects. It is much to be regretted, that a blind zeal, attended with a total want of curiosity, in the *Mohammedan* governors of this country, have been so hostile to the preservation of *Hindoo* monuments and coins. But a spirit of inquiry among *Europeans* may yet perhaps be successful; and an instance, which relates to the place above described, though in itself a subject of regret, leaves room to hope that futurity may yet have in store some useful discoveries. The *Kauzy* of *Madras*, who had often occasion to go to a place in the neighbourhood of *Mahâbalipoor*, assured the writer of this account, that within his remembrance a ryot of those parts had found, in plowing his ground, a pot of gold and silver coins, with characters on them which no one in those parts, *Hindoo* or *Mohammedan*, was able to decypher. He added, however, that all search for them would now be vain, for they had doubtless been long ago devoted to the crucible, as, in their original form, no one there thought them of any value.

The inscription on the Pagoda mentioned above, is an object which, in this point of view, appears to merit great attention. That the conjecture, however, which places it among the languages of *Siam*, may not seem in itself chimerical, the following passages from some authors of repute are here inserted, to show, that the idea of a communication having formerly subsisted between that country and the coast of *Choromandel*, is by no means without foundation; nay, that there is some affinity, even at this day, between the *Balic* and some of the *Hindoo* languages: and that the same mode of worship seems formerly to have prevailed in the *Deckan*, which is now used by the *Siamese*.

MONSIEUR DE LA LOUBERE, in his excellent account of *Siam*, speaks thus of the origin of the *Balic* language.

"The Siamese, says he, do not mention any country where the "Balic language, which is that of their laws and their religion, is at "present in use. They suppose, indeed, on the report of some "among them, who have been on the coast of Choromandel, that it "bears some resemblance to some of the dialects of that country; "but they at the same time allow, that the character in which it is "written is not known but among themselves. The secular Mis-"sionaries settled at Siam believe that this language is not entirely "a dead one; because they have seen in their hospital a man from "the neighbourhood of Cape Comorin, who mixed several Balic "words in his discourse, declaring that they were in use in his "country, and that he himself had never studied nor knew any "other than his mother tongue. They at the same time mention, "as matter of certainty, that the religion of the Siamese comes from "those parts; as they have read in a Balic book that Sommonaco-"dom, the idol of the Siamese, was the son of a King of Ceylone*."

The language of the man mentioned in this passage, who came from the neighbourhood of *Cape Comorin*, could be no other than the *Tamulic*; but the words here alluded to may very possibly have been derivatives from the *Shanscrit*, common to both that and the *Balic*.

* "Leis Siamois ne nomment aucun Pais, ou la langue Bali qui est celle de leurs loix et "de leur religion, soit aujourdhuy en usage. Ils soupconnent a la verite, sur le rapport de "quelques-uns d'entre eux, qui ont ete a la côte de Coromandel, que la langue Balic a quelque "resemblance avec quelqu'un des dialects de ce pais la: mais ils conviennent en même temps "que les lettres de la langue Balic ne sont connues que chez eux. Les Missionaires séculiers "a Siam croyent que cette langue n'est pas entierement morte; parce qu'ils ont vu dans leur "hopital un homme des environs du Cap de Comorin, qui metoit plusiers mots Balis dans "son langage, assurant qu'ils etoient en usage en son pais, et que luy n'avoit jamais etudié, et "ne savoit que sa langue maternelle. Ils donnent d'ailleurs pour certain que la religion des "Siamois vient de ces quartiers la, parce qu'ils ont lu dans un livre Balic que Sommonacodom "que les Siamois adorent, etoit fils d'un Roy de l'isle de Ceylone."

In another part of the same work, where the author treats of the history of *Sommonacodom* at large, on the authority of the *Balic* books, he says:

"The father of Sommonacodom, according to the same Balic "book, was a King of Teve Lanca, that is to say of the famous "Ceylone*."

Here it is observable, that, while the country of *Siam* seems to be utterly unknown, both to the natives of *Ceylone* and *Hindostan*, *Ceylone*, should nevertheless be so well known to the *Siamese*, and under the same appellation it bears in the *Shanscrit*. An epithet is also here prefixed to it, which seems to be the same as that used by the *Hindoos* in speaking of that island; for they also call it, in *Shanscrit*, *Dêve Lanca*, or *the Sacred Lanca*. From several passages in the same work it also appears, that the *Shanscrit* word *Mahâ*, which signifies *great*, is constantly used in the *Balic* language in the same sense. And the names of the days of the week are most of them the same in *Shanscrit* and in *Balic*, as may be seen in the following comparison of them.

Shanscrit.	*Balic.*	
Aditta-vâr,	Van Athit,	Sunday.
Soma-vâr,	Van† Tchân,	Monday.
Mungela-vâr,	Van Angkaan,	Tuesday.
Bouta-vâr,	Van Pout,	Wednesday.
Brahspati-vâr,	Van Prahout,	Thursday.
Soucra-vâr,	Van Souc,	Friday.
Sany-vâr,	Van Sâoa,	Saturday.

The same author gives, in another place, an account of a pretended print of a foot on a rock, which is an object of worship to the *Siamese*, and is called *Prabât*, or the venerable foot. For *prâ*, in *Balic*, he says, signifies *venerable*, which agrees with *prâper* and *pramesht* in *Shanscrit*; and *bât* in the same tongue is a foot, as *pâd* in *Shanscrit*. After which he goes on to say:

"We know that in the island of Ceylone, there is a pretended "print of a human foot, which has long been held in great venera-

* "Le pere de Sommonacodom etoit, selon ce mesme livre Bali, un Roy de Teve Lanca, cést a dire un Roy de la celebre Ceylan."

† Here one *Hindoo* word is substituted for another; for *Tchân* in *Hindostany*, and *Tchânder* in *Shanscrit*, signify the moon as well as *Soma*.

"tion. It represents, doubtless, the left foot; for the Siamese say "that Sommonacodom set his right foot on their *Prabat*, and his left "foot at Lanca*."

From KNOX'S History of *Ceylone* it appears, that the impression here spoken of is upon the hill called, by the *Chingelays*, *Hamalell;* by *Europeans*, *Adam's Peak;* and that the natives believe it to be the foot-step of their great idol *Buddou;* between the worship of whom, as described by KNOX, and that of *Sommonacodom*, as related by M. DE LA LOUBERE, there is a striking resemblance in many particulars, which it may be proper here to enumerate.

1st. Besides the foot-steps above mentioned, there is a kind of tree (which, from description, appears to be the *Pipel* tree, so well known in *India)* which the *Chingelays* hold sacred to *Buddou*, and the *Siamese* to *Sommonacodom;* insomuch that the latter deem it meritorious to hang themselves upon it. The *Chingelays* call it *Bogahah;* for *gahah*, in their language, signifies a tree; and *bo* seems to be an abbreviation of *Bod* or *Buddou;* and the *Siamese* call it, in *Balic*, *Pra si Mahà Pout*, which, according to DE LA LOUBERE'S interpretation, signifies the tree of the great *Pout*†. This he supposes to mean *Mercury;* for he observes that *Pout*, or *Poot*, is the name of that planet in the *Balic* term for *Wednesday;* and in another place, he says, *Pout* is one of the names of *Sommonacodom*. It is certain that *Wednesday* is called the name of *Bod*, or *Budd*, in all the *Hindoo* languages, among which the *Tamulic*, having no *b*, begins the word with a *p*, which brings it very near the *Balic* mode of writing it. It is equally certain that the days of the week, in all these languages, are called after the planets in the same order as with us; and that *Bod*, *Budd*, or *Pood*, holds the place of *Mercury*. From all which it should appear that *Pout*, which, among the *Siamese*, is another name for *Sommonacodom*, is itself a corruption of *Buddou*, who is the *Mercury* of the *Greeks*. And it is singular that, according to M. DE LA LOUBERE, the mother of *Sommonacodom* is called, in *Balic*,

* "On fait que dans l'isle de Ceylan, il y a un pretendu vestige de pié humain, que "depuis long temps y est en grande veneration. Il represente sans doute le pie gauche; car "les Siamois disent que Sommonacodom posa le pie droit a leur *prabat*, et le pie gauche a "Lanca."

† In vulgar *Siamese* they call it *Ton-pô*.

Maha-mania, or the *great Mania*, which resembles much the name of *Maia* the mother of *Mercury*. At the same time that the *Tamulic* termination *en*, which renders the word *Pooden*, creates a resemblance between this and the *Woden* of the *Gothic* nations, from which the same day of the week is denominated, and which, on that and other accounts, is allowed to be the *Mercury* of the *Greeks*.

2dly. The temples of *Sommonacodom* are called *Pihân;* and round them are habitations for the priests, resembling a college; so those of *Buddou* are called *Vihâr*, and the principal priests live in them as in a college. The word *Vihâr*, or, as the natives of *Bengal* would write it, *Bihâr*, is *Shanscrit;* and FERISHTAH, in his History of *Bengal*, says, that this name was given by the *Hindoos* to the Province of *Behâr*, because it was formerly so full of *Brahmins*, as to be, as it were, one great *seminary of Learning*, as the word imports.

3dly. The *Siamese* have two orders of priests, and so have the worshippers of *Buddou*. Both the one and the other are distinguished by a yellow habit, and by another circumstance, which must be mentioned in the words of the respective authors. KNOX says of the *Buddou* Priests, "They have the honour of carrying "the *Tallipot* with the broad end over their heads foremost, which "none but the King does." And M. DE LA LOUBERE says of the *Siamese* priests, "To defend themselves from the sun they have "the *Talapat*, which is their little umbrella, in the form of a "screen*."

The word here used is common to most of the *Hindoo* languages, and signifies *the leaf of the Palmyra tree*. M. DE LA LOUBERE mentions it as a *Siamese* word, without seeming to know its origin or primary signification.

4thly. The priests of *Buddou*, as well as those of *Sommonacodom*, are bound to celibacy, as long as they continue in the profession; but both the one and the other are allowed to lay it down and marry.

5thly. They both eat flesh, but will not kill the animal.

* "Pour se garentir du soleil ils ont le Talapat, qui est leur petit parasol en forme "d'ecran."

6thly. The priests of either nation are of no particular tribe, but are chosen out of the body of the people.

These circumstances plainly show that this is a system of religion different from that of the *Vèds;* and some of them are totally inconsistent with the principles and practice of the *Brahmins.* And, indeed, it is manifest, from KNOX'S whole account, that the religion of the *Chingelays* is quite distinct from that which prevails at this day among the *Hindoos,* nor does it appear that there is such a race of men as that of the *Brahmins* among them. The only part in which there seems to be any agreement is in the worship of the *Debtahs,* which has probably crept in among them from their *Tamulian* neighbours; but that is carried on in a manner very different from the *Brahminical* system, and appears to be held by the nation at large in very great contempt, if not abhorrence. KNOX'S account of it is this: "Their temples (i. e. those of the *Debtahs*) are, he says, "called *Covels,*" which is the *Tamulic* word for *Pagoda.* He then goes on to say, "A man piously dis-"posed, builds a small house at his own charge, which is the *temple,* "and *himself becomes priest thereof.* This house is seldom called "*God's House,* but most usually: *Jacco,* the *Devil's.*" But of the prevailing religion he speaks in very different terms, and describes it as carried on with much parade and splendour, and attended with marks of great antiquity. "The pagodas, or temples of their gods, "says he, are so many that I cannot number them. Many of them "are of rare and exquisite work, built of hewn stone, engraven "with images and figures; but by whom, and when, I could not "attain to know, the inhabitants themselves being ignorant therein. "But sure I am, they were built by far more ingenious artificers "than the Chingelays that now are on the land. For the Portu-"guese, in their invasions, have defaced some of them, which there "is none found that hath skill enough to repair to this day." In another place, he says, "Here are some ancient writings, engraven, "upon rocks, which puzzle all that see them. There are divers great "rocks in divers parts in *Cande Uda,* and in the northern parts. "These rocks are cut deep with great letters for the space of some "yards, so deep that they may last to the world's end. No body "can read them, or make any thing of them. I have asked Mala-"bars and Gentoos, as well as Chingelays and Moors, but none of "them understood them. There an ancient temple, Goddiladenni "in Yattanour, stands by a place where there are these "letters." From all which the antiquity of the nation and their religion is sufficiently evident; and from other passages it is plain, that the worship of *Buddou*, in particular, has been from remote times a very eminent part of that religion; for the same author, speaking of the tree at *Anurodgburro*, in the northern part of the island, which is sacred to *Buddou*, says, "The due per-"formance of this worship they reckon not a little meritorious; "insomuch that as they report, ninety Kings have reigned there "successively, where, by the ruins that still remain, it appears they "spared not for pains and labour, to build temples and high "monuments to the honour of this God, as if they had been born "to hew rocks and great stones, and lay them up in heaps. These "Kings are now happy spirits, having merited it by these labours." And again he says, "For this God, above all other, they seem to "have an high respect and devotion," &c.

And from other authorities it will appear, that this worship has formerly been by no means confined to *Ceylone*, but has prevailed in several parts of *India* prior to that of the *Brahmins*; nay, that this has been the case even so late as the ninth and twelfth centuries of the *Christian* Æra.

In the well-known* *Anciennes Relations*, translated from the *Arabic*, by that eminent orientalist EUSEBIUS RENAUDOT, that the *Arabian* traveller gives this account of the custom of dancing-women, which continues to this day in the *Decan*, but is not known among the *Hindoos* of *Bengal*, or *Hindostan* proper.

"There are in India public women, called *women of the idol*, "and the origin of this custom is this: when a woman has made "a vow for the purpose of having children, if she brings into the "world a pretty daughter, she carries it to *Bod*, (so they call the "idol which they adore,) and leaves it with him †."

This is a pretty just account of this custom, as it prevails at

* Anciennes Relations des Indes et de la Chine, de deux Voyageurs Mohametans, qui y allerent dans le neuvieme Siecle. *Paris* 1718, 8vo.

† " Il y a dans les Indes des femmes publiques, appellés, femmes de l'idole, l'origine de " cette coustume est telle: Lors qu'une femme a fait un voeu pour avoir des enfans, si elle " met au monde une belle fille, elle l'apporte au *Bod*, c'est ainsi qu'ils appellent l'idole qu'ils " adorent, aupres duquel elle la laisse, &c. Anc. Rel. p. 109.

this day in the *Decan ;* for children are, indeed, devoted to this profession by their parents, and when they grow up in it, they are called, in *Tamulic, Devadâsi,* or *female slaves of the idol.* But it is evident they have changed their master since this *Arabian* account was written, for there is no idol of the name of *Bod* now worshipped there. And the circumstance of this custom being unknown in other parts of *India,* would lead one to suspect, that the *Brahmins,* on introducing their system of religion into that country, had thought fit to retain this part of the former worship, as being equally agreeable to themselves and their new disciples.

The same *Arabian* travellers give us an account of a very powerful race of *Hindoo* kings, according to them, indeed, the most powerful in *India,* who then reigned on the *Malabar* coast with the title of *Balhâra.* Their dominion appears to have extended over *Guzerat,* and the greatest part, if not the whole, of the ancient kingdom of *Visiapoor.* For the *Arabian* geographer quoted by M. REN UDOT, makes *Nahelvârah* the metropolis of these princes, which is, doubtless, *Nahervalah,* the ancient capital of *Guzerat ;* though M. RENAUDOT seems not to have known that place ; and the rest of the description sufficiently shows the great extent of their dominion southward. M. D'ANVILLE speaks of this race of kings on the authority of the *Arabian* geographer EDRISI, who wrote in the twelfth century, according to whom it appears, that their religion was, even so late as that period, not the *Brahminical,* but that of which we are now speaking. M. D'ANVILLE'S words are these : "Edrisi acquaints us with the religion which this Prince "professed in saying, that his worship was addressed to *Bodda,* "who, according to St. Jerome and Clemens Alexandrinus, was "the founder of the sect of the Gymnosophists, in like manner as "the Brahmins were used to attribute their institution to Brahma*."

The authority of CLEMENS ALEXANDRINUS is also cited on the same subject by RELANDUS in his 11th Dissertation, where, treating of the language of *Ceylone,* he explains the word *Vehâr,* above spoken of, in these terms.

* "L'Edrisi nous instruit sur la religion que professoit ce Prince, en disant que son culte "s adressoit a Bodda, que selon St. JEROME and St. CLEMENT D'ALEXANDRIE, avoit ete "l'instituteur des Gymnosophistes comme les Brachmanes rapportoient a Brahma leur "institut." Ant. Geog. de L'Inde, p. 94.

"Vehâr signifies a temple of their principal God Buddou, who, "as Clemens Alexandrinus has long ago observed, was worshipped "as a God by the Hindoos*."

After the above quotations, the following extract from the voyage of that inquisitive and ingenious traveller M. GENTIL, published in 1779, is given as a further and very remarkable illustration of this subject.

"This system is also that of the Brahmins of our time; it forms "the basis of that religion, which they have brought with them into "the southern parts of the Peninsula of Hindostan, into Madura, Tanjore, and Maissore.

"There was then in those parts of India, and principally on "the Coast of Choromandel and Ceylone, a sort of worship, the "precepts of which we are quite unacquainted with. The God, "Baouth, of whom at present they know no more in India than the "name, was the object of this worship; but it is now totally "abolished, except that there may possibly yet be found some "families of Indians, who have remained faithful to Baouth, and do "not acknowledge the religion of the Brahmins, and who are on "that account separated from and despised by the other casts.

"I have not, indeed, heard that there are any such families in "the neighbourhood of Pondichery; but there is a circumstance "well worthy of remark, which none of the travellers that have "treated of the Coast of Choromandel and Pondichery seem to "have noticed. It is this, that at a short league's distance to the "south of this town, in the plain of Virapatnam, and pretty near "the river, we find a statue of granite very hard and beautiful. "This statue, which is from three feet to three and a half in heighth, "is sunk in the sand to the waist, and weighs doubtless many thou-"sand weight; it is, as it were abandoned in the midst of this "extensive plain. I cannot give a better idea of it, than by saying, "that it exactly agrees with and resembles the Sommonacodom "of the Siamese; its head is of the same form, it has the same "features, its arms are in the same attitude, and its ears are exactly "similar. The form of this divinity, which has certainly been

* "*Vehâr*, templum dei primarii Buddoe βουττα quem Indos ut Deum venerari jam olim "notavit Clemens Alexandrinus. Strom. lib. 1. p. 223. Rel. Diss. pars tertia, p. 85.

" made in the country, and which in no respect resembles the pre- " sent idols of the Gentoos, struck me as I passed this plain. I " made various inquiries concerning this singular figure, and the " Tamulians, one and all, assured me that this was the God Baouth, " who was now no longer regarded, for that his worship and his " festivals had been abolished ever since the Brahmins had made " themselves masters of the people's faith*."

M. GENTIL then goes on to say a good deal more upon this subject, in the course of which he supposes, that this Deity is the *Fo* of the *Chinese*, whose worship, by their own accounts, was brought from *India*. And, indeed, the abridgment of the name *Pout*, mentioned in a note of this paper, which the vulgar *Siamese* reduce to the single syllable *Po*, seems to countenance this opinion. But as this is foreign to our present purpose, and the above passages, it is hoped, are sufficient to establish what was proposed, it seems high time to take leave of this subject, with an apology for that prolixity, which is inseparable from this kind of discussion.

17th june, 1784.

* " Ce systeme est aussi celui des Brames de nos jours ; il fait la Base de la religion qu'ils " ont aportee dans le sud de la presqu'isle de l'Indostan, le Madure, le Tanjaour, et le Maissour.

" Il y avoit alors dans ces parties de l'Inde, & principalement a la Côte de Coromandel & " a Ceylan, un Culte dont on ignore absolument les Dogmes : le Dieu Baouth, dont on ne " connoit aujourd'hui, dans l'Inde, que le Nom, etoit l'objet de ce Culte ; mais il est tout-a- " fait aboli, si ce n'est qu'il se trouve encore quelques familles d'Indiens séparés & méprisées " des autres Castes, qui sont restées fideles à Baouth, & qui ne reconnoissent point la religion " des Brames.

" Je n'ai pas entendu dire qu'il y ait de ces familles aux environs de Pondichery ; cepen- " dant, une chose tres digne de remarque, & a laquelle aucun des Voyageurs qui parlent de la " Côte de Coromandel & de Pondichery, n'ont fait attention, est que l'on trouve a une petite " lieue au sud de cette Ville, dens la plaine de Virapatnam, assez pres de la Riviere, une statue " de *Granit* tres-dur & tres-beau : cette statue, d'enveron trois pieds a trois pieds & demi de " hauteur, est enfoncée dans le sable jusqu' a la Ceinture, & pese sans doute plusieurs Milliers ; " elle est comme abandonnée au milieu de cette vaste plaine : je ne peux mieux en donner une idée, " qu'en disant qu'elle est exactement conforme & ressemblante a *Sommonacodom* des Siamois ; " c'est la même Forme de Tête, ce sont les mêmes traits dans le Visage, c'est la même attitude " dans les Bras, & les Oreilles sont absolument semblables. La forme de cette divinite, qui " certainement a été faite dans le pays, & qui ne ressemble en rien aux divinités actuelles des " Gentils, m'avoit frappélorsque je passai dans cette plaine ; je fis diverses informations sur " cette figure singuliere, les Tamoults m'assurerent tous que c'etoit Baouth qu' on ne regardoit " plus ; que son Culte & ses fêtes etoient cessées depuis que les Brames s'etoient rendus les " Maitres de la Croyance du peuple."

John Forbes Royle

Illustrations of the Botany of the Himalayan Mountains. **London: WH Allen, 1839**

ILLUSTRATIONS

OF THE

BOTANY OF THE HIMALAYAN MOUNTAINS.

THE introductory observations having enabled us to appreciate the extent and general nature of the territories comprised within the boundaries of India, and shown the general uniformity, or rather almost insensible gradation of temperature, on which so greatly depends the natural distribution of animal and vegetable forms, as well as those which are the product of art, we now proceed to the more immediate object of this work; that of illustrating the Flora of the Himalaya Mountains. Here we shall find the changes in climate more rapid at successive elevations, and the modifications in plants correspondingly great, whether we ascend the great mountain ranges near the Southern extremity of India or those towards its most Northern limits. It is necessary only to enumerate the sources whence our information has been drawn, to show that these have been sufficiently extended to allow some reliance being placed on the inferences which are deduced.

The situation of the Honourable Company's Botanic Garden at Saharunpore in 30° of Northern latitude, one thousand miles to the north-west of Calcutta, elevated as many feet above the level of the sea, and placed nearly at the head of the extensive plain which forms the great Gangetic valley, was admirably adapted for enabling an observer to obtain a knowledge of the Flora of the plains of Northern India, as well as of the Himalayan Mountains, it being within thirty miles of the commencement of the successive ranges which form that great barrier between the dominions of the British and the territories of the Chinese.

The herbarium consists of at least 3,500 species; collected, 1st, in the plains which form some of the north-western provinces of India, from 28° to 31° of N. lat. or from about Delhi to the banks of the Sutledge; 2d, of plants growing in the mountainous tract included between the latter river and the Ganges, or between 30° and 31½° of

N. lat. from the level of the plains up to the Snowy Passes; with these may be enumerated the plants of Cashmere, which can only be considered a valley of the Himalaya; the third portion consists of plants from Kunawur, a country which being beyond the influence of the periodical rains, has its climate, and consequently many of its animal and vegetable productions, sufficiently modified to entitle them to a separate consideration.

The researches both in the hills and the plains having been carried on at all seasons for a series of years, the collection may be considered as giving (with the exception of the lower tribes of *Cryptogamic* plants) a very fair idea of the Flora of that part of India.

The plants from Cashmere were obtained in 1828, 1829, and 1831, by means of native plant collectors sent with the northern merchants, on their return to that valley after disposing of their annual investments of fruit and shawls in the plains of India. Along with dried specimens, seeds and living plants were also brought down, and grown either in the Saharunpore Botanic Garden or in the Experimental Nursery in the Hills. This collection can only be considered as giving a general idea of the nature of the Flora of that far-famed valley.

The collection from Kunawur, consisting of several hundred species from a cold and arid country, made in two years during the seasons of vegetation, will give a very good idea of the nature of the Flora of that tract. The first collection was made for me in 1825, by the late Lieutenant Maxwell, of his Majesty's 11th Dragoons, and the second by my plant collectors in 1831. With these, through the kindness of the distinguished Mr. Brown, I have had an opportunity of comparing a collection in his possession, made by R. Inglis, Esq. of Canton, in the year 1830, as well as a small collection in the British Museum made by that adventurous traveller the late Mr. Moorcroft, in his journey beyond the Himalaya; a few specimens from the same tract of country sent to Dr. Wallich by Messrs. Webb, Moorcroft, and Gerard, may be seen in the East-India Herbarium.

That attention may not appear to have been confined to too limited a portion of the Himalaya, the magnificent herbarium formed by Dr. Wallich, and presented by the Honourable the Court of Directors of the East-India Company to the Linnean Society, has been constantly consulted, for the purpose of showing either analogy or difference in the vegetation of different portions of the Himalayas. The plants of these mountains in the above collection consist of specimens from Dr. Wallich's plant collectors in Kemaon, a portion of the Himalaya extending from the Ganges to the Gogra, together with many sent by Drs. Govan and Gerard, from Garhwal and Sirmore. The great proportion, however, consists of plants collected by Dr. Wallich himself in Nepal and its mountains, together with some from the same country collected by Dr. Buchanan Hamilton. The most southern and also most western point from which any considerable collection has been obtained by Dr. Wallich's plant collectors is from the mountains above Silhet and Pundooa,—so that the space whence the several collections have been formed extends over ten degrees of latitude and nearly twenty of longitude.

Though there is no intention, in the present work, of treating of the Botany of India in general, yet as it is proposed particularly to note, not only the difference in the vegetation of the Hills and of the Plains and the distribution of particular families, but also for what other plants, chiefly the useful products of similarly constituted countries, India is peculiarly adapted, it may not be improper to remark, that the observations respecting the distribution of different tribes will be deduced from the collections and works of Drs. Roxburgh and Buchanan, Wallich and Wight; as well as from the author's own collections made in the most northern provinces of India.

It is hardly necessary, after the liberality with which Dr. Wallich placed his treasures in the hands of the Botanical World, to mention, that previous to his departure for India he expressed his most anxious desire that every possible use should be made of that portion of his collection which he had not himself had an opportunity of publishing, and joined in an application to the Honourable the Court of Directors, that his unpublished drawings should be placed at the disposal of the author for the purpose of selections being made for the present work. Major-General Hardwicke has also most kindly placed in the author's hands ten volumes of drawings made in the plains of Northern India, and also while travelling nearly thirty years ago in the Himalayas. These, when so used, will be duly acknowledged, but the greater portion of the illustrations will be from drawings made under the author's own direction. These were executed by the Honourable Company's painters, who during Dr. Wallich's absence in England were by the orders of the then Governor-General of India, the Earl of Amherst, sent from the Botanic Garden at Calcutta to that of Saharunpore.

Some explanation may perhaps be expected upon the preference given to the publication of the illustrations according to the natural families, as well as upon the particular series which has been adopted. For the latter no better reason than that of convenience can be assigned, as the celebrated De Candolle is the only botanist who has attempted an arrangement of all plants according to their natural families. For the adoption of the natural method of classification, no apology is in the present day necessary, as the advantages have been so frequently displayed ever since the illustrious Mr. Brown proved them in his Prodromus of the Plants of New Holland, and has so often illustrated them by his luminous observations on the Flora of different countries; a course which has been followed by the great Humboldt and other celebrated botanists. For whether we consider the structure, classification, geographical distribution, properties, or uses of plants, in every way does the natural method afford numerous advantages, particularly as our observations, instead of being confined to species and genera, may in general be made applicable to whole tribes of plants.

This we shall see to be more particularly the case in noticing the geographical distribution and uses of different families of plants, and in making the application to India of the result of our observations; for no where is the field more extended, and at the same time more favourable for acclimating the useful productions of different countries. In the peninsula of India, and in the neighbouring island of Ceylon, we have a climate capable of producing cinnamon, cassia, pepper, and cardamoms. The coffee grown on the Malabar Coast is of so superior a quality as to be taken to Arabia and re-exported as Mocha coffee; the Tinnevelly senna brings the highest price in the London market; and there is little doubt that many other valuable products of tropical countries may be acclimated, particularly as several are already in a flourishing condition in the Botanic Garden at Calcutta, such as the cocoa and nutmeg, as well as the camphor, pimento, cajeput, and cashew-nut trees. In the Neelgherries a favourable site might without doubt be found for the cinchona, as well as the different kinds of ipecacuanha; and as the potatoe has been introduced into almost every part of India, equal success and considerable benefit would probably result from introducing the different kinds of arracacha, so much prized for their roots as food for the natives of South America.

Along the coasts of the Bay of Bengal the cocoa and areca-nut palms flourish and abound, and the continent every where produces indigo, cotton, tobacco, sugar, and opium. The first, hardly of any note as an Indian product thirty years ago, is now imported in the largest quantities into England. The cotton, though indigenous to India, has not been in any way improved, though many provinces seem peculiarly well adapted for the culture, particularly Malwa, and those to the north-west. The tobacco brought home by Dr. Wallich from Martaban was pronounced by competent judges in England to be equal to the best from America; while the Persian tobacco, the produce of a peculiar species, the *Nicotiana persica* of Dr. Lindley, is celebrated, and commands a high price both in India and Europe. This, there is every probability in considering, would succeed well in the N.W. provinces which are nearest its native country. The opium of Patna is preferred in China, and that of Malwa bids fair to rival Turkey opium in the European market. The sugar-cane is cultivated in every part of India, but very inferior sugar has hitherto been produced; lately, however, a manufactory has been established near Calna, a new mine opened in the Burdwan coal formation, and very superior specimens of sugar sent home. Here the occurrence of sugar at the surface of the soil, and coal only a few feet below it, in a country where labour is so cheap, ought to be attended with decidedly favourable results. If from these we turn our attention to other products, we shall still see that there are great capabilities even where we should least expect them: for though India is generally looked upon chiefly as a rice country, wheat has been imported into and sold at a profit in England from the northern provinces, and flour for making starch is now one of the annual exports from Calcutta. Of dyes, medicinal drugs, resins, and gums, there are great varieties, and more might be successfully introduced. Timber of every kind is every where abundant, the coasts producing teak, ebony, and many others; the interior, saul, sissoo, bamboos, and rattans, while a great variety of plants, though but little known, yield excellent material for cordage.

The northern provinces and the hills forming the more immediate object of this work, will be more fully considered in the sequel; it is sufficient at present to observe, that at one season they grow European grains and at another those which are peculiar to the tropics: and that many perennials of both these two climates seem to succeed equally well in the northern provinces of India; here, therefore, many of the useful products of Persia, Arabia, and Barbary, might be grown.

The hill provinces enjoy nearly similar advantages; the forests are formed of oaks and pines, and the hill-men make their strongest ropes for crossing rivers with hemp, which every where abounds and is of the finest quality; opium, rhubarb, and turpentine, form articles of commerce, as well as musk, Thibet wool, and borax from the other kingdoms of Nature.

Somewhere in the valleys at the foot of these hills, or at moderate elevations, the more generally useful productions of European countries might be successfully introduced, as the olive and the hop; the latter would be particularly beneficial, as a brewery has been established in the hills, where the climate is excellent.

Here also, as I have recommended in a report to Government, there is considerable prospect of success in the cultivation of the tea plant, for the different elevations allow of every variety of climate being selected, and "the geographical distribution of this plant is sufficiently extended to warrant its being beneficially cultivated."

The above few examples will be sufficient to show that in the climates where these varied productions grow, others from different countries may be successfully introduced. It is not to be expected that equal success will attend every attempt, but where so many circumstances are favourable there is little probability of failure in many, if the proper means are adopted for ensuring success; and these consist chiefly in applying to one country our knowledge of the climate and productions of another, where any similarity of circumstances occur; and I entertain sanguine expectations that, with moderate attention and proper encouragement, the products of India may be still more varied, almost indefinitely increased in quantity, and very much improved in quality. Hitherto, instead of endeavouring to call forth the resources of the country, it seems rather to have been wished to repress its energies, by charging upon articles of well-known inferior quality a higher duty if imported from the East-Indies than from other parts of the world.

Having mentioned that considerable uniformity of temperature and of vegetable productions occurs over a very great expanse of Indian territory, we proceed to adduce specimens from some of the most northern parts as an indication of the truth of the observation. Delhi, the capital of Northern India, situated on the western bank of the Jumna, nearly at the upper part of the inclined slope which forms the plains of India, is elevated about eight hundred feet above the level of the sea. The soil is barren and remarkable for its saline efflorescence, and the wells for the brackishness of their water. The rocky soil, always exposed to the solar rays, absorbs much heat, and a high temperature with considerable dryness is produced in the hot weather; but from the openness of the country, and exposure to winds which pass over extensive lakes in the vicinity, a greater degree of cold is produced in winter than we should otherwise expect. We do not therefore find in the Flora round Delhi such plants as *Guttiferæ*, *Anonaceæ*, and *Strychneæ*, which requiring moisture with heat, flourish in the southern provinces of India. But the climate in general being favourable, and the minimum of cold not long continued, we find many of the plants which are common in warmer parts of India, but which are not found at Saharunpore. Among these may be enumerated *Ailantus excelsa*, *Prosopis spicigera*, and *Salvadora persica*, with *Capparis aphylla*, and species of *Hibiscus*, *Grewia*, and *Flacourtia*, as shrubs, together with such herbaceous plants as *Anisochilus carnosus*, *Ærua Javanica*, *Elytraria crenata*, *Fagonia Mysoriensis*, *Lepidagathis cristata*, *Acanthus Madraspatensis*, *Echinops echinatus*, *Cenchrus echinoides*, also species of *Cocculus*, *Leucas*, *Aristolochia*, *Polygala*, and *Ionidium*. *Cochlearia flava* spreads along the banks of the Jumna, nearly up to Delhi. A species of *Farsetia* and *Linaria ramosissima* are found; the latter only enumerated in the Flora of more southern parts of India; while a *Salsola*, which is common, indicates the saline nature of the soil. *Balanites Ægyptiaca*, *Alhagi maurorum*, *Salvadora persica*, and species of *Ethulia*, *Heliotropium*, &c. are remarkable as occurring all over the Northern provinces of Hindostan, and being equally common in Egypt, while the presence of a species of *Picnomon* and one of *Kentrophyllum* is interesting, as forming a point of resemblance to the Flora of the South of Europe.

Most of the plants which have been enumerated, I also found on the hills near Lohargaon and Mirzapore; several were recognized by Dr. Wight as occurring in the most southern parts of the peninsula, and nearly all have been described by Dr. Roxburgh as occurring in the neighbourhood of Samulcottah.

To show the effects of protection and culture, *Xanthochymus dulcis* may be adduced as a remarkable instance; this tree, which is found only in the southern parts of India, and which would not live in the more exposed climate of Saharunpore, exists as a large tree in the garden of the King of Delhi; but here, surrounded by the numerous buildings within the lofty palace wall, in the midst of almost a forest of trees, with perpetual irrigation from a branch of the canal which flows through the garden; an artificial climate is produced which enables a plant even so sensitive of cold as one of the *Guttiferæ* to flourish in the open air at Delhi, where it is highly prized, and reported to have milk thrown over its roots, as well as its fruit protected from plunder by a guard of soldiers.

The animal kingdom does not present many peculiarities to distinguish this district from that of India in general. The Lion is however almost peculiar, being found beyond Hansi on the edge of the desert. The Neel-gae is common in the plains, and the Porcupine and a species of Hedgehog which I have called *Erinaceus Indicus*, and the short-tailed Manis, are common about Delhi.

In crossing the Jumna in the latitude of Delhi, and entering the Doab or flat country between that river and the Ganges, a considerable difference is observed in the vegetation, the arid-looking thorny shrubs having disappeared, and the trees become more luxuriant; this is consequent chiefly upon a change of soil, and is more observable as we approach Meerut and Saharunpore;—if we take the latter as an example, we shall obtain a fair specimen of the Flora of the plains of northern India.

The district is flat with but slight inequalities, intersected by several rivulets and watered by the Doab canal. The soil is generally clayey with a proportion of sand, having a substratum in many places of hard and retentive brick clay, and in some situations *kunkur*, imbedded in masses sometimes large enough to be used in the erection of tombs, but is generally employed only for making a coarse kind of lime. Below this, small gravel is brought up in digging wells. A part of the district is rather more elevated than the rest, therefore drier; and water being more distant from the surface, the wells are deeper; this tract is called *khadir*, while towards the hills and beyond Kheree, the ground being low, moist, and frequently overflowed, is called *bangur* land.

The climate has been described as being that of India in general; but modified by the more northern position of Saharunpore, as the cold commences earlier, continues later, and is succeeded by a short spring in February and March, when the deciduous trees come into leaf, and the greater number into flower; the heat in May and June is considerable, and the rains plentiful. The periods of occurrence of the maximum and minimum temperature (105° and 37° in June and January) being remote, the rise and fall very gradual and divided between several months, a degree and continuance of cold weather is produced, which allows of the growth of many annuals apparently incompatible with the Flora of the country; while the great rise of temperature in the hot months, and the influence of the periodical rains, permit the successful cultivation of tropical plants, which appear equally at variance with the European-like cultivation of the cold-weather months; as the great heat, however, is never very long continued, nor the cold excessive, many perennials both of tropical and temperate climates thrive here in the open air, and this latitude may be considered as being nearly the northern limit of the Flora of India, as well as the southern boundary of that which is called the Oriental or Persian region.

Tropical plants cannot easily extend beyond this, for though they can resist a moderate degree of cold in a dry atmosphere, in the north-western provinces there is always a good deal of rain about Christmas, when the cold, much increased in consequence of the freer radiation which ensues on the clearance of the atmosphere, combined with the moisture, is injurious to many plants, which have besides to undergo great vicissitudes of temperature instead of the equality of the tropics. Hence in valleys and in the midst of thick forests, where the climate is moister, the radiation less free, and the range of the thermometer less extensive, we find the same plants reaching a much higher latitude than in the open plains. This we shall see strikingly exemplified as we pass through the belt of jungle in ascending the Himalayas from the plains. With respect to perennials of more temperate climates, though many thrive, others, as well as most from alpine situations, suffer, not so much from the great heat, which when shaded from the direct rays of the sun they resist, nor from the equable moisture of the rains, but from the clear weather which succeeds, when there is always a good deal of moisture, with great heat during the day and considerable cold at night: a state of the atmosphere which is not only hurtful to plants, but injurious to the human frame; we cannot therefore expect to find, either in a wild or cultivated state, such plants as the *Guttiferæ*, impatient of the least degree of cold; for even the mangoe, though flourishing as a tree and producing fine fruit, requires when young to be defended from the cold by a covering of grass; the same may be said of the custard apple (*Anona squamosa*), of which indeed old plants are frequently killed by the cold of winter. The plantain, covered by sheathing petioles, is enabled to resist a greater degree of cold, and survive through the winter, while the more delicate *Papaya* is generally killed. The pine apple does not flourish, but the *Agave* is as vigorous as in more southern latitudes, and *Pandanus odoratissimus* is only kept alive in the shade of trees. The arboreous vegetation is the same as generally found in the plains of upper India, consisting almost entirely of Dicotyledonous trees, which lose their leaves in the cold weather as completely as trees in more northern climates. The Monocotylenous trees consist only of *Phœnix sylvestris*, and of the almost stemless *Phœnix humilis*. The most common trees are *Dalbergia sissoo*, *Acacia Serissa*, *Arabica*, and *Farnesiana*, *Cedrela Toona*, *Butea frondosa*, *Ægle marmelos*, *Feronia elephantum*, *Nageia Putranjiva*, and species of *Melia*, *Ficus*, *Morus*, *Trophis*, *Bauhinia*, *Cordia*, *Gmelina*, and *Premna*. Of shrubs, species of *Zizyphus*, *Capparis*, *Carissa*, *Vitis*, *Vitex negundo*, *Buddleia Neemda*, *Guilandina Bonduc*, and *Cratæva religiosa*. The smaller herbaceous plants consist chiefly of species of *Cassia*, *Hedysareæ*, *Justicia*, *Barleria*, several *Cucurbitaceæ*, *Euphorbiaceæ*, *Sida*, *Carduus*, *Cirsium*, *Chondrilla*, *Cæsulia*, *Cotula sternutatoria*, *Ocymum*, *Leucas*, *Cissampelos*, *Vallaris pergulana*, *Cardiospermum Halicacabum*, *Plumbago Zeylanica*, *Gisekia pharnacioides*; also of *Corchorus*, *Achyranthes*, *Portulacca*, *Trianthema*, *Celsia*, *Trichodesma*, *Heliotropium*, *Boerhaavia*, *Aneilema*, *Aloe*, *Anthericum*, *Gloriosa superba*; *Costus Nepalensis* is the only one of the *Scitamineæ*, which escapes to any distance from the hills, and *Zeuxina sulcata* the only *orchideous* plant found in the arid plains, and this is spread all over India, from Ceylon to Saharunpore. The bamboo is only found in a cultivated state; the other *gramina* consist of *Sporobolus*, *Polypogon*, *Eragrostis*, *Rottboellia*, *Saccharum*, *Andropogon*, and *Anthistiria*, with species of *Panicum*, *Paspalum* and *Elytrophorus*.

In the vicinity of water and in moist situations, many of the same plants, that are common in other parts of India in similar situations, are found here. *Herpestis monniera*, *Gratiola juncea*, *Hydrolea Zeylanica*, *Sphenoclea Zeylanica*, *Limnophila gratioloides*, *Jussiæa repens*, *Marsilea quadrifolia*, together with species of *Coix*,

Leersia, *Sagittaria*, *Pontedera* and *Butomus;* and with these along the edges of streams we generally find species of *Polygonum*, *Rumex* and *Tamarix*, and as aquatics *Nelumbium speciosum*, *Euryale ferox*, *Damasonium Indicum*, *Trapa bispinosa*, several species of *Nymphæa*, *Utricularia*, *Potamogeton*, *Lemna*, one *Typha* and *Vallisneria;* along with these *Ranunculus sceleratus* and *aquatilis* are found; the former in every part of India, but the latter I have only met with in the Northern provinces. Here we have a good instance of the equalizing effects of water in producing uniformity of temperature, for we have in one situation many of the same kind of plants which occur in more northern latitudes, as well as in the most southern parts of India.

The plants hitherto enumerated are either those which, from being perennial, give the character to the Flora, or occurring in the rainy season, assimilate it more to that of tropical countries. But in the cold weather, or from November to March, when the temperature becomes low, and the ground as well as the atmosphere dry, species, generally only single ones, of colder latitudes, elevated sites, or of European genera, make their appearance, as of *Potentilla*, *Campanula*, *Arenaria*, *Spergula*, *Lithospermum*, *Tradescantia* and *Poa*. The following plants appear to be identified with those found in northern latitudes; some have no doubt been spread with the *Cerealia*, others have crept down from the hills, or spread themselves from more northern latitudes: *Malva rotundifolia*, *Veronica hederifolia*, *Fumaria Vaillantii*, *Anagallis cærulea*, *Sonchus oleraceus*, *Antirrhinum Orontium*, *Silene conoidea*, *Saponaria vaccaria*, *Avena fatua* and *Lolium temulentun*; *Verbena officinalis* and *Zapania nodiflora*, more extensively diffused, are also found here; *Peganum Harmala* is found a little to the north of the district near the Sutledge, and also in the vicinity of Agra, but it has probably been introduced into the latter, as its seeds still continue to be used in medicine by the natives of India.

From the foregoing enumeration it is evident that, with the trifling exceptions mentioned, there is great uniformity in the vegetation of different parts of the widely extended plains of India, as several of the plants found in the northern parts of the Continent are equally so in the southern parts of the Peninsula, as well as in the island of Ceylon, and some even, as enumerated by Mr. Brown, on the eastern coast of New Holland. *Aloe perfoliata*, *Guilandina Bonduc*, and *Gisekia pharnacioides*, occur in Africa, as well as in every part of India; while species of *Cratæva* are found in both, as well as in America. *Lantana* is generally considered an American genus; but there is no doubt that one, if not more species, are indigenous to India, as I have found it common in the north-western provinces, and Dr. Wallich in Rohilcund. He had also a species sent him from the Neelgherries; and *L. nivea* of Ventenat was also most likely obtained from the Peninsula, while Forskaol met with *L. viburnoides* in Arabia. *Cactus Indicus*, *Roxb.*, another plant common about Saharunpore, and indeed over all India, is the only species, not only of the genus, but of the family found out of the New World; though Dr. Roxburgh has also a *Cactus Chinensis*, but it is doubtful whether the former may not have been introduced into India.

Having seen that both the climate and vegetation partake at different seasons of the year of the nature of both temperate and tropical parts of the world, we shall be less surprised at finding the cultivation likewise participating in this double nature, and the northern enjoying, like the southern parts of India, two crops during the year: the one called the *khureef* or rain crop, sown in May and June and reaped in October; the other sown in October and reaped in March and April, called the *rubbee* crop.

The latter, embracing the months which approximate in temperature to that of the seasons of cultivation in colder countries, corresponds with them also in the nature of the grains cultivated; as, for instance, of *gramina*, wheat, barley, oats, and millet; of leguminous plants, peas, beans, vetch, tares, chick, and pigeon peas; of *cruciferæ*, species of *Sinapis* and allied genera cultivated for oil seeds; and of the *umbelliferæ*, the carrot, coriander, cummin, species of *Ptychotis* and *Fœniculum panmorium;* as well as of other tribes, tobacco, flax, safflower, and succory. Hemp exists in abundance in a wild state, but is only used for making an intoxicating drug. Almost all the esculent vegetables of European countries succeed remarkably well in the cold weather in India.

In the rainy season a totally different set of plants engages the agriculturist's attention, as rice, cotton, indigo, maize; *Holcus Sorghum*, species of *Panicum*, *Paspalum*, and *Eleusine;* of leguminous plants, species of *Phaseolus* and *Dolichos;* many of the *Cucurbitaceæ*, as well as *Sesamum*, and the species of *Solanum* for their esculent fruit. Ginger, turmeric, and *pan*, or betel leaf, do not extend quite so far to the northward. The *Crotalaria juncea* and *Hibiscus cannabinus* are every where cultivated for the purpose of yielding fibre for rope-making.

As we have seen with perennials of other kinds, so it is with those yielding fruit of an edible nature; many, both of tropical and temperate climates, succeed nearly equally well in the northern parts of India; so that, taking the Saharunpore garden as an example, we have collected in one place, and naturalized in the open air, the various fruit-trees of very different countries, as of India and China, Caubul, Europe, and America.

Of those belonging to hot countries, we have the plantain, custard-apple, shaddock, orange, lemon, and guava, with the mangoe, tamarind, and others, which are common in every part of India. Of Chinese fruits, the *Leechee, Loquat, Longan, Wampee,* flat peach, and digitated citron, are perfectly naturalized. Of fruit-trees from more northern countries, as Caubul and Cashmere, and from the Hills or Europe, there are the almond, peach, nectarine, apricot, plum, pomegranate, grape vine, apple, pear, quince, mulberry, fig, and walnut. Of useful trees of cold countries, which thrive in what is at some seasons so hot a climate, pines, oak, maple, dog-wood, service-tree, holly, juniper, and box. Of American trees, besides those first enumerated, the logwood, mahogany, *Parkinsonia aculeata* and *Acer negundo* may be instanced as perfectly naturalized.

That to hope for success in the cultivation of a still greater number of the useful plants of other countries is not chimerical, is evident from the result which has already attended the attempts which have been made, particularly when we take into consideration that countries which have many valuable productions of their own, have already possessed themselves of those which were originally peculiar to India. It is of some parts of China and Japan, as well as of America, New Holland, and the Cape, parts of Persia, Arabia, and the north of Africa, corresponding in latitude and a good deal in climate, particularly in having hot summers and rather cold winters, that it would be the most desirable to acquire the productions, whether these be the gift of Nature, or the result of the successful application of Art.

The distribution of the animal kingdom does not present any thing requiring particular notice, except in those which are migratory, for the others being always subject to the influence of temperature, partake of the uniformity in distribution all over India, which we have seen to characterize the climate and vegetation.

The camel, buffalo, and bullock form the beasts of burden; the latter alone used for agricultural purposes; though the climate and soil being dry, and the pasturage good, the district is favourable to horses, and the breed has been of late years much improved by means of the Company's stud. Tigers were formerly common in the very centre of the district, but the increase of cultivation has removed the jungles, with its inmates, to the outskirts: now the antelope roams over the plains, and the peacock is found near most villages where there are groves of trees. The other *Mammalia* are those common in almost every part of India. The otters, which are very abundant near all the rivulets, are perhaps less common in the southern provinces. The *rattel* is considered only a variety of that found at the Cape, while the *caracal* is identical with that found in Persia and the north of Africa. With regard to the feathered creation the variety is greater, as they have the power of changing their habitation according to the seasons. In the rains numerous *Grallæ* and *Anseres* make their appearance; among the latter the pelican, with many, towards the close of the season and in the cold weather, which are well known as English ducks and teal. The Chinese *jacana* and purple gallinule are also seen, as well as coots and rails; together with the ibis, curlew, bittern, and egret. The different kinds of game, as black and grey partridge, quail and snipe, and among the latter, *Scolopax capensis*. The starling, oriole, and cuckoo, make their appearance chiefly in the spring. The insects met with are those common in every part of India, and several have been recognized in my collection by Mr. Wilson Saunders as also found by him at Calcutta and Madras. Of these may be instanced the fire-fly, which attracts every one's attention, as well as several of the Coleoptera, as the *Copris Molossus, Lamia rubus*; and of butterflies, *Papilio Epius, Vanessa Almana, Pieris hyparote, Terias Hecabe, Eublæa Plerippus,* and *Phalanta antica,* are among others which are common in the northern, as in the most southern parts of India.*

* These, together with some hill specimens, have been examined and named by Mr. Samouelle, of the British Museum, to whom I feel much indebted for his kindness.

It is generally well known that the bases of the mountains in India are every where covered with a thick, and often impenetrable jungle, and that a broad strip of this nature extends along the whole foot of the Himalaya from Chittagong to the Sutledge. This gradually diminishes in breadth and density the further we proceed to the northward, until in the country beyond the Jumna it is scarcely perceptible.

The greater portion of the land occupied by this tract of jungle is low, and being inundated during the rainy season, as well as by the hill streams frequently overflowing their banks, is generally in a moist state, and has hence been called the *Turrai*, or moist land. The powerful rays of a nearly vertical sun beating upon this, and a dense mass of vegetation, where there is little circulation of air, produce a heated and moist atmosphere highly favourable to the production of tropical plants. From the southern and eastern parts of this tract, on the confines of Silhet and Chittagong, Drs. Roxburgh and Wallich obtained their splendid specimens of tree-ferns, and numerous species of *Scitamineæ*, of *Epiphytal Orchideæ*, of *Piperaceæ*, *Ebenaceæ*, *Bignoniaceæ*, *Myrtaceæ*, *Byttneriaceæ*, *Malvaceæ*, *Guttiferæ*, *Dipterocarpeæ*, *Anonaceæ* and *Dilleniaceæ*.

According, however, as we approach the north-western limits of this tract, so do we find that, as the same causes operate in a less degree, so does the jungle diminish in breadth and density, the country becomes drier, and the atmosphere less moist. In consequence, however, of the increased cold of the winter months, the more strikingly tropical forms disappear, and some of a European type by degrees make their appearance; but as there is still considerable heat combined with moisture, so do we find many of the plants which are common in Bengal and Silhet, in the Peninsula, and even in Java, creeping to a much higher northern latitude along this favourable tract, than they can do in the open plains.

In the most northern parts, the jungle consists generally of large trees and long grass; the latter is annually burnt down for the purpose of allowing cattle to feed upon the young blade, which immediately shoots up on the removal of the old grass. The low range of hills is covered with trees and herbaceous vegetation, and the valley of Deyra, in the uncleared parts, with dense and almost impenetrable forests. It is unnecessary at present to take separate notice of the distinctions in the Flora of these low hills and of the valley, as there is between them a general uniformity, adapting each for the support of many of the animals and plants which occur in perfection in more southern latitudes. For though the rhinoceros and wild buffalo are not found to the northward of the Ganges, the elephant here reaches his most northern limit. Tigers, leopards, hyenas, lynxes, and bears are common, as well as *Simia rhesus* and *Entellus*, together with the stag, the spotted and hog deers, with the four-horned antelope. The jungle fowl, *florikin* and *leek* (*Otis Bengalensis* and *auritus*), horn-bill, and a green pigeon (*Columba Javanica*), with *Picus Bengalensis*, are common as birds; and the *Papilio parakekte* is remarkable as a butterfly found also by Dr. Horsfield in Java. A species of Boa constrictor is found in the lower hills as well as in those of Central India. As indicating the vicinity of a cooler climate, a species of pheasant

(*P. leuconotus*) may be noticed as existing with the jungle fowl in these hills, and the woodcock is occasionally shot in the Doon in winter.

According as we have seen to be the case in the plains of Upper India, so do the valleys at the foot of the Himalaya enjoy a climate and vegetation partaking at different seasons of both the temperate and torrid zones. At Deyra, elevated about two thousand feet, with a maximum and minimum temperature of 101° and 37°, where snow occasionally falls, we find many of the plants of Lower India more flourishing than in the neighbouring plains. As, for instance, *Artocarpus integrifolia*, *Psidium pyriferum*, and different kinds of limes and plantains. Rice, with many of the smaller grains, forms the chief cultivation, though wheat and barley are not neglected, but very little *gram* (*Cicer arietinum*) is cultivated. This difference in a cooler climate can only be ascribed to the greater moisture, as well as to the less free radiation which takes place during night in these valleys than in the open plains.

As arboreous vegetation is characteristic of tropical countries, so we find in the doons or valleys at the foot of the Himalaya a profusion of trees, many of which are common in more southern parts of India; and arborescent species of genera, of which herbaceous ones are found in colder parts of the world, as of *Terebinthaceæ*, *Semecarpus anacardium*, *Buchanania latifolia*, *Spondias mangifera*, *Boswellia glabra*, *Garuga pinnata*, *Odina Wodier;* of *Leguminosæ*, arborescent species of *Cassia*, *Bauhinia*, *Dalbergia*, *Pongamia; Bauhinia corymbosa* and *Robinia macrophylla* exist as immense climbers, and the *Acacia Catechu* in great abundance, affording its extract as one of the articles of commerce; while *Cathartocarpus fistula*, *Butea frondosa*, and a species of *Erythrina* when in flower, form the great ornaments of the forest. Of *Malvaceæ* and *Tiliaceæ*, several species of *Hibiscus* and *Grewia; Byttneriaceæ*, species of *Sterculia* and *Kydia; Aurantiaceæ*, *Murraya*, *Glycosmis* and *Citrus; Bombax heptaphyllum*, with its trunk supported by great buttresses. *Myrtaceæ*, *Eugenia* and *Careya; Combretaceæ*, species of *Terminalia*, *Conocarpus* and *Pentaptera;* species of *Nauclea* and *Hymenodictyon*, *Rondeletia*, with *Coffea Bengalensis*, and others exist as species of *Rubiaceæ;* of arborescent *Boragineæ*, species of *Ehretia;* and of *Euphorbiaceæ*, *Phyllanthus Emblica*, species of *Rottlera*, *Briedelia*, and frutescent species of *Euphorbia;* of *Urticeæ*, *Artocarpus lacucha*, numerous species of *Ficus* and of *Trophis*. Among the other trees worthy of notice *Diospyros Embryopteris* and *Moringa pterygosperma* may be mentioned, as well as the *Saul* or *Shorea robusta*, with its durable resinous wood, shining leaves, and showy clusters of flowers, forming in many places a forest extending for many miles without the interposition of any other tree. *Marlea begonifolia*, *Pogostemon plectranthoides*, *Panax odora*, *Psoralea corylifolia*, *Biophytum sensitivum*, and *Smithia sensitiva* may be instanced as plants found in the most southern parts of India, and some even in Java. Of herbaceous plants the forms are also very tropical, consisting of species of *Curcuma*, *Zingiber* and *Globba*, as well as of *Pothos*, *Piper* and *Begonia; Platanthera gigantea*, and *Saccolabium guttatum* may be taken as specimens of the *Orchideæ*. *Cyrtopera obtusa* and *flava*, with *Eulophia herbacea* occurring in the valley within the hills, and the last also in the Kheree Pass. Bamboos are common at the foot of the hills, and the plantain seems to be wild in some places. It is not the least interesting feature in the Flora of the northern portion of this tract that the palms here attain their highest limits, a species of *Calamus* being found in the valley itself; and a *Phœnix*, which I have called *humilis*, from its never attaining above a few feet of elevation, exists alongside of the *Pinus longifolia*, which is the only one of the Indian *Coniferæ* found at so low an elevation as two thousand feet. The existence of European and tropical forms in juxtaposition is an interesting fact for the Geologist, particularly when it is considered that the vicinity of lofty hills affords a still greater number of the former, while the valley is filled with the latter.

That it is not, however, devoid of other characteristics of a more temperate climate, we observe, from finding species, generally only single ones, of the following genera: *Pinus*, *Ulmus*, *Salix*, *Gentiana*, *Campanula*, *Geranium*, *Rosa*, *Rubus*, *Clematis*, *Viola*, and *Galium*.

That similar vegetation characterises the forests further to the eastward may be seen in the accounts, by General Hardwicke and Mr. Traill, of that passed through in entering Kemaon, which is described by the latter as consisting of *Saul*, *Sissoo*, and bamboos, and called in Bishop Heber's Journal "the belt of death." If we proceed still further in the same direction, the low land lying between Nipal and the plains of India will be found of the same nature, both with regard to climate and vegetation. Dr. Buchanan describes it as hot and unhealthy, the vegetation the same as in other parts of India, and similar to what we have already seen characterizing the tract between the Ganges and Jumna. Bounding this on the north is a region of nearly the same breadth, consisting of small hills covered with numerous trees, which, according to Dr. B., resemble those of Goalpara; and from the instances given, likewise those found in the hills near Hurdwar, as we find among them *Saul*, *Sissoo*, *Toon*, *Catechu*, and *Pinus longifolia*. The nature of the vegetation in the most southern part of this tract has already been indicated as occurring in the districts of Silhet and Chittagong, where the several Palms are found with the Tree-fern.

As in ascending mountains, the same decrease of temperature is observed as in receding from the equator, so do we observe a similar change in vegetation; and it has been remarked, that the same families and genera which approach nearest to the poles, are those which attain the highest elevations in mountainous regions. This is no where better exemplified than when we depart from the tropical vegetation of the plains of India, and passing through the intermediate changes which may be observed in proceeding from the equator to either pole, we attain a moderate elevation, and find a mild temperature, with the climate and many of the productions, both of the animal and vegetable kingdoms, of the temperate zone. At a still greater elevation, where from the late melting of the snow in summer, and its early fall in autumn, the season of vegetation is as short as in polar regions, we have in place of either an Indian or a European one, a perfectly Alpine Flora. But as the decrease of temperature is gradual, so is the disappearance of Indian forms, and we continue for some time to meet plants with which we are familiar in every part of the plains, many of which indeed must originally have been derived from the bases of these mountains. Among these may be mentioned *Butea frondosa, Carissa sepiaria, Justicia Adhatoda, Nyctanthes arbor tristis, Grislea tomentosa, Sterculia villosa, Kydia calycina,* and *Leea aspera. Nerium Oleander* is found at the base of these mountains; and as in Syria and Barbary, along the banks of streams; *Bassia butyracea,* to which the *shea* tree of Bruce is probably allied, is indigenous in the neighbourhood of Almora, while the other species are found in warmer parts of India. The mangoe, though its fruit does not ripen, is found as high as four thousand feet, near Deyra, as well as at Nahn: and *Gloriosa superba* attains an equal elevation, but it only exposes its annual shoots during summer, while the subterranean situation of its tubers protects them from the great vicissitudes of temperature.

An European, on his first arrival in a tropical country, is struck by the magnificent peculiarities of its vegetation; but to one who has long resided in such a clime these become familiar, and his attention is more quickly excited by the re-appearance of forms with which he was familiar in his youth, and which characterize the more humble and verdant, but not less beautiful Flora of temperate climates. In proportion as we ascend these mountains, the plants of India disappear, and we are delighted at finding the increase in number and variety of those belonging to European genera. At first we see only a few straggling towards the plains, which in a more temperate climate would be their favourite resort; and it is not until we have attained a considerable elevation that, having apparently lost all traces of tropical vegetation, we enter a forest of pines or oaks, and lofty rhododendrons, where none but European forms are recognizable. The genera of which species descend to the lowest levels, are chiefly *Clematis, Berberis, Viburnum, Hypericum, Rhus, Euonymus, Rubia, Geranium,* and *Viola.*

This disappearance of tropical forms is not so complete as would appear at first, on visiting the mountains in the spring or summer months; for the southern slope of the Himalaya being within the full influence of the tropical rains, a peculiarity of atmospherical phenomena is induced, which favours the existence of a series of forms not otherwise to be expected in a climate of which the mean temperature is so low.

For the attainment of greater precision in our ideas respecting the peculiarities of vegetation as connected with the climate of successive elevations, it is proposed to divide the slope of the Himalaya into three several belts, and take separate notice of each. The first has been already considered, and may be supposed to extend to between four and five thousand feet of elevation, as several tropical perennials extend to the latter, and snow does not usually fall below the former. The second belt may be conceived to embrace the space between five and nine thousand feet of elevation, as the winter's snow is always melted from such elevations before the accession of the rainy season, and the upper is nearly the limit to which the herbaceous plants of tropical genera extend. The third belt may be taken from this elevation up to the highest limits from which snow melts away on the southern face of the Himalayan Mountains. The bounds are in a great measure arbitrary to which each of these belts have been restricted, for the changes, both in temperature and vegetation, are so gradual, that it is impossible to draw any line where the peculiarities of one can be so clearly defined as not to interfere with those which are considered characteristic of another; and this difficulty is further increased by the change which is continually taking place in the climate and productions of similar elevations the further we penetrate into the Himalayas, for even where the mean temperature is the same, the range of the thermometer is greater, and the line of perpetual congelation higher in the internal than in the external ranges of these mountains. A further difficulty is also produced by the great difference in the vegetation of the northern and southern faces of the very same range or mountain, so that frequently a straight line running along the summit of the ridge may be seen dividing the luxuriant arboreous and shrubby vegetation of the northern face from the brown, barren, and grassy covering of the southern slope. This difference has been observed by all travellers, and may be ascribed in part to the greater depth of the soil on the northern face; but chiefly, I conceive, to the less direct influence of the solar rays on this than on the southern side.

The stations of Simla, Mussooree, and Lundour having been much resorted to for health, their climate and vegetation attentively observed, and offering an altitude of seven thousand five hundred feet, will afford a good illustration of the peculiarities of the central belt. The details of meteorological phenomena being confined to the introductory chapter, it is sufficient here to remark, that with a range of the thermometer of 53°, from 27° to 80°, and a mean temperature of about 55° observed at this elevation in 30° of N. lat., we could not expect the existence of any plants either belonging or allied to tropical genera; and certainly we do not meet with them in the clear dry months of the autumn, spring, or summer, but only in the rainy season, when a moderate and uniform degree of evaporation, in a moist, mild, and equable atmosphere, is favourable to the growth of plants usually considered indicative of a tropical climate. These generally consist of only a few species of genera belonging to such tribes as have perennial roots and annual stems or their tuber-like stems secure in the earth from the cold of winter.

The families and genera of which the species come into flower when the mild temperature and moist atmosphere are so congenial, consist of *Scitamineæ*, *Canna*, *Hedychium*, *Roscoea*, and *Globba;* *Orchideæ*, *Habenaria intermedia*, *pectinata*, and *marginata*, species of *Platanthera*, *Pleione*, *Herminium*, and *Satyrium Nepalense;* *Commelineæ*, species of *Commelina* and *Tradescantia;* and of *Graminæ* a few species of *Panicum*, *Eragrostis*, and *Andropogon;* of other tribes *Begonia*, *Osbeckia*, *Drosera*. Almost every rock is covered with species of *Cyrtandraceæ* and *Platystemma Violoides*, and the ground with *Balsamineæ;* of *Acanthaceæ*, a few species of *Justicia* and *Ruellia* are found; the

Leguminosæ consist of a few shrubby *Indigoferæ, Acaciæ*, and *Desmodia*, as well as of small species of *Cassia* and *Crotalaria*. Species of *Vitis* are found in the valleys and at moderate elevations; of *Tiliaceæ, Corchorus* and *Grewia*; of *Apocyenæ, Alstonia*; of *Asclepiadeæ*, a few species of *Cynanchum, Oxystelma, Marsdenia*, and *Hoya*; and of *Myrsineæ*, two or three shrubby species of *Myrsine* and *Bæobotrys*.

That the arboreous vegetation corresponds almost entirely with that of temperate climates, will be evident from a mere enumeration of the plants which constitute the forests at elevations of from seven to eight thousand feet. These consist almost entirely of *Rhododendron arboreum*, and species of *Quercus, Acer, Ulmus, Carpinus*, with, more frequently on the northern aspect, the different Himalayan Pines. Of smaller trees, there are species of *Cornus, Benthamia, Euonymus, Rhamnus, Rhus, Ilex, Andromeda*; and of shrubs, *Berberis, Buxus, Daphne, Cratægus*, and *Coriaria*, with others of the *Rosaceæ, Caprifoliaceæ*, and *Smilaceæ*. Among the trees which produce edible fruits, now cultivated in almost every part of the world (here growing apparently wild, but some may have been introduced from the mountains of Caubul and the hilly regions further to the north-westward), we have *Juglans regia, Armeniaca vulgaris, Persica vulgaris*, and *Punica Granatum*, with species of *Pyrus, Cerasus, Rubus*, and *Morus*. Species of *Abelia* and *Stauntonia* are interesting, as the only other species are found in China; and species of *Deutzia, Kadsura*, and *Hovenia* are found here, in Nipal, and Japan, as well as *Boehmeria frutescens, Daphne cannabina, Cleyera ochnacea*, and *Lonicera japonica*. *Senacia nepalensis* is remarkable as belonging to a genus of which the other species are found in Mauritius, and the rest of the family scattered from New Zealand in the southern to Madeira in the northern hemisphere, nearly in the same latitude, to which the Himalayan species of *Senacia* extends. Many of the trees and shrubs belong to the same genera as those of the northern parts of America, but the genus *Triosteum* is peculiar in being confined to North America and to parts of the Himalaya. So also *Onoseris nepalensis* and *Leucomeris spectabilis* belong to genera of which the rest of the tribe are South American.

But as the climate has been shewn to correspond in so many respects with that of the temperate zone, so do we find the distinguishing characteristic of this mid region of the Himalaya to be that which is the most pleasing feature of climes where man, as De Candolle observes, attains the greatest perfection. Here, in a rich thick sward, numerous delicate annuals are found, of which the congeners are so abundant in European countries, and which to enumerate at present would be tedious and out of place: but they may be described in general terms as belonging to the great European families of *Ranunculaceæ, Umbelliferæ, Saxifrageæ, Crassulaceæ, Caryophylleæ, Hypericineæ, Geraniaceæ, Violaceæ*, and a few *Cruciferæ*. Among the monopetalous tribes, *Campanulaceæ, Plantagineæ, Dipsaceæ, Valerianeæ*; and of *Compositæ*, species of *Carduus, Echinops, Lactuca, Hieracium*, and *Mulgedium*, as well as of *Solidago, Diplopappus, Aster, Achillea, Artemisia, Gnaphalium, Carpesium*, and *Senecio*; together with species of *Stellatæ, Gentianeæ, Primulaceæ, Pediculares*, and *Labiatæ*. The monocotyledons consist of *Irideæ, Junceæ,* herbaceous *Asphodeleæ, Liliaceæ, Aroideæ.* The *Gramineæ* consist of species of *Agrostis, Polypogon, Trisetum, Poa, Festuca, Brachypodium, Kœleria,* and *Vilfa;* with of *Cyperaceæ* several species of *Carex.* Of *Rutaceæ,* a single species, *Ruta Albiflora* is extremely abundant. *Oxalis Corniculata* and *Centranthera hispida,* as well as other plants, are found both in the hills and the plains. This is accounted for by observing that the cold weather of the latter and the warm weather of the former approximate much nearer the same degree of temperature than would at first be supposed, and these are the respective seasons of vegetation of many of these plants.

It is not necessary to be more minute on the present occasion, but some plants may be more particularly alluded to, as they are remarkable on account of their geographical distribution; as for instance, we have among the herbaceous, as among the shrubby vegetation, an affinity to the Flora of China and Japan, in *Ophiopogon spicatus* and *Japonicus, Pardanthus Chinensis,* and *Houttuynia cordata* being found here as well as in those countries. With reference to the Flora of North America, analogous species of *Podophyllum, Monotropa, Phytolacca, Ampelopsis,* and other genera have been found, and the specific identity of American and Himalayan specimens of *Panax quinquefolium, Phryma leptostachya,* and *Datura Stramonium* has been ascertained; while *Chaptalia gossypina* is a Himalayan species of a South American genus and tribe. But what is still more remarkable, a species of *Sclerocarpus,* which does not seem to differ from *S. africanus,** has been found at Mussoree and at Simla as well as in Africa, while a species of *Melianthus,* a genus belonging to the Cape of Good Hope, exists also in Kemaon. With respect to the Flora of Europe, the number of identical species already ascertained is more numerous, and others I have no doubt will be determined to be so in the families which remain to be examined. Of those already ascertained, it will be sufficient to mention *Ranunculus arvensis, Thlaspi arvense, Capsella Bursa Pastoris, Hedera Helix, Galium Aparine, Leontodon Taraxacum, Acorus Calamus, Alisma Plantago, Prunella vulgaris, Carduus nutans, Phleum alpinum, Alopecurus geniculatus, Phalaris canariensis, Cynodon Dactylon, Poa annua, Lolium temulentum. Samolus Valerandi* is a remarkable instance of a plant found in many parts of the world, but in no part of India except at moderate elevations in moist situations in the interior of the Himalaya.

In the same way that we have seen the plains, from their northern latitude, and from being also within the influence of the periodical rains, enjoying the benefits both of an European and a tropical climate, with respect to the seasons and the nature of their cultivation; so do we find the hilly regions, with their cool summits and heated valleys equally deluged by the same rains, partaking of the same advantages; and we may sometimes, at the same time, see wheat being cut on the top of a mountain and rice sown in the valley at its base: or immediately that the former is removed, the ground prepared

* This plant was recognised in my collection by Mr. David Don, who informs me that he had also seen a specimen in a collection formed by the Countess of Dalhousie at Simla.

prepared for the reception of the latter. On account both of the climate and the facilities for irrigation, rice is generally cultivated in the valleys, though not restricted to them; particularly the variety which does not require irrigation, as this is sown at elevations of five thousand feet on the terraced flats of the mountain side, where, as soon as the wheat is ripe, the ears are merely picked off, the straw burnt on the ground for manure, and the rice sown immediately after the first shower of rain, of which there are generally some falls in the months of April and May. Maize, millet, *Eleusine coracana*, and many of the other small grains, constitute, as in the plains, the rain crop; together with species of *Amaranthus, Polygonum*, and an *Arum*, of which the root is much in use as the ordinary food of the hill people. Capsicum, turmeric, and ginger, the last as high as four thousand feet, are also cultivated, and form articles of export to the plains. Mr. Traill describes the little cotton that is produced in Kemaon, as " superior to that of the plains in softness of texture, gloss of colour, and length of fibre." Hemp is also cultivated, of excellent quality for the manufacture of both cloth and cordage. The cold weather cultivation of moderate, and the only one of higher elevations, consists chiefly of wheat, barley, buckwheat, peas, opium, and a little tobacco: the last only in small quantities, but the opium of very superior quality. As few of the villages extend above this central belt, so is there little cultivation to be found beyond it. I have not myself seen wheat and barley at a greater elevation than eight thousand feet on the sides of Urukta, and higher on this than on Choor, a more exterior mountain; but no where have I seen finer crops than at seven thousand feet on the shoulders of the latter. Mr. Gerard has seen wheat at ten thousand feet, and Captain Webb at twelve thousand feet of elevation, still on the southern slope of the Himalaya; but these being included within the limits of a higher belt, will be afterwards considered. The mustard tribe is also cultivated as oil seeds, which is also afforded in large quantities, of a very fine quality, by the kernels of the apricot at the highest villages. It may not be uninteresting to remark, that at some of these, where fodder is with difficulty or not at all to be procured in the winter months, the cattle are fed upon the leaves of trees which have been stacked for that purpose in the autumn. The kinds preferred are species of *Grewia, Ulmus*, and *Quercus;* but those of the *Coniferæ* are also employed: first, as bedding for their cattle, and afterwards as manure for their fields. Since the introduction of the potatoe its cultivation has been much increased, and the quality, which had deteriorated, much improved by renewing the stock from seed. It is fortunate, both for growers and consumers, that the Hill potatoes are not ready until those cultivated in the plains are either spoilt or expended.

The animal forms which are associated with the foregoing vegetation display alike the powerful influence of climate and the admixture of European with Tropical forms. Of the monkeys, the *Entellus* alone ascends in the summer months as high as nine thousand feet, where may also be seen one of the *Scitamineæ*, which, though not entirely agreeing with the generic character, I have called *Roscoea alpina:* but this makes its appearance only with the first showers, while its tubers, as well by the depth to

Henry Piddington

'Fifth Memoir. Madras Hurricane of May 1841'. *Journal of the Asiatic Society of Bengal* 11 (1842)

Names of Men.	*Names of Women.*
Chakla,	Phagooni,
Sunka,	Bisaje,
Balasache,	Bisahawa,
Deringa sache,	Furgunnic.
Poojoon,	
Esula,	
Puharoo,	
Oonti,	
Jenti tokla,	
Mhedla,	
Secuta.	

A. CAMPBELL.

Art. II.—*Researches on the Gale and Hurricane in the Bay of Bengal on the 3rd, 4th, and 5th of June,* 1839; *with reference to the Theory of the Law of Storms in India. By* Henry Piddington.

PART II.

That the hurricane part of the tempest which we are considering was blowing in tolerably well defined circles, has been, I think, clearly shewn in the foregoing part of this memoir. The object of this second part, is to adduce evidence, which shews that it was at the same time both a *gale,* i. e. a strong wind blowing in with tolerable steadiness from one quarter of the compass; and a *hurricane*, namely, a violent wind blowing in a circle or vortex of greater or less diameter. At present too it seems probable, from the dates, that the gale produced the hurricane. We may consider that this storm was one of those which usually occur at the change of the moonsoon from NE. to SW., which in various parts of the Bay may be said to take place between the 15th May and 15th June. It is from the 1st to the 15th June that we look for the rains in Calcutta, though sometimes, as in this year, they may be said to have begun in April. It will be borne in mind then, that whatever follows, whether facts or hypotheses, relates only to the beginning of the SW. monsoon. Future observations will inform us, whether the October Gales as they are called,—though they sometimes occur in November,—are subject to the same or different laws. (The European reader will recollect, that October is the epoch at which the NE. monsoon takes the place of the SW. one.)

If we look at the Bay of Bengal, Map No. II, we shall be struck with the fact, that while it is bounded on the East by the mountain range which stretches from the Malay peninsula to Bootan, often approaching very near the shores, and rising to the height of from 3000 to perhaps 5000 feet on the Arracan coast; it is also bounded, on the West, by the Coromandel range, which supports the Eastern side of the elevated table lands of the Deccan. At the valley of the Mahanuddee (the river of Cuttack) however, at its junction with the Vindiya range, it turns suddenly to the North-Westward and Westward, leaving thus between it and the mountains of Arracan, the wide opening from Point Palmiras to Chittagong, which, to use an orientalism, is the *gate* to the plains of Bengal.

The salient angle, formed by the corner where the Vindiya and Coromandel ranges meet, and the entering one, where the Bootan, or Himalaya, and Arracan and Cachar ranges join (leaving however the valley of Assam as an opening for the great Burrumpooter to flow through,) thus form, as it were, an angular channel; through which all the lower strata of the current of the SW. monsoon may be supposed to find their way over the plains of Bengal and up the valley of the Ganges; and this is their natural course. But we may suppose that the SW. monsoon when urged to any great force at the mouth of the Bay, about Ceylon, must strike against the mountain ranges of Arracan in about from lat. 16°, which is that of Cape Negrais, to lat. 20° or 21°; or about that of Arracan; and, being deflected thence, must turn off in a paraboloidal line towards the great opening offered by the low lands at the head of the Bay, and thence proceed up the valley of the Ganges as before.

But when the head of the Gale is thus deflected, it may meet also with that portion of the monsoon which has blown along the Coromandel range and coast—called the "long-shore wind," by the old navigators —which has a much shorter distance to travel; and there occasion an eddy of variable winds, whirlwind or hurricane, according to the force of the first impulse—and this again influenced too, doubtless, by many causes to which we are yet strangers.

If this theory be true for these tempests, we should look to find points, about the meeting of the two currents, varying in position according to their respective forces, at which, during these gales, it should be comparatively calm, or blowing but moderately; and it is curious that at Balasore, in latitude 21° 28′, and at the Black Pagoda in 19° 62′ N. this comparative calm is found to have existed. My authority for this is the following letter.

Balasore, July 31*st*, 1839.

DEAR SIR,—I should have been much at your service in giving you all the requisite information concerning the gale here, had any taken place, but we had only strong gusts of wind at NE. to SE. with uncommon heavy rain on the 5th, 6th, and part of the 7th of June, which even to this day has kept back the rice crops. The thermometer fell to 81½°, and unluckily my barometer was broken a few days prior, so that we could only foretel a gale coming on by the blackness of the heavens to the Eastward; which gale did not reach from the Northward of Point Palmiras to Balasore, but blew hard from Point Palmiras to below Pooree to the Southward. No vessels were lost in the Balasore roads; but to the Eastward they may have been lost, as a Telingah topgallant mast was picked up, besides pieces of deal boxes, supposed to have contained glass-ware, marked "*Protector*," which vessel was lost to the Eastward, between the reefs, last October.

Gales at Kedgeree, though blowing dead to windward of us, distant seventy-five miles, do not always reach this coast; as in the May Hurricane of 1833, when the "*Duke of York*" was blown from her moorings at Saugor across to Hidgelee, and became a wreck, yet the gale did not reach here, although the bank to the Eastward in the heavens so plainly indicated a gale, that every person here barred up their doors and nailed them. We only had a good topgallant breeze.

The Neilgherry Hills appear to influence the winds much on the coast north of Point Palmiras, as the winds are generally throughout the SW. monsoon, SW. to W. in the morning to 7 A. M., veering round to S. and SE. P. M.; and in the NE. monsoon, W. to NW. veering round to NE. after 8 A. M.

(*Signed*) A. BOND.

Mr. Richardson, Branch Pilot, informs me, moreover, that during the fury of the Gale of 1833, in which the "Duke of York" was wrecked, and he himself was driving about with all his anchors down, some passengers whom he had previously landed at the Black Pagoda were upon the top of it, and felt no excessively violent wind, though they *saw* the horizon very black, and the sea dreadfully agitated to the North Westward of them.

The slow rate at which our vortices travel onwards is very remarkable, but seems, if future observation should confirm it, to afford countenance to this theory; for, as before said, we may consider them as pent up between the current passing round the vortex of the parabola and the Coromandel range; and no doubt to feel, as water in similar channels would do, the repulsion from these last. It is clear, as shewn in p. 576, by the log of the "Indian Oak," that the monsoon was blowing up along the coast as far as Vizagapatam, from between which and Ganjam, to Point Palmiras, the Hurricane was probably felt. Its limit to the North we well know to have been between Point Palmiras and Balasore, but I could obtain no intelligence from Ganjam to fix a limit to the South.

We should also find that, as the current of air proceeds up the valley of the Ganges to the North Westward, it should give rise to an Easterly Gale, which has also in this instance occurred, as will be seen by the following extracts, the first being from a very able and interesting letter from Mr. Ravenshaw, of the Civil Service, dated Chuprah in Behar, lat. 25° 46′ N. long. 84° 46′ E.

Chuprah, July 17th, 1839.

Dear Sir,—Having observed in the Newspapers that you are desirous of obtaining information connected with the Gale which occurred in the Bay of Bengal from the 3rd to the 5th June inclusive, I have the pleasure to contribute my mite to the stock of facts which you are engaged in collecting. The enclosed extract from my Register will shew the height of the Bar. and Ther. at 10½ A. M. during the Gale, and for some days succeeding it. I regret that my official duties prevented me from taking observations at 4½ P. M.; but I hope the small amount of information afforded will not be without use, in shewing the direction and duration of the Gale of this district, inland from the Bay of Bengal. It will be remarked, that the Gale did not commence here until the 4th instead of the 3rd June, and that it terminated on the 7th instead of the 5th. The Bar. kept falling during the continuance of the Gale, and strange to say did not reach its minimum until the day after the violence of the Gale had ceased, i. e. the 8th. The direction of the Gale was nearly due East, but on the 8th the wind shifted to the SW. and West, and on the 9th blew as furiously from the latter quarter as it had previously done from the East; towards evening, however, it shifted to the NE. On the 10th it changed to SE., on the 11th to SW.; and the following day to the West. On the 14th and 15th it again veered to the NE. and EbN. until on the 16th it resumed its old position of East, which is the usual direction from which it blows at this season of the year. From the above it would appear that the wind, after the violence of the Gale had subsided, acquired a rotatory motion and turned twice round the compass in a Southerly direction before it recovered its equilibrium. By letters received at the time from Mootebarry, 60 miles North of Chuprah, and from Gyah, about 90 miles South of this station, I learnt that the Gale occurred with equal violence at those places. The breadth of the column of air put in motion was therefore at least 150 miles, and probably much greater. It would be interesting to ascertain the exact limits of this Gale inland as well as at sea, which object might be effected by your addressing a circular letter to the residents at each of the principal stations in the Western Provinces e. g. Allahabad, Cawnpore, Agra, Delhi and Saharunpore. Information from these points would probably give the extreme length to which the Gale extended, as information obtained from Jubbulpore, Gwalior, and Ajmere, would shew the extreme breadth. I do not recollect at present from what direction you stated the Gale to have blown in the Bay of Bengal, but if from the SW., the usual course of the monsoon, it is difficult to account for its blowing here from the East, unless we suppose the column of air to have been driven against the Assam and Himalaya Mountains, and by them turned in a Westerly course. In this event, it is probable that the Gale may have subsequently followed the direction of the mountains NW. perhaps as far as Hurdwar.

I conclude that it is not your intention to confine your observations and inquiries to the Gale under consideration, but to all storms of magnitude in the Bay, or its vicinity. The Gale which seems to occur almost annually in the Bay of Bengal in the month of October, would, from its regular recurrence, form an excellent subject for observation. It was felt at Chuprah during the two years that I have been stationed here. On the first occasion it blew (to the best of my recollection) from the East, whereas last year it came from the West.

It appears to me very desirable that either Government or some public body like the Asiatic Society, should take measures for securing an uninterrupted official record, not only of the periodical and occasional storms which extend generally over large tracts of country, but also of local atmospherical peculiarities—the changes in the direction of winds and storms occasioned by mountains and the larger rivers—also of the general character of the seasons in different parts of the country—the paucity or abundance of rain—the minimum rise of the Ganges, Burrumpooter, &c.—the price of grain as affected by the seasons—the date of the commencement and termination of the rains—of the hot winds—or of any other prevailing winds.

The Asiatic Society through its numerous members might, I should imagine, without difficulty obtain information on the points adverted to from all the principal stations in India, which should be annually digested and published in their *Journal*. These again will be compared and generalized every 10 years or so by a Meteorological Committee of the Society. The Asiatic Societies of Madras and Bombay might be requested to adopt the same system throughout their respective Presidencies, so that the observations might embrace the whole of India. Such a combination of laborers in the cause, and the consequent accumulation of facts, assisted by the rapid progress of science in these days, would almost justify the hope that we may ultimately arrive at the discovery of some general laws by which the seasons are regulated; and by which we may be able to foresee and to guard against both inundation and famine, in a country where their ravages are often so destructive to life and property.

(*Signed*) E. RAVENSHAW.

1839.	Bar. at 10½ A. M.	Ther. attached	Bar. at 4½ P. M.	Ther. attached	Bar. at 10 P. M.	Ther.	Remarks.
June 4th	No observation.		....	....	....	....	Strong and continued gale from East, with occasional rain.
5	29·50	86	....	....	....	....	
6	29·42	86½	....	....	....	....	
	29·32	83	....	....	....	....	
8	29·30	84	....	....	....	....	Rain; wind SW. shifting to West.
9	29·34	81½	29·32	82½	....	....	Ditto, W. do. to NE.
10	29·40	82	....	....	....	....	Ditto, Wind SE.
11	29·39	83	....	....	....	....	Ditto, SW.
12	29·38	85	....	....	....	....	Ditto, W.
13	29·38	85	....	....	....	....	Ditto, W.
14	29·47	87	....	....	....	....	Ditto, NE.
15	29·58	87	....	....	....	....	Ditto, EbN.
							East, the usual direction of the wind at this season.

N. B. This gale extended in ***breadth*** from Mootebarry, 60 miles North of Chuprah, to Gyah, 90 miles South—and perhaps further, but of this I have no authentic intelligence.

As far then as our present knowledge extends, and referring to the state of the Gale in the Southern part of the Bay, we find that the impulse, which may be said to begin to be violently felt on the 31st by the *Susan,* did not reach Chuprah till the 4th, when it produced an Easterly Gale, terminating on the 7th, shifting to the South-West and West on the 8th; the counter-gale and eddies, if we may so call them, being only the irregular movements of the various currents produced by this great derangement of the usual equilibrium of the aerial currents, which, as is remarked, are usually from the East at this season; affording also a proof towards the theory which I have ventured to offer. When the monsoon slackens the Southerly and South-Westerly gales, and currents may find their way as far inland as this place. The dates show that the Gale did not begin at the point to which it blew, but that it was a progressive impulse travelling about the direction which I have laid down. Assuming this theory as a *guide* only, let us now see how it accords with the facts we already possess here. By referring to the Map, No. II. we see that though along the coast from Madras to Vizagapatam, by the Indian Oak's log at Masulipatam, by the Master Attendant's report from Coringa, and up to the 3rd at noon by the Laurel Amelia's log, it was fine, though threatening; yet from the 31st May to the 5th June, by the logs of the Lady Macnaghten, Petrel, Susan, Jumna, and Laurel Amelia—to which too we might add those of the Nine, Eden, and Mobile—a severe gale was blowing between WbS. and SW. diagonally across the Bay, in lines about parallel to one drawn from the centre of Ceylon to Cape Negrais, the termination of the Arracan coast. We find that at Cheduba on the

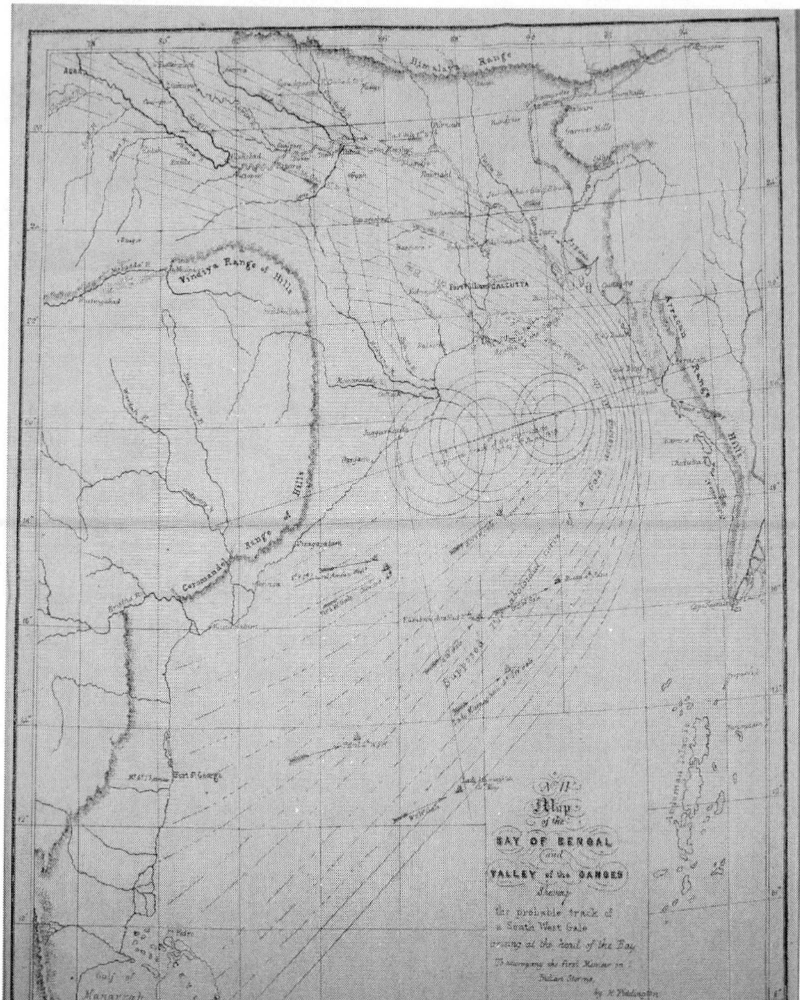
No. II
Map
of the
BAY OF BENGAL
and
VALLEY of the GANGES
Shewing
the probable track of
a South West Gale
arising at the head of the Bay
To accompany the First Memoir on
Indian Storms
by H. Piddington
Himalaya Range
Vindiya Range of Hills
Coromandel Range of Hills
Arracan Range of Hills
Fort William CALCUTTA
Fort St George
Gulf of Manarrah
AGRA

2nd, and part of the 3rd, the John William Dare had a severe gale from S. to SSE. the gale being then deflected by the mountains of that coast. At the harbour of Akyab No. 27. we find that our meagre notices give us "Easterly winds with hard gales" on the 2nd; on the 3rd, and 4th, "brisk;" on the 5th, "gales;" and on the 6th, SW. winds.

At Dacca* Dr. Lamb's Register gives as follows:—

	Winds.	Bar. 10 A. M.	Ther. Noon.
June 1st.	SE. East SE.	29·68	90
2nd.	SS. East,	,, 64	90
3rd	East South SE.	,, 64	91 3 inches of rain.
4th.	East SE. South,	,, 68	88½ 6 inches of rain.
5th.	South SE. SbE.	,, 71	85

So that here the winds were varying between South and East.

At Jellinghee, in lat. 24° 8′, long. 88° 42′ E. about 140 miles WbN. of Dacca, and about 100 NbE. of Calcutta, at the spot where the river of that name branches off from the great Ganges, a memorandum informs me as follows:—

June 6th, strong Easterly gales with frequent showers.
,, 7th, ditto ditto.
,, 8th and 9th, Frequent showers and cloudy weather.

The following is an extract of a letter and memorandum from H. B. Beresford, Esq. Deputy Collector, Purneah.

"The observations from 4th to 10th inclusive, in the following memorandum, were made on the Ganges, some miles south of Purneah—at least so I understand Mr. Palmer to say:"

Transcript of Extract of Day Book, 1839.

June 1st. Wind E. blew hard and rained in the morning.
2nd. Wind E. a warm clear day.
3rd. Wind E. clear morning, rained heavily in the afternoon, and blew hard from South at night.
4th. Wind E. blew fresh.
5th. A strong gale from the East—rained a great deal—a wet rainy night.
6th. Blew hard the whole day from the East, and squalls accompanied with rain came frequently.
7th. Wind SE. in the morning—East at noon; died away in the afternoon, rained a little.
8th. Wind S. and SE.
9th. Wind East—rained a great deal and blew fresh.
10th. Wind ESW. and E. again—rained a great deal.

* The Indigo planters of the district of Dacca and the Eastern part of Jessore are well aware of the tendency of strong Easterly winds to cause rapid rises of the river, and severe loss to them by inundating their plant. If we suppose the Easterly gale to be a Southerly and South Westerly one in the Bay, we obtain an additional reason for this, to the common one of the Easterly gale being partly against the current of the Ganges; i. e. the waters of the ocean are driven up into the NE. corner of the Bay.

"The inclosed notes I made in original, and regret not having it in my power to comply more fully with your request."

June, 1839.

June 1st. Light airs from NE. to E. cloudy at times.
2nd. Ditto, Ditto.
3rd. ENE. cloudy, or slight showers from ESE.
4th. Ditto, ditto light fresh breezes with slight showers.
5th. Heavy ENE. wind, very cloudy with light showers.
6th. Ditto ENE. with constant sleet and rain.
7th. Heavy ENE. with sleet, wind veered S. to SSE. occasional showers.
8th. Heavy ENE. veering round to South with rain—night, Northerly.
9th. Fresh ENE. cloudy with heavy showers.
10th. Rain almost all day—clouds flying from East—Light airs from West, a great deal of rain has fallen, the nullahs rising very high, threatening to overtop their banks.*

At Ghazeepore lat. 25° 35′ N. long. 83° 33′ E. and 41 miles East of Benares and 84 miles W.½S. from Chuprah, Dr. Jackson kindly forwards me a journal for the month of June, from which the following is an extract, which I copy to the 11th, to shew how remarkably they agree with those of Mr. Ravenshaw from Chuprah, in the sudden change of the wind, from ESE.—which we may call its average from the 1st to the 7th,—to SW. on the 8th. The subsequent changes seem to indicate, as before said, that the more direct current of the monsoon had for a short time forced its way upwards; for the remainder of the month the wind is variable from E. to W. with sultry weather, as usual there in the month of June.

Date.	Winds.	Ther	*June*, 1839.—*Remarks, &c.*
1	ESE.	98	Pleasant breezes, fair weather, 11 A. M. cloudy with a few drops of rain, hot and sultry.
2	ESE.	98	Light breezes, fair weather, hot and sultry.
3	ESE.	99	Fresh ditto, cloudy, at intervals hot and sultry; at 1/30 P. M. a squall, no rain.
4	ESE.	96	Fresh breezes, cloudy at intervals, with hard squalls, fair weather.
5	ESbE.	92	A. M. cloudy and showery, hard gales with showers at intervals.
6	SEbE.	86	Hard gales, dark cldy. weather, showers at intervals, night rainy.
7	SEbE.	86	Ditto ditto ditto ditto with heavy rain, 7 P. M. wind shifted to the SW.
8	SW.	80	Dark cloudy rainy weather, with hard squalls of wind, 6 P. M. fair and continued during night.
9	SW.toESE.	80	Morning dark, cloudy and fair, which continued throughout, 5 P. M. wind shifted to the ESE.
10	ESE.	84	At 3 A. M. dark and cloudy with drizzling rain, at 5 fair, moderate breezes.
11	WSW.	88	A. M. dark and cloudy, with thunder, lightning and rain, at 8 fair moderate breezes, passing clouds.

GHAZEEPORE,
September 14th, 1839.

J. JACKSON,
Civil Surgeon.

* In the Northern parts of the district much more rain fell, both the Coosey and Mahanuddee were uncommonly high for the time of the year.

From Gorruckpoor, in lat. 26° 45′ N. long. 83° 22′ E. I learn by one letter that it blew a gale from the East on the night of the 5th and 6th June; strongly from the East during the 6th, and until the afternoon of the 7th, when it was NE., also blowing strongly; on the morning of the 8th it was NW. strong, and towards the afternoon it shifted to the East and moderated. The rain commenced at noon on the 6th and continued night and day till the afternoon of the 8th, when it ceased.

From Gorruckpoor I have also by the kindness of Mr. Vicars the following memorandum.

Gorruckpoor, 23rd September, 1839.

At the request of Mr. Bridgman, I send you an extract from my Meteorological Journal, it is a very unfortunate circumstance that I should have neglected to register the barometer and thermometer until the 7th of June, I however, noted the direction of the winds and the **maximum** of the Thermometer, which is better than nothing, and perhaps may answer your purpose; there was a storm from the East with rain on the 31st May.

Yours sincerely,

N. VICARS.

	10 A. M.			4 P. M.			*Remarks.*	
ate		Alt. Ther.	Detch.	Bar.	Alt. Ther.	Detch. Ther.	A. M.	P. M.
1	Max.	of	ther.	91·0	min.	89·2	Estly. moderate, none.	Easterly.
2	Do.	....	Do.	91·2	....	....	Easterly (minimum of Bar. 28·873)	None.
3	Do.	....	Do.	92·0	....	....	Easterly, moderate.	Storm rain, no wind.
4	Do.	Do.	....	91·5	....	....	Easterly, strong.	Easterly, strong.
5	Do.	Do.	....	88·0	....	....	Easterly, showers.	Easterly, strong.
6	Do.	....	Do.	86·0	....	....	Easterly, stg. hvy. rain (min. of Bar. 28·808)	Easterly, strong.
7	28·970	....	81·0	28·750	....	80·0	Estly. stg. rain all day.	Easterly, strong.
8	28·788	77·5	78·5	28·777	79·5	77·8	Easterly, strong, heavy rain till 4 P. M.	Easterly, strong.
9	28·902	80·7	80·2	28·940	...	84·0	Easterly, strong, cloudy.	Easterly.
10	28·964	81·0	81·0	28·800	82·8	83·0	Easterly, cloudy.	Variable.

From Mirzapore lat. 25° 10′ N. long. 85° 35′ E. I am indebted to Mr. Stuart for the following memorandum of the weather, from 1st to 10th June, 1839.

1st June, Thermometer,	.. 88·	..	Fresh Easterly Breeze.
2nd ditto, ,,	.. 86·	..	Morning wind Easterly. Noon dreadfully hot and blowing strong from the NW.
3rd ditto, ,,	90·	..	Not a breath of wind, until 6 A. M.
4th ditto, ,,	.. 88	..	Sultry night—strong Easterly wind.

5th ditto,	,,	87· ..	Blowing heavy from the East, showers, noon blowing very fresh and weather wild looking.
6th ditto,	,,	80·	A regular gale from the East with drizzling rain, noon gale increasing and more rain, evening stormy and wet.
7th ditto,	,,	80· ..	Severe squalls through the night from the East with heavy and incessant rain, noon blowing heavier, rained more Northerly, evening raining very hard.
8th ditto,	,,	80·	Very wet morning, cleared up about nine.
9th ditto,	,,	80·	Gloomy morning with distant thunder.
10th ditto,	,,	80·	Heavy Squalls through the night, torrents of rain, cleared up at 8 A. M. noon close, calm and sultry.

My attention was drawn to this theory while endeavouring to trace some barometric curve, and some relation between it and the magnetic equator,* and withal some law which might theoretically account for the paraboloidal course of the West Indian and American hurricanes, as shown by Mr. Redfield and Col. Reid ; and the singular difference shown by the track of our Hurricane led me to suppose that it might perhaps move in the axis of the parabola ? Mr. Ravenshaw's letter shortly afterwards gave much credit to these views, and subsequent facts serve to justify our asserting that for this time at least it has done so.

If we describe, as I have done on the Map No. II, a great parabola, one branch of which stretches towards Ceylon, and the other up to the valley of the Ganges towards Agra, the vortex being towards Arracan, and the axis in the line of the supposed track of the Hurricane; it will be found that the focus of such a parabola falls in about lat. 19° 36′ N. long. 88° 10′ E. which was about the centre of the Hurricane on the 4th. These sort of lines are of course arbitrary, but still the coincidence is novel and curious ; whether we look upon the whirls of the Hurricane to have been produced by the mere dynamic action of the streams of air, like the eddies within the bends of a river flowing through a curved channel, or suppose that these vortices are Thermo-electric Phænomena, produced by the sudden transfer of great volumes of the caloric and moisture of the stream of air from the warm equatorial regions to the colder ones toward and beyond the tropics. The remarks on the warmth of the weather in the logs, and the thermometrical

* It may be worth remarking that while this hurricane seems to have travelled from East to West or nearly parallel to the direction of the Magnetic Equator as laid down by Biot, those of the West Indies seem for the most part to come from the South Eastward, which is also there the direction of the plane of the Magnetic Equator. The "Raleigh's" Hurricane in the China Seas seems too to have travelled in this direction.

register, with the peculiar state of the atmosphere so well described in the remarks of Captain Paterson, of the H. C. S. *Amherst*—and her track from Akyab we must remember was almost in the direction of the path of the hurricane till it overtook her at the Sand Heads—are well worth considering.

These are but vague theories, it will be said, but it will not be forgotten that theories on a new subject, like torches in exploring dark caverns often lead us to the passage we seek ; though not by the road we expected. "We have only to be ready to lay them aside when they have served our turn,"* and if I venture to introduce this one here it is to point attention to the importance of obtaining electric observations if possible.

The slow rate at which the vortex appears to have travelled also seems to show, as before remarked, that it was, as it were, pent up between the great stream of air blowing along the Arracan range and the Coromandel Hills. We see analogous instances to this in the small bays at the sides of rivers, where while there is one part of the stream turning round the shores of it and another flowing from point to point, we see the eddies are from time to time found almost stationary about the middle of the bay.†

I wish to be understood here however as suggesting probable comparisons rather than advancing a theory.

Col. Reid and Mr. Redfield give from ten to thirty miles per hour for the rates at which the centres of their different vortices have probably travelled onwards. If our centres are correctly laid down ; and I think there is good evidence that at least those of the 4th and 5th are so; it appears that from the 3rd to the 4th the Hurricane travelled onwards only about 100 miles, or say 4-16 per hour, and from the 4th to the 5th about 70 or 83 miles per hour. This again is conformable to what we observe in the bends of a stream where the eddies seem to start from some point, and move onwards with more rapidity in the first part of their course than latterly. Should future experience confirm this instance of the slow progress of our Hurricane, it will become an important element in any calculation to be made by the seaman for avoiding their violence.

* Sir John Herschel.

† In the rivers of India banks are often formed at these points, which ending by choking the stream as the river becomes lower, changes its channel in succeeding years.

I have quoted at p. 563 an opinion expressed in my hearing, that it was thought by the individual that "they would not make much of it." Few I think who have perused the preceding pages, will be inclined to repeat this, but still as the plain man and the practical seaman may not so readily arrive at *all* the conclusions to be drawn from the knowledge we have collected of this single tempest, I have been induced to sum them up here.

My original intention was to delay doing this, and even the publication of this memoir, until I could collect also what was to be gleaned from the records now existing of our former gales and hurricanes, and then accompany the whole with practical deductions; but it was suggested to me by Professor O'Shaughnessy, that by the delay which this would occasion, we should loose the opportunity of exciting public attention to the subject before the approach of the autumnal gales, and moreover, that even by publishing our knowledge in this yet imperfect state, we might nevertheless, possibly, avert mischief. This I thought sound counsel, and therefore propose to make our former Indian tempests the subject of a future memoir.

It will then be recollected that what is here said is merely the amount of our *present* knowledge, and that what is said is rather meant as a suggestion than as a rule. I shall however distinctly state the grounds from which the various inferences are drawn, and it will be for every man to exercise his own judgment thereupon; I shall also acknowledge when I borrow from Colonel Reid, or other writers.

Clearly to comprehend this theory of gales and hurricanes, let us begin with the *words*. As I have elsewhere said, the words are not to be used so much with relation to the force of the wind in a storm, as to its motion.

A *storm*, or tempest, may mean either a Gale or Hurricane, but it always means a storm of *wind*, and not, as frequently used by landsmen, one of thunder and lightning only; unless so expressed.

A *gale* means a storm of wind, the direction of which is tolerably steady for a long time, sometimes not only for days but for weeks.

A hurricane means a *turning* storm of wind blowing with great violence, and shifting more or less suddenly, so as to blow half or entirely round the compass in a few hours.

With this explanation of our words we shall better understand the things treated of.

The present state of our knowledge seems to show that for the West Indies, Bay of Bengal, and China Sea, the wind in a hurricane has two motions, the one a turning or veering round upon a centre, and the other a straight or curved motion forwards, so that it is both turning round and rolling forward at the same time. It appears also that it turns, when it occurs on the North side of the Equator from the East, or the right hand, by the North, towards the West; or *contrary* to the hands of a watch; and in the Southern hemisphere, that its motion is the contrary way, or *with* the hands of a watch. The foregoing memoir with the charts and diagrams shew that this rule holds good at least for our storm of June last; and that the wind was really blowing in great circles in a direction as described; i. e. against that of the hands of a watch. We assume then for the present, that the hurricanes in the Bay of Bengal *always* follow this law. We do not yet positively *know* that such is the case, but it is the most probable opinion.

If we describe on a piece of paper a few concentric circles, like those in the diagrams, and marking a little compass with its *fleur de lis* to the North in the middle make four arrows at the top, bottom, and two sides, writing against them as in the diagram, East-wind, North-wind, West-wind and South-wind, and then cut this out with scissors, we shall have what is called a *Hurricane-circle* or *Hurricane-card.*

The use of this is to lay it down upon any part of a chart. We may also cut out a little spindle-shaped piece to represent our ship, and place this in that quarter of the card at which the wind is found.

The card may be supposed to represent a circle of fifty or of five hundred miles in diameter, as we please; and one which would fill up the head of the Bay of Bengal would show, on our map No. II, the wind South on the Arracan coast, East at the Sand-Heads, North on the coast of Coromandel, and West across the Bay.

We have now to judge of three important points, What is the track of the hurricane if it is to be one? In what direction does it bear from us now? How far are we from its centre?

We do not yet know what is the usual track of our Indian hurricanes. We know from Col. Reid's and Mr. Redfield's researches that those of the West Indies begin about the Leeward Islands, travel to the WNW. and then round the shores of the Gulf of Mexico, and following the Gulf Stream, are lost in the Atlantic between the Bermudas and Halifax; and they have investigated a sufficient number to show that this may be taken as a general rule. Those also of the Mauritius seem to come from the Eastward. All we yet know positively here is the course of this single tempest; and hence the great necessity of further observation and research, to which I shall perhaps farther allude. We may however, in the absence of better knowledge, take it as a supposition, that the hurricanes in the Bay of Bengal travel from the Eastward to the Westward,* and it may be quite safe to calculate upon their blowing in a circle from right to left.

We must then *assume* this point, and supposing we have the wind at ESE. we are then *somewhere* upon the line leading from the NNE. point of the hurricane-circle to its centre.

If the wind now veers to SE. and SSE. we can easily understand that the centre has passed somewhere to the Southward of us, and that we are upon the *right* hand side of its track.

But if the wind had begun at North, and veered to the N. West and West we can also understand that the hurricane is passing somewhere to the Northward of us, and that we are upon the *left* hand side of its path. At what distance we are from the centre can only be judged of by the quickness with which the wind veers round; and it will be clear that if a ship stood exactly still with the hurricane coming direct towards her, she might have the wind always in one direction till the centre passed her, when she would probably have a shift exactly in the opposite direction.†

The seaman will now understand how it is that he may be running into a Hurricane or scudding in company with one—which no one of course desires to do—and how important it is that a knowledge of their usual paths should be obtained; for they seem to have in all countries tracks which we may call their usual paths.

As an example how a vessel may run into a hurricane, let us suppose upon our Chart, the Amherst, bound across the Bay from Chittagong to Coringa. It is clear that her course then lies across the track of the Hurricane, and that, if ignorant of what we now know, she might with a little alteration of time, and tempted by the fine Easterly Gale, run into the middle of it; for till now, though a falling Barometer would teach the seaman that he was to expect a tempest, he was quite ignorant, or had only some general rules derived from very partial experience, to inform him where it was beginning, how it would blow, and how he could escape it. We shall know this as I have said before, when we know the usual path of our Indian Hurricanes.

* In an able review of Col. Reid's work in No. 23 of the *Madras Journal of Literature and Science* by T. G. Taylor, Esq. H. C. Astronomer at Madras, he says, "The East India Gales appear invariably to travel from the coast of Arracan towards the West, the curves conforming gradually to the slope of the shore until in about the latitude of Madras when their course is due South, after which the curve binds again towards the West, the violence of the storm seldom extending below Cuddon or Porto Novo." Mr. Taylor speaks here of a *gale*. He does not observe that he has described the curve which a hurricane (i. e. a turning gale) would make on three sides of its circle.

† Col. Reid, p. 8.

The question of scudding or heaving to must it is evident depend upon the commander's judgment as to the position in which he is, his sea-room and the like; but the tack on which he ought to heave to is so clearly indicated by Col. Reid's directions that I cannot do better than extract them; he says page 425,

" *Rules for laying Ships to in Hurricanes.*—That tack on which a ship should be laid to in a hurricane has hitherto been a problem to be solved; and is one which seamen have long considered important to have explained.

" In these tempests when a vessel is lying to and the wind veers by the ship's head, she is in danger of getting stern-way* even when no sail is set; for in a hurricane, the wind's force upon the ship's masts and yards alone will produce this effect, should the wind veer ahead, and it is supposed that vessels have often foundered from this cause.

" When the wind veers aft as it is called, or by the stern, this danger is avoided, and a ship then ***comes up*** to the wind instead of having to break off from it.

" If great storms obey fixed laws, and the explanation given of them in this work be the true one, then the rule for laying a ship to follows like the corollary to a problem already solved. In order to define the two sides of a storm, that side will be called the right hand semicircle which is on the right of the ship's course, as we look in the direction in which it is moving, just as we speak of the right bank of a river. The rule for laying a ship to will be, when in the ***right-hand*** semicircle to heave to on the ***starboard*** tack, and when in the left-hand semicircle on the larboard tack in both hemispheres."

As an example of this on our own diagram. If a line be drawn across those of the 4th and 5th N. 76° E. and S. 76° W. or about WbS. ½ S. and EbN. ½ N., which is the track we have supposed for the hurricane; it will be seen that all the vessels above it, or to the right hand of the hurricane's path, had the wind veering from NE. to South, and were thus safe upon the starboard tack, and all

* From being taken aback. This taking aback in a tempest we all know to be most dangerous, not only on account of the getting stern-way here mentioned; being pooped, dismasted, and the like; but from another danger which is not sufficiently adverted to I think; and this is, that a vessel, may in one of the terrific gusts which accompany these sudden shifts of wind be thrown on her broadside in the trough of the sea ***with her deck towards the sea!*** In such a case she is in the position of a vessel on a reef which has fallen over to seaward; and there is every chance that her hatches would be beaten in; which would swamp her. A parallel case to this is mentioned in Col. Reid's work, page 221, of the H. C. S. Diana, when part of the upper fore-hatchway was stove in by the weight of the water above it, and the vessel nearly swamped in consequence. Hatches, particularly those of the upper deck, should not only be made stouter then they usually are (they might for lightness be lined with sheet copper or iron) but moreover two extra strong fore and aft-pieces should be made to ship parallel with the middle piece, halfway between it and the side, so as to afford additional support in cases like this. I shall be told that we know of very few instances of this accident. This may arise from few escaping to tell the tale. The number of well-found, stout ships, ably manned and commanded, which disappear induce us to believe that, apart from fire, there are storm-dangers which we can only guess at. I think this may reasonably be supposed to be one of them. H. P.

those below it,* or on the left hand side, had the wind veering from N. to SW. and were thus safe on the larboard tack. The vicinity of the shore, or the necessity of wearing to ease the masts, if the rigging has stretched too much upon one tack, may oblige the seaman to vary from this rule; and close to the centres of the hurricanes anomalies may be found; but it will be seen at once, I think, without further explanation, of what great value it must ultimately prove to him.

I annex here a public order recently issued by the Government of India, and a memorandum by the Lords of the Admiralty and by Lord Glenelg, which will assist in shewing both the seaman and landsman what we require in the way of information on this subject.

Calcutta: Wednesday, 11th September, 1839.—NOTIFICATION.—The importance of investigating the course and Phænomena of Storms has been brought to the notice of Government by the Hon'ble Court of Directors; and the Hon'ble the President in Council is in consequence desirous of obtaining local Registers of these Phænomena taken simultaneously at as many stations of India as may be found possible. The public Officers of the different settlements and stations of India are accordingly invited and requested, upon the occurrence of any Hurricane, Gale or other Storm of more violence than usual, to note accurately the time of its commencement, the direction from which the wind first blows, whether in gusts or regular, and whether accompanied with rain, thunder and lightning or other Phænomena. Also to note, with as much accuracy as possible, the changes of direction in the wind, and the time of the occurrence of each, and lastly, the duration of the Gale and in what quarter the wind is when it ceases. The variations of the Thermometer and Barometer at each period noticed will also be of importance if the means are forthcoming of making such observations.

The President in Council refrains from making it the business of any particular Officer to note the above circumstances, but relies on the known desire of all enlightened persons to promote objects of scientific and useful enquiry that the public Officers will arrange in such manner as to ensure that the observations will be taken by some one in the vicinity of each station.

Reports upon matters of the description comprehended in this Order may be forwarded to the Secretary to Government in the General Department, free of postage, (superscribed "Storm Report.")

A scientific gentleman in Calcutta has obligingly undertaken to combine all reports that may be so received into a synopsis for exhibition of the results in the manner adopted and recommended by Colonel Reid, R. E.

By Order of the Hon'ble the President of the Council of India in Council.

H. T. PRINSEP,
Secy. to the Govt. of India.

* The places of the Justina and Eden, by an oversight, are unfortunately omitted in the diagram of the 5th. It will be seen that they had the wind at SW. and SWbW. on that day.

MEMORANDUM.

Admiralty, Dec. 28th, 1838.

The Lords Commissioners of the Admiralty having had under consideration the general utility of recording with clearness and precision, in the log books of all Her Majesty's ships and vessels of war, the actual state of the winds and weather, have thought fit to order that henceforward in each page of the log book two columns should be introduced, wherein the force of the wind and the appearance of the atmosphere, shall be every hour registered according to the annexed scheme, a copy of which shall be pasted into each book, and painted on the back of every log board or log slate: and two more columns shall likewise be given for the purpose of entering the heights of the barometer or simpiesometer, and thermometer, when such instruments may be on board.

By command of their Lordships,

C. WOOD.

To all Captains, and commanding officers
of Her Majesty's ships and vessels.

FIGURES TO DENOTE THE FORCE OF THE WIND.

0 denotes Calm.		
1 Light Air, ...	just sufficient to give	Steerage way.
2 Light Breeze, ..	with which a well-conditioned man-of-war, under all sail, and clean full, would go in smooth water, from	1 to 2 knots.
3 Gentle Breeze, ..		3 to 4 knots.
4 Moderate Breeze,		5 to 6 knots.
5 Fresh Breeze, ..	in which the same ship could just carry, close hauled, ..	Royals, &c.
6 Strong Breeze,		Single-reefs and top-gallant sails.
7 Moderate Gale,		Double reefs, jib, &c.
8 Fresh Gale, ...		Triple reefs, courses, &c.
9 Strong Gale, ..		Close reefs & courses.
10 Whole Gale,	with which she could only bear ..	Close reefed main top-sail and reefed fore-sail.
11 Storm, ..	with which she would be reduced to	Stay-sails.
12 Hurricane, ..	to which she could shew	No canvas.

LETTERS TO DENOTE THE STATE OF THE WEATHER.

b Blue sky—whether with clear or hazy atmosphere.
c Cloudy—*i. e.* Detached opening clouds.
d Drizzling rain.
f Fog—f thick fog.
g Gloomy dark weather.
h Hail.
l Lightning.
m Misty or hazy—so as to interrupt the view.
o Overcast—*i. e.* The whole sky covered with one impervious cloud.
p Passing showers.
q Squally.
r Rain—*i. e.* Continuous rain.
s Snow.
t Thunder.
u Ugly threatening appearance in the weather.
v Visibility of distant objects—whether the sky be cloudy or not.
w Wet dew.
. Under any letter denotes an extraordinary degree.

By the combination of these letters, all the ordinary phænomena of the weather may be recorded with certainty and brevity.

EXAMPLES.

b c m Blue sky, with detached opening clouds, but hazy round the horizon.

g v Gloomy dark weather, but distant objects remarkably visible.

q p d l t Very hard squalls, and showers of drizzle, accompanied by lightning, with very heavy thunder.

Nautical Magazine,—March, 1839.

Memorandum respecting the Records to be kept of the state of the Weather in the British Colonies.

The Captains of Ports, Harbour-Masters, and Keepers of lighthouses, or, where those officers do not exist, some other competent public functionary, should be required to keep journals of the weather, on the principle of the log books of ships. A column should be specially reserved for inserting the height of the barometer. Under the head of 'Remarks,' should be entered all meteorological observations considered worthy of particular notice. When the keeper of a journal may hear that a vessel has encountered a storm, he will enter in it any information on the subject which he can rely on, together with the name of the ship, of her owner, and of the port to which she may belong. With the view of tracing the course of storms, the Trinity Board of London have given directions for the adoption of measures to obtain a more accurate record of the weather, than has hitherto been kept, at the lighthouses of Great Britain and Ireland. The keepers of these lights having the opportunity of taking their observations by night as well as by day, great advantage may be derived from employing them in this manner. Officers in charge of Colonial lighthouses should be instructed to keep similar journals. In noting the wind's force, both in the Harbour-Master's journals and in the lighthouse reports, it is desirable that the officers should adopt the numbers for noting the strength of the wind now in use at Greenwich Observatory, and about to be introduced at the lighthouses under the Trinity Board. In the cases of St. Helena and Ascension, it is desirable that more precise information should be obtained by observation, respecting the 'Rollers' at those islands. As the object of H. M's. Government in instituting these inquiries is the advancement of knowledge in science generally, the Governors of the several British Colonies will consider how far it may be in their power to obtain useful information bearing on the subject, from countries adjoining to their Governments in the possession of foreign powers, or how far it may be useful to the study of meteorology, to exchange the observations made within their Governments, for those of other countries in the neighbourhood. If at any time desired, there would be no objection to the publication in the Colonial newspapers of extracts from the journals.

(*Signed*) GLENELG.

There is little to be added to these ample directions, but I may be allowed here to repeat what has been said in another place,*—that every European in India, may be said to have a direct personal interest in this matter; for, though unconnected with commercial speculations, he probably looks one day to cross the ocean himself on his return home; or has those who are dear to him doing so; or he may be sent to sea for his health. It is superfluous to allude here to that general interest which the feelings of humanity must awaken in every man's mind when he hears of a new branch of knowledge, which may so much contribute to disarm the tempest of its terrors; and which careful, common-sense accounts of storms may so very essentially assist us in perfecting.

In closing this first memoir, which, in the absence of abler labourers in the field, I propose to follow by others as I can find materials, I ought to apologize for its imperfections. I have mentioned in Part I. some of the difficulties I experienced in collecting information, and that, by the advice of a friend, I published earlier than I originally intended, to attract attention to the October Gales. When I add to this, that I am far from being master of my own time, I trust due allowance will be made for its defects, by those who are not aware of these circumstances. To solicit information on any question of natural history is often fruitless enough in all countries, but upon meteorological questions, and in India, where the public mind has not yet been roused to attention on this head, and where observers are so few, is absolutely at times, to use a Gallicism, *désespérant*. I trust however this little essay will shew how much every trifle, insignificant as it

* Englishman, 17th September, 1839.

might be thought by the possessor, may contribute to the end we seek. Mr. Hudson's valuable barometrical observations on board the Hope Floating Light, I have alluded to at p. 589; and I may state here, that those of the Hurricane of October, 1832, quoted by Col. Reid p. 269, as taken at Chandernagore, are my own; and both prove to be of far more utility than was at the time supposed by the observers. We may indeed, if allowed to speak metaphorically on such a subject, say, that as the great pyramids of human knowledge must be built of separate stones, no man can say, before he brings his to the builder, that it may not become "the head stone of the corner!"

Art. III.—*Extracts from Mr. M'Clelland's paper on Indian Cyprinidæ. As. Res. Vol.* xix. *Part* II.

For such of our readers as do not subscribe to the Researches of the Society, we take this opportunity of extracting such parts of the 2nd part of the 19th vol. just published, as may be separated, without disadvantage from the rest of Mr. M'Clelland's paper. The utility of Ichthyology is set forth in the following remarks.

"Utility will always be found to depend more on the degree of attention paid to any subject connected with science, than on the nature of the subject itself; yet it is a common remark that this, or that, is important or frivolous, according as we happen to be acquainted with it. When we find any branch of science regarded as useless, we may be assured that, contrary to ordinary expectation, it will prove the most productive field we can enter. Science, indeed, can only be useful where it has been cultivated, and its principles worked out; practical results will then follow in proportion to the pains taken to develop them.

"The moral interest of Ichthyology having been sufficiently attended to throughout the preceding paper, I shall here pass it over, merely remarking, that in common with other branches of natural science it is calculated to improve the mind as well as the condition of society, while its cultivation need not interfere with any duty, public or private; and few who are placed on our coasts, or on the banks of any of the noble rivers of India, who might not with amusement to themselves, and advantage to science, communicate many observations no-

John Goldingham

'The Great Trigonometrical Survey of India'.

The Calcutta Review 38 (1863)

ART. II.—1. *Journal of the Asiatic Society of Bengal.*

2. *Proceedings of the Royal Geographical Society of London.*

3. *Description of China, Chinese Tartary &c. &c. translated from the French of* P. DU HALDE, printed by T. Gardner. Bartholomew Close, London: A.D. 1738.

4 *Results of a Scientific Mission to India and High Asia. By Herman, Adolphe and Robert De Schlagintweit. Vol.* 1, LEIPZIG: F. A. Brockhaus. London: Trübner & Co. 1861.

5. *A Series of Papers on Mountain & other local attraction in India and its effect on the calculations of the Great Trigonometrical Survey.* By JOHN H. PRATT M. A. Extracted from the Transactions of the Royal Society for 1854, 1855, 1858 & 1861. Calcutta: 1862.

6. *Asie Centrale—Recherches sur les Chaines de Montagnes, et la climatologie comparée.* Par A DE HUMBOLDT. Paris: Gide, Lebaire Editeur, 1843.

IN former numbers of this Periodical* we have given accounts of the Great Trigonometrical Survey of India, and traced its operations continuously from its commencement in 1800 by Captain Lambton—the Father of Indian Geodesy—to the year 1850, when the Blue Book, containing Colonel Waugh's able analysis of the proceedings of the Survey was published. We entered at length on the long contested question of the relative value of Astronomical Observations in comparison with Trigonometrical, for the basis of an operation of such magnitude as the Topographical delineation of the British Indian Empire. We would, however, again return to this subject, to shew that the

* No. VII. Sept. 1845. Art. 3. and No. XXXII. Dec. 1851. Art.8.

arguments in favor of Trigonometrical operations are almost as valid in the present advanced stage of Astronomy, as they were of old in the infancy of the Trigonometrical Survey of this country.

There is much that is very tempting and charming in Astronomical observations. They give absolute values of the two important elements Latitude and Longitude, of the place at which they are taken, and it would seem at first sight to be far preferable to employ them to determine the positions which are to become the origins and termini of future Surveys, than to undertake the very tedious and laborious process of connecting these points by Triangulation. They have often an appearance of very great accuracy; numerous repetitions give results which for the most part coincide very closely, and consequently have very small Mathematical 'probable errors'. Under such circumstances, none but a hardened unbeliever would venture to suggest the possibility of the existence of a large actual error, due to some mysterious and unknown cause, which is beyond the ken of the Astronomer, and not subject to his control.

Most persons are agreed that very accurate and satisfactory determinations of latitude may be obtained with ordinary means. In our last notice of the Trigonometrical Survey, we expressed an opinion, which we are now anxious to qualify, that thirty or forty observations with a good sextant ought to determine the latitude certainly within 200 feet of the truth. Granting that the results would be within 200 feet of the value given by the most refined measurements, with the most powerful instruments, they may still be some way off from the truth, for there is a source of error which affects all such observations alike, independently of the instrument by which they may be taken; it ever exists to a greater or less extent, and cannot be eradicated, or even measured with absolute certainty. We mean the tendency of the plumb line to deviate from its normal direction, in consequence of local irregularities in the Earth's crust. The plummet is attracted by mountains, and repelled by oceans, the former by the excess of matter which they bring to bear on it, the latter by the deficiency which results when water takes the place of land. Even on level plains remote from hills and seas, deflection exists when the rocks and strata below are of unequal densities, on opposite sides of the plummet.

In the memorable experiment which was made at the mountain of Schiehallien, in Perthshire, for the purpose of measuring the amount of its attraction on the plumb line, the meridional distance of two stations on opposite sides of the mountain was found to be 4364·4 feet, or 42″·9, as computed by a process of triangulation, while by Astronomical observations it was apparently 54″·6 or 5551·7 feet. The difference, amounting to more than one-fourth of the entire distance, is wholly attributable to the Astronomical observations, the plumb line at the station on the south of the hill being attracted northwards, while at the opposite station it was attracted southwards, thus causing the Astronomical arc to be larger than the Terrestrial by the sum of the deflections. Half this quantity is the mean effect of the mountain in disturbing the plumb line at either station, but whether the attraction is greater at one than the other, and by what amount, are questions which are undeterminable with absolute accuracy, and probably will ever remain to baffle and perplex the Geodesist.

A contour survey can give the magnitude of the superficial irregularities, and assign their relative excess or defect in the neighbourhood of each plumb line, but it is also necessary, for a complete solution of the amount of attraction, to know the density, not only of the superficial masses, but also of the subjacent strata, to a depth far beyond the reach of the Geologist.

Thus even the determination of latitude is not so easy a problem as appears at first sight;—Archdeacon Pratt tells us in his able investigations of the effects of attraction on the operations of the Trigonometrical Survey, that the whole of India may be as much as half a mile north of the position assigned it on the maps of the Survey. At Kalianpùr the origin of latitudes, where it was necessary to make Astronomical observations, and refer the operations to the faithless zero of an erratic plumb line, the Archdeacon has shown that the probable error caused by the Himalayas is one fourth of a mile, and by the Ocean about one sixth, which may be increased by variations of density in the strata below. He demonstrates that it affects all the triangulation and the maps in an equal degree, and consequently the whole of the relative distances are correct, which would be very far from being the case if they had been based on Astronomical observations instead of Trigonometrical.

If we now turn to the subject of longitudes, we find a far wider margin allowed for possible inaccuracies. But even here the difficulties of the operations are in general greatly underrated. There is scarcely a Ship-Captain but believes that with a few sextant observations of lunar distances he can find his longitude whenever he pleases within five miles, and is inclined to ascribe to his lunar observations the successful guiding of his ship to port, which is due in far greater measure to his older allies, the lead and look-out. Like the man who maintained that nothing was easier than to predict eclipses, for one had but to take them out of the almanac, he will say 'what is the difficulty? one has but 'to compare his lunar observations, after they have undergone 'certain well known corrections, with the data which are given 'ready to hand in the Nautical Almanac, to obtain the requisite 'longitude'. Granting that the observations are perfectly accurate, which is highly improbable, the errors of the Almanac have still to be taken into consideration, and that *they* are not small, may be more clearly understood from the following example of their practical operation, than from any further explanation.

The longitudes observed at Lake Memphramagog in 1845 by the Royal Engineers sent out to determine the boundary between the United States of America, and British Canada were as follows, in terms of the data given in the Nautical Almanac for that year.

August	14th	4 H.	48 M.	26·86
"	15th	4 "	48 "	38·07
"	16th	4 "	48 "	24·58
"	17th	4 "	48 "	26·97
"	20th	4 "	48 "	7·53
	Mean	4.	48.	24·80

After correction for the presumed errors of Nautical Almanac as determined by observations at Greenwich, taken on the dates in question, these values become.

August	14th	4 H.	48 M.	38·17
"	15th	"	"	53·07
"	16th	"	"	35·86
"	17th	"	"	48·25
"	20th	"	"	23·51
	Mean	4	48	39·77

Showing a difference of 15· seconds in time which is nearly equivalent to 4 miles, on the parallel of Madras, and arises from causes entirely beyond the control of the observer.

There is even said to be a doubt of 1″ in the difference of longitude between the splendid and long established Observatories of Paris and Greenwich, for the re-determination of which special Trigonometrical operations are now on foot.

'There is nothing new under the sun'. More than a century and half ago, a few French Jesuits who had settled in China with the laudable object of converting the inhabitants of that vast empire to Christianity, managed to impress the Emperor Kanghi, with the accuracy and advantages of the European methods of mapping, and were consequently engaged by him to construct maps of all the provinces of his empire. Animated by the hopes of securing the protection of the Emperor, 'which was necessary to favor the progress of Christianity,' the Jesuit fathers set to work most rigorously and conscientiously, adopting, after due consideration, the method of triangles in preference to any other.

Our readers will not require us to apologize for placing before them the following brief description of this grand undertaking, which Père Regis, writing in the commencement of the 18th century, rightly called 'the greatest geographical work that ever was performed according to the rules of art'.

Our extracts are taken from the account sent by the Father to France in the name of the Missionaries who were associated with him, as given in the preface to Père Du Halde's work on China, in the English translation which is quoted at the head of this article.

'I can assure you', says he, 'that we have omitted nothing re-'quisite for rendering our work perfect. We have ourselves 'visited all the places, even those of least consideration, through-'out the Provinces; èxamined the maps and histories of each 'city preserved in their tribunals; made enquiries of the Man-'darins and their Officers, as well as the principal inhabitants, 'whose territories we passed through; in short, by measuring as 'we advanced, we still had measures ready to serve the Trian-'gles, formed by such points as were to be fixed.

'For after mature deliberation we thought it best to use the 'method of triangles, all others appearing to us not only too 'tedious, considering the vast extent of the countries, of which 'the Emperor wanted the map, but scarcely practicable on ac-'count of the towns being so near one another, since it is certain 'that the least error, occasioned by the pendulum going wrong, 'or the immersion of one of Jupiter's Satellites not being ac-'curately observed, would cause a considerable error in the lon-'gitude: for instance, the mistake of a minute in time would 'produce an error of 15 minutes in longitude, which are equi-'valent to four or five leagues according to the difference of the 'parallels: so that it might happen, that according to the ob-'servation, two towns would be made contiguous, at the same 'time that there would be really some distance, though not much, 'between them.

'This inconvenience is not to be feared in the method of 'triângles: for how is it possible to err four leagues in the 'distance between two places no farther asunder, when by a 'measure that always follows us, and semi-circles accurately 'divided, we fix divers points between the two terms, which 'joined together make as it were a chain of triangles? On the 'other hand, nothing is so difficult as to avoid a small error in 'time; the best pendulums are put out of order by travelling, 'and to prevent erring, even in a single minute, the observations 'must be repeated several days; a task which would be extreme- 'ly fatiguing.

'The observations of the Satellites require not only more 'time and accuracy, but also Telescopes of the same size, and, 'if I may so speak, the same eyes in the observer, and his corres- 'pondent; for, if the one sees them ever so little sooner than the 'other some error will inevitably happen, which must not be 'suffered in determining small distances. And if observations 'of a Satellite, made in the same place, by the same person, 'differ so in time as to cause a small variation in the longitudes, 'and oblige us to take a middle difference among them (supposing 'the difference to become insensible by the greatness of the dis- 'tance) the results will be still more uncertain when there are 'several observers, who have neither the same instruments nor 'address; so that the difference arising between the observations, 'renders the position of places lying near one another doubtful, 'nor can it be fixed but by the rules of Geometry, which shews 'the necessity of having recourse to the method of triangles 'at last.

'This method when continued without interruption, has one 'farther advantage, as it gives not only the longitude, but 'also the latitude of the towns to be inserted; which being 'afterwards examined by the Meridian altitudes of the sun or 'Polar stars, serves to correct the preceding operations. This 'course we took as often as we were able, and commonly found 'no sensible difference between the observation of the latitude, 'and the determination by triangles. If sometimes we dis- 'covered variations, we did not think ourselves thereby obliged 'to lay aside this method, since we find as many in the observa- 'tions of the Polar altitudes, made by the best Astronomer in 'the same place. Although the theory, whereon such observa- 'tions are grounded, is certain, nevertheless the practice depends 'on so many little circumstances, which must all be attended 'to in order to obtain perfect accuracy, that the operations cannot 'be always exact, but must vary something more or less. However, these little defects always appear, and may be often corrected in large works, by connecting the points fixed by Trigonometry with those whose position is under examination.

'Another method which we judged ought to be employed for great precision was to return to the same point, already determined, by different ways, from a considerable distance, working according to rules. For if by the last essay you find the same situation, the exactness of the preceding operations will be proved in some measure to a demonstration. When in measuring we could not return to the same point, our method was, as we passed near the great towns already marked down, or other fit places, to look out for the remarkable towns or mountains that commanded them; and from time to time we measured to see if the distance, resulting from the operations (when corrected) agreed with the actual measures.

'All these precautions and many more, too tedious to enumerate, appeared to us necessary when executing a work in a manner worthy the trust reposed in us by a wise Prince, who judged it of the greatest importance to his state. Moreover, the hopes of meriting his protection, which was necessary to favor the progress of Christianity in his empire, supported us amidst those dangers and crosses that are unavoidable by those who have to do with such a variety of tempers, and are engaged in so laborious an undertaking: nay, we were willing for our own satisfaction, to have repaired again both to the Eastern and Western Frontiers, as well as to some places within the kingdom, situated at convenient distances, there to examine the longitudes by repeated observations of eclipses; but as the work was finished, and the Emperor appeared satisfied with it, we did not think it proper to engage him in a new, and not altogether necessary affair. We therefore contented ourselves with observations of the moon and satellites of Jupiter made before our time in several cities by members of our society, though we rejected a few because they did not agree with our measures on account of some small error as to time in the observation, which but too often happens to the most experienced. Not but that we ourselves observed some eclipses of the moon, and found no other difference in our observations than is usual in such cases; where we had any doubt we chose the mean difference.

'Thus having first made use of the method of triangles for determining the distances between the several cities, and afterwards compared it with that of eclipses observed in places, 'remote from Pekin, we flatter ourselves that we have fol-'lowed the surest course; and even the only one practicable in 'prosecuting the greatest Geographical work that ever was per-'formed according to the rules of art.'

The Surveys of the Fathers extended from the Eastern frontier of the Chinese Empire as far west as the meridian of Pegu, embracing the Provinces of Yunnan, Szuchuan, and the rest of China proper, and the portion of Eastern Tartary lying between the Chinese frontier and the Saghalian Ula or River Amoor. A map of Korea was met with in the palace of the king of that country, which on examination was found to be so accurate that it was incorporated by the Fathers into their own survey without revision,—a singular circumstance, suggestive of a higher civilization in Korea than at Pekin, for we are led to believe that it was the want of a map of the country around Pekin which prompted the Jesuits to construct one in order to excite the interest of the Emperor, and obtain his favor and support by inducing him to employ them in making a survey of the whole of his dominions. It is to these operations, executed nearly a century and a half ago, that we owe our present admirable maps of China, which are a source of surprise to all who are ignorant of their origin, and only know how jealously Europeans have been excluded from the interior of the Empire. There, or at least in China proper, there is no *terra incognita* to reward future explorers. The recent enterprising expedition of Colonel Sarel and Captain Blakiston up the River Yang-tse-Kiang, which has afforded so much valuable information on numerous subjects, has not, we believe, made any additions to our knowledge of Chinese geography; the noble river up which they ascended, and the chief cities and towns on its banks, being mapped out in their chart pretty much as it was mapped by the Jesuits 150 years ago. We trust that at no very distant date the officers of the Trigonometrical Survey of India will be able to connect their triangles with those of the Jesuit Fathers.

When we last reviewed the operations of the Survey, we stated that on the completion of the great meridional series of triangles which extends from Cape Comorin to the Dehra Dhoon, and is now well known in the scientific world as the Great Arc of India, being the longest and probably the most accurate of the several arcs which have been measured in various parts of the world to determine the figure of the earth, the Survey establishments were deputed to execute series of triangles on successive meridians eastwards from the great Arc, at distances of about one degree apart, as far as the meridian of Calcutta. These triangulations emanate from a longitudinal* series which had been carried eastwards from the Seronj base line in Central India to Calcutta, in the years 1826—32, before Colonel Everest revised and extended the great Arc. This series was executed with rapidity through a wild and difficult tract of country, at an insignificant cost, barely one fourth the ordinary expense of such operations. Unfortunately the only instruments then available were of a secondary order, the system of operations was deficient in rigor and accuracy, and very inferior to what was subsequently introduced by Colonel Everest, which is much to be regretted, because all the meridional series between the great Arc and Calcutta are necessarily based on it, and their final values cannot be determined until the Calcutta longitudinal series has been revised. The late Hon'ble Court of Directors authorized the revision to be undertaken as soon as the triangulation had been well advanced over the rest of India.

The last of the meridional series between Calcutta and the great Arc, to the north of the longitudinal series, was completed in 1852; and now the greater portion of the Trigonometrical operations to the west of the great Arc, the axis of Indian Geography, are finished. A western longitudinal series extends from Seronj to Karachi in continuation of the Calcutta longitudinal arc; a north west Himalayan series from Dehra Dhoon to Attok; and the Indus series from Attok to Karachi, following the course of the frontier of our Indian empire towards Persia and Affghanistan. These, with the great Arc, form a vast quadrilateral figure at whose four corners base lines have been measured with the set of compensating bars and microscopes which was constructed on the model of the apparatus invented by Colonel Colby for the measurement of the base lines of the Ordnance Survey of Great Britain, and brought out from England by Colonel Everest in 1830.

The bases at Dehra Dhoon and Seronj were measured by Colonel Everest in the course of the great Arc; those at Attok and Karachi in the seasons 1853-54 and 54-55 by Colonel Waugh.

The western longitudinal series was commenced at the close of 1848 by Captain Renny Tailyour B. E., assisted by Captain Strange of the Madras Cavalry. After having successfully started the work, Captain Tailyour returned to his duties at the head quarters of the Surveyor General, leaving Captain Strange to go

* So called because it is carried in an east and west direction, and measures the distance between successive meridians of longitude.

on with the triangulation. Great difficulties were met with in the course of these operations; first, the Arabulli range, formidable for its ruggedness rather than its height, had to be crossed, and afterwards the extensive salt desert which intervenes between those mountains and the Indus, and forms the northern flank of the Runn of Cutch.

Captain Strange describes the Arabulli mountains as 'an extensive tract, having a general north and south direction composed of ridges and peaks which though attaining no elevation greater perhaps than 5,500 feet above the sea, yet exhibit in the details that compose them all the boldest features of the most stupendous mountain scenery. The traveller at the end of his day's journey attains perhaps an elevation but little greater than that from whence he departed; but he has in its course more than once ascended with great labor high acclivities only to plunge again and again through dense forests and across rugged beds of mountain torrents into precipitous valleys of equal depth. In many parts of this very peculiar tract where but slight communication and no traffic exists, it may be said that there are no roads whatever. Nothing meets the eye but vast blocks of granite towering aloft, and jungles almost impenetrable obstruct every step. The habitations of men are seldom met with, and man himself as here found roams a lawless savage.

'In addition to the physical difficulties presented by the Arabulli mountains, the impediments were enhanced by the unwillingness of the inhabitants to render assistance. Great interruptions would have been experienced from this cause but for the services of a native officer of the Meywar Bheel Corps, Subadar Chutter Tewaree, who was obligingly deputed by his commanding officer Captain Brooke to accompany Captain Strange. Having been long and extensively employed in recruiting from the Bheel population, and in promoting order and civilization among them, he had been recognized as a benefactor to whom they readily on all occasions accorded obedience. His influence was extraordinary, and a word from him always sufficed to collect strong gangs of carriers, when no persuasion from any one else was listened to.'

The tract crossed by the triangulation between the Arabulli mountains and the Indus comprises three distinct kinds of ground:—

First, a succession of gentle sandy undulations dotted with thick stunted jungle, appertaining chiefly to the Jodhpore and

Palampur states;—thinly populated and but little cultivated, with a scanty supply of water, which is only to be found in wells of great depth, and is usually brackish, this is altogether a miserable country, and is described by Capt. Strange as 'interesting only from its physical deficiencies.'

Next comes the Desert, commonly known among the natives as the Thur; it is throughout composed of sand hills whose general form is long straight ridges, which seldom unite but stand at close and regular intervals parallel to each other; like the ripple on the sea shore. Some of them are perhaps a mile long and vary from 50 to 300 feet in height, their sides being deeply channelled by rain and their general appearance fiom a distance differing little from that of ordinary low hills. There is more jungle than might be expected, but it is low and almost leafless. The whole desert in the cold season is clothed with grass, and is then much resorted to for pasturage by herdsmen. The population is scanty, the villages small and far apart, consisting merely of a few conical huts, scarcely a man's height, which are rudely constructed of twigs and grass.

Where the desert ends, the plains of Sind begin, and the transition is surprisingly sudden. In a space of one hundred yards, the traveller leaves sands and dunes, and the stunted vegetation of the desert, and enters a perfectly flat country with a firm, black loamy soil, Inhabitants, customs, language, and vegetation are exchanged with the same strange, startling abruptness. The soil is hard and grassless. Jungle is plentiful and thick, the country populous and well cultivated, and intersected in every direction by irrigation canals. Such a country is, however, very much more difficult for Trigonometrical operations than the preceding inhospitable tracts of sand hills and undulations. In them the chief difficulty was to provide food and water for the officers and men employed. But depots for grain and other supplies were established at various places, and replenished periodically from Deesa and Hydrabad; and the water of the desert, though brackish and most unpleasant, was drinkable without any deleterious effects. The sand hills afforded excellent stations for the Trigonometrical operations, being just sufficiently high to overtop the lower murky strata of the atmosphere, and not too high to make their ascent a matter of difficulty. They only needed the construction of a small pillar and platform of masonry to mark the site of the station. Scarcely a single ray had to be cleared to open the view between the Stations at its extremities. And thus the operations proceeded without check or hindrance, and with greater rapidity than had ever previously been attained in any part of the Trigonometrical Survey.

But when the convenient sand hills were passed, and the plains of Sind were reached, it became necessary to construct towers for stations of observation. Most of our readers are probably aware that the limited distance at which ordinary objects are visible on a plain is due to the curvature of the earth. If we walk over a perfectly level plain away from an object twenty four feet high, we find that at the distance of six miles, only as much of it will be visible as equals the height of the observer's eye above the ground. The height which it is necessary to give a tower, to overtop the earth's curvature for any given distance, is determined by the well known rule, that it must equal, in feet, two thirds of the square of the distance, in miles. The towers of the Trigonometrical Survey are usually made from 24 to 30 feet in height; thus each has a command of about six miles, and they are consequently mutually visible at double that distance, when there is nothing but the curvature to be surmounted. Other obstacles must be removed, or overtopped by increasing the height of the towers.

These structures consist of a central pillar of brick and mortar tapering upwards to a diameter of three to four feet at top, on which the Theodolite employed for the principal triangulation is rested. A mass of masonry of unburnt bricks cemented with clay is erected, so as to afford a platform of about twelve by sixteen feet on a level with the top of the pillar, to give room for the Observatory tent, and the heliotropers who are required to flash to and arouse the signallers at the adjacent stations. The summit is reached by a substantial flight of steps. The central pillar is separated from the surrounding platform by an annulus, in order that the instrument may be unaffected by the movements of the observer and his attendants. The pillar is perforated vertically to allow a plummet suspended from its summit to be adjusted over the markstone, which is fixed in its base at the ground level, lest the tower should become accidentally deflected.

These structures cost on an average only Rs. 250 each, or 10 Rupees for every foot in height, but the time occupied in the selection of suitable sites, and afterwards in the erection of the towers, and in carefully clearing the rays between them of all obstacles, causes much delay, and greatly impedes the operations. Progress is further retarded by the bad signals which are presented on all sides to the observer; being so close to the ground their rays are most irregularly refracted in all directions, lateral as well as vertical, during their passage through the thick dust and vapours in the lower strata of the atmosphere. Under such circumstances the measurement of the angles proceeds very slowly, and numerous repetitions are entailed. Captain Strange, whose progress over the Arabulli mountains and across the desert had been a series of successes, encountered his first check on the plains of Sind, being delayed at one station no less than twenty-five days, in taking a set of observations similar to what had rarely occupied him as many hours on the sand hills of the desert.

West of the Indus, the triangulation again reached a hilly tract of country, and then advanced with rapidity to Karachi, where, in the month of April 1853, it was brought to a termination on Colonel Waugh's base line. The field operations thus occupied five seasons in all; they comprise 173 principal triangles arranged in quadrilateral or polygonal figures in order that each link of the chain of triangles may be self-verificatory. The average triangular error was 0″·79 or about eight-tenths of a second. Numerous secondary triangles were measured, and the positions of all the principal places in the vicinity of the operations were fixed.

The extent of the measured arc of longitude is 10° 37′, equivalent to 668 miles in length, and the area covered by the principal and the secondary triangles is 20,323 square miles, the average cost per square mile being Rs. 6-13. The operations involved 117 principal stations, of which only twenty-two were towers, or the expense of the operations, and the time they would have occupied, must necessarily have been considerably greater.

At Kurachi, Lieut. Tennant took a series of observations for latitude with one of the large Astronomical circles brought out from England by Col. Everest for the great Arc, and a set of azimuthal observations on circumpolar stars with the great Theodolite.

The Astronomical latitude of Karachi Observatory on Bath Island thus deduced is	24°49′49″·27
The computed value brought up from Kalianpoor Observatory near Seronj is	24° 49′50″·15
Difference	0″·88

The Astronomical azimuth of referring mark is 179°59′57″·43

That brought up from Kalianpoor is ... ...179° 59′57″·74

Difference 0·31

The small differences between the Astronomical and computed values indicate that, whatever may be the deviation of the plumb line at Kalianpoor in Central India, it is deflected by nearly the same amount at Karachi on the Sea coast.

The N. W. Himalaya series was commenced at a side of the great Arc near Dehra Dhoon in the season 1847-48 by Major Du Vernet of the Madras Army. The following year an insurrection broke out in the Saon or Jaswan Dhoon, which drove the whole party from the field. Major Du Vernet with a large theodolite narrowly escaped capture, and one of the sub-assistants was made a prisoner by the rebels, who plundered his property and destroyed his instruments; he was marched off bound to the Rajah of Amb, but after eight days was released by a detachment sent for his rescue. The rebellion was soon extinguished and operations were resumed. Two years afterwards they were again stopped because the Maharajah of Kashmir took umbrage at the occupation of the Mountain of Trikote as a survey station on the plea of its being sacred.

Thus the principal triangulation progressed somewhat slowly, but a large amount of secondary triangulation was executed to lay down the positions of the hill peaks and the chief towns of the Jullundur and Baree Doab and the Cis-Sutlej states.

Simultaneously a topographical survey of the Himalayas was commenced in connexion with the triangulation, being the first time that the members of this survey were ever employed in filling in the details of the ground they had covered with their triangles. These interesting operations were originated under the superintendence of Major Du Vernet, who had been long employed in the topography of Hydrabad and other parts of the Madras Presidency. In the six years between 1848 and 1854, a map of the belt of hills between the Ganges and the Beas River, and the parallels 31 and 33 of latitude, was completed on the scale of four miles to one inch. It has been recently published in degree sheets, lithographed in colors in the office of the Surveyor General, Calcutta, and is now available to the public.

While Major Du Vernet was employed in topography, the triangulation of the N. W. Himalaya series was extended to Attok by Mr. Geo. Logan, who had recently completed the North East longitudinal series, through the Terai at the base of the eastern Himalayas, under circumstances of very great difficulty, owing to the unhealthy nature of the tract of country passed through. Mr. Logan's principal triangulation reached Attok in 1853, supplying the requisite elements for the Topographical Surveys of the Rawul Pindi and Jhelum districts, and the northern Trans-Indus frontier, which were commenced in connexion with the Trigonometrical Survey, shortly after the annexation of the Punjab.

The N. W. Himalaya series consists of seventy seven principal triangles arranged in quadrilaterals and polygons, extending over a direct distance of 416 miles. The triangulation, principal and secondary, embraces an area of 33,000 square miles, including snow peaks, and was executed at a cost of Rs. 3-5 per square mile. The stations being all on hills or high mounds, no towers had to be constructed, and the cost of the work per square mile was much diminished by the large areas included in the triangles to the snow peaks. The area topographically surveyed was 33,700 square miles, at a cost of Rs 3-10 per square mile.

The Indus series extends from Attok to Karachi, and is 706 miles in length, the longest of any series of this Survey from base line to base line. Its extremities rest on the hills of Lower Sind and of the Rawul Pindi and Bunnoo districts. But the Soolimani Range to which the triangulation runs parallel, was inaccessible for political reasons. Even the Tukhti Sooliman, the fabled throne of the 'weary King Ecclesiast', whose summits survey a vast extent of country hitherto untrodden by Europeans, the surveyors were reluctantly obliged to turn away from, and leave the frontier without attempting to visit. The Trigonometrical stations had to be restricted for a distance of about 470 miles to the flat and monotonous plains bordering the river Indus, which are rarely relieved by an undulation, or a mound suitable for the Triangulation.

It thus became necessary to construct towers at no less than 113 out of the 148 principal stations, and to clear 230 sides of triangles, whose united length amount to upwards of 2400 miles. The observations were almost entirely taken with the great Theodolite constructed by Messrs. Troughton aud Simms for Colonel Everest. Each angle was measured on five zeros 'face right,' and the same number 'face left', three repetitions being taken on each zero; the instrument having five horizontal microscopes, the value of each angle was thus obtained from fifty measures on equidistant parts of the limb, 7° 12′ apart. There are in all 205 triangles arranged in self-verificatory quadrilaterals and polygons ;—their average triangular error is 0″·47. The area embraced by the principal and secondary operations is about 35,000 square miles, and the cost Rupees 9-4-0 per square mile.

In connection with the Indus series, a set of levelling operations with the spirit level was instituted with a view to determine the heights of the base lines of the Trigonometrical Survey with accuracy. Values of height had already been approximately afforded by the vertical observations between the principal stations of the triangulation. But such a method of levelling, though susceptible of a high degree of accuracy in a hilly or mountainous region, is beset with many difficulties in a flat country. For it is evident that an object to be correctly observed must first be truly seen. But when both object and observer are low down or only slightly raised, the rays of light they interchange graze the surface of the ground and traverse a medium which is subject to many variations, being sometimes dense and heavy with moisture, at other times rarified by the heat radiated at mid-day from the surface of the ground. Thus the apparent position of the object varies within wide limits, according as the soil is dry or moist, barren or cultivated, baked by the sun or chilled by night dews; the rays of light being generally refracted more or less upwards, because the denser strata of the atmosphere are usually lowermost, though for a few hours before and after noon, if there are no clouds, the heated ground rarifies the strata of air in its immediate proximity, the denser strata then float some feet above, and rays of light passing below them are necessarily bent downwards and have their paths concave to the ground; the refraction is then called negative.

The following extract from a set of vertical observations taken in the Sind Saugor Doab with one of the great instruments of the Trigonometrical Survey, will serve to show how distant objects, seen over a plain, rise and fall to an extent that is probably little imagined. At the tower of Nar thirty feet high (lat 32° 27′; longitude 73° 19′;) the observations to the station of Goonia, distant 10.53 miles were as follows :—

Date	Hour			Vertical Angles ° ′ ″
22nd November 1855	2-35	(P. M.)	Depression	0 5 45·6
	2-48	„	„	0 5 34·5
	3-5	„	„	0 5 32·1
	3-37	„	„	0 5 25·2
	4-30	„	„	0 4 52·6
	10-50	„	Elevation	0 2 24·0

Here the signal rose 20″, equivalent to 5·4 feet between 2h. 35m. and 3h. 37m; 33″, or 8·9 feet in the following interval of 53 minutes, and. 7′17″ or 117·8 feet in the next 6½ hours; the total observed change of altitude being equivalent to 132 feet, during little more than eight consecutive hours!

The law is invariably the same; objects are seen at a minimum elevation between 1 and 3 o'clock P. M; they then rise, at first gradually, afterwards very rapidly as the sun sinks and the dew begins to fall, attaining a maximum elevation when the air is most saturated with moisture, which is usually before day-break. As the sun rises the phenomena are repeated in the reverse order, and the object sinks, rapidly at first, but more slowly as the time of minimum refraction approaches. The limits between which the oscillation takes place will of course vary with the amount of moisture in the atmosphere, the nature of the soil, whether favorable or not to the deposition of dew, the heat of the sun's rays, and the aspect of the sky, whether clear or cloudy.

A few feet of difference in the height of a station of observation on the plains have a great effect on these phenomena. The nearer the rays of light are to the ground the greater and more irregular is the range through which they are refracted. Grazing rays are therefore always objectionable. But it is often impossible to avoid them without a more minute reconnaissance of the ground to be triangulated than is for other reasons allowable. Usually the survey stations in the plains are from eleven to twelve miles apart, at which distance, when raised twenty-four feet above the ground level, they become just high enough to overtop the curvature of the earth, to which the line joining their summits will be a tangent. The instrument and signal stand five feet high on the towers, and thus their mutual rays of light pass on an average five feet over the ground midway, sometimes well above, at other times grazing so closely as to be liable to the extremes of positive and negative refraction. The following figures show how the refraction varies with the height of the rays. At Futti station (latitude 31°52′; longitude 73° 32′;) consecutive observations were taken to the signal on the Moogoo tower, and to an auxiliary signal erected perpendicularly over the other at a distance of 16·53 feet. The towers being 10·74 miles apart, the two signals should have subtended an angle of 60″·1; but their apparent subtenses were as follows:—

				″
7th February 1856. at	2h.	33 m.	P.M.	73.9
	2	43	”	69.8
	4	16	”	58.1

7th February 1856. at	4h.	33m.	P.M.	48″·9
	4	43	,,	41·7

shewing that when the day was hottest the negative refraction in the lower ray combined with the positive in the upper to exaggerate the apparent distance of the signals, while towards sunset the excess of positive refraction in the lower ray over that in the upper produced the opposite effect. On another occasion two signals similarly adjusted, and having a true subtense of 49″5, appeared to subtend at sunset on an evening after long continued dry hazy weather, an angle of 16″·5, and at sunset of the next day after a fall of rain 35″·6.

Wherever the heat, radiated from the surface of the ground, is capable of rarifying the air immediately incumbent on it, there must necessarily be a stratum of the atmosphere floating at some height above, through which rays of light will pass in straight lines, while on either side they will be bent upwards or downwards.

Thus for a short interval daily, near the time of maximum heat, a distant signal, whose rays graze the ground, will appear in its true position, unrefracted as a zenith star. This is the time of minimum refraction. If the exact moment of its occurrence could be predicted, one of the Geodesist's greatest difficulties would cease, and Astronomers might envy the freedom of his observations from refraction. But the time is rendered variable and uncertain by causes innumerable. A cloud before the sun will cause an object dimly visible in the horizon to start up, sharply and well defined, over all intermediate objects, only to sink down again and perhaps disappear altogether, when 'the wind passeth and cleanseth' the cloud, and the 'bright light' behind again exerts its influence. At this time moreover the air is not in the state of calm repose which comes on towards sunset, but is boiling and seething under the sun's rays, thus giving distant objects an appearance of dancing wildly up and down, and often of gyrating in circles. A signal formed by reflecting the light of the sun from a mirror through a disk of only one inch aperture, which at the distance of ten miles appears no larger than a star when the atmosphere is calm, may be seen magnified nearly a thousand times in the heat of the day, the rays being repeatedly reflected and refracted through the dancing vapours, until they form an apparent column of fire completely concealing the tower on which they are exhibited and often rising to double its height!

Enough has been stated to show the difficulties which beset

vertical triangulation over the plains of India and the sources of inaccuracy to which it is liable. Great as they are, it is now known that they can be practically overcome by the system, first introduced by Colonel Waugh, of taking vertical angles between 1 and 3 P. M. the hours which limit the period of minimum refraction. But until the Trigonometrical levels had been rigorously tested by a series of spirit levels, they were a source of much anxiety and uncertainty, because, if erroneous, the lengths of the base lines and of all operations emanating therefrom would be affected. The heights of the Ordnance Survey of Great Britain are all based on spirit levels, though that survey has peculiar facilities for checking its levels by reference to the sea, from which no part of England is more than ninety miles distant. In this country, on the contrary, the triangulation extends over a distance of upwards of 2000 miles from sea to sea, without external check of any kind.

Thus the measurement of lines of independent verificatory Spirit Levels became a necessity for the Indian survey. They were commenced on the Indus series, and in two field seasons were carried up to Attok, from the mean sea level of Karachi, which was determined in the Manora Harbour, by a set of tidal observations extending over two semilunations. Numerous precautions were adopted to guard against cumulative and accidental errors on so long a line of operations. The instruments were large and of superior construction, and fitted with delicate levels furnished with finely divided scales on which the deflection of the instrument from horizontality was measured, and a correction applied, as with Astronomical instruments, in preference to the usual method of attempting to correct by hand. The staves were invariably set up at equal distances from the instruments. They were divided on both sides, one painted white with black divisions numbered from 0 to 10 feet, the other black with white divisions from 5·55 to 15·55, in order to check accidental errors of reading; for the successive readings on the two faces should differ by the constant quantity 5·55, so that it is impossible to make the same mistake in both readings, and any error is immediately shown up by the difference in the results obtained from the two sets of faces. As an additional check two observers were invariably employed on the same line, each with his own instrument and staves, one following the other at a convenient distance, station by station.

These operations have now connected the base lines at Attok, Dehra Dhoon, and Seronj with the sea, and have satisfactorily established the fact that heights deduced from Trigonometrical verticals rigorously observed with regard to the time of minimum refraction, are not liable either to large or cumulative error. Thus from the Sea at Karachi to Attok, 706 miles, the

Trigonometrical height is ... ... +1011·36 feet
The levelled height is ... ... +1014·60 feet

From Attok to Dehra Dhoon, 416 miles. The
Trigonometrical difference of height is ... + 948·11 feet
The levelled ... ... + 943·05 feet

From Dehra Dhoon to Seronj, 429 miles, the
Trigonometrical difference of height is ... — 430·10 feet
The levelled ... ... — 428·30 feet

And from Seronj to Karachi, 669 miles. The
Trigonometrical difference of height is ... —1531·36 feet
The *deduced* levelled difference ... ... —1529·35 feet

On the other hand, there are errors of from 70 to 115 feet in the Trigonometrical heights which were measured before the necessity for limiting the observations to the time of minimum refraction was discovered.

The spirit levelling operations of the Survey are now being employed to connect together all the different lines of levels executed in this country by Canal and Railway Engineers, which will thus be reduced to the mean sea level as their common datum. This very desirable measure was recommended by the late Special Cholera Commission, because in their recent visits to various Military stations in the Punjab and N. W. Provinces, they had found much difficulty in forming a correct opinion as to the merits of existing or proposed works for drainage or water supply, on account of the absence of systematic sets of levels. The suggestions of the commission met with the approval of Government, and orders have been issued for the connexion of levels over the whole of India. The fact is singular, but not wholly uncharacteristic of Anglo-India, that a Geodesical undertaking of such interest and importance and such vast dimensions, should have its origin in a source which would seem to be so utterly incapable of affinity or alliance with Geodesy as Cholera.

The Kashmir Triangulation* originates on a side of the North West Himalaya series, between Sealkote and Goordaspore. It was commenced in the Spring of 1855 by Captain Montgo-

---

* We are indebted to the unpublished reports of Colonel Sir Andrew Waugh and Capt. Montgomerie, for much of the information which we are able to give on the subject of the Kashmir Survey.

merie of the Bengal Engineers, whose name has been so often before the public of late years in connexion with the interesting and extensive operations entrusted to his superintendence, which embrace not only the triangulation but also the topography of Kashmir and Ladak, and of the whole tract of mountains between the British frontier and Chinese Turkestan.

The Instrument employed in the principal triangulation was a 14 inch Theodolite by Troughton and Simms, the largest of the class of instruments suited for being carried over the stupendous Himalayan ranges.

In the first season the Pir Punjal was crossed under circumstances of great difficulty, the two stations thereon being respectively 15,000, and 13,000 feet high, and the range itself being liable to heavier falls of snow, and more constant clouds and mists than the inner and higher mountains, because it receives in the first instance and arrests the greater portion of the moisture which southerly winds exhale from the Indian ocean to deposit on the summits of the Himalayas. Thus at one station no less than twenty two days elapsed before all the necessary observations were completed, the party engaged thereon being exposed to the most inclement weather, and harassed by constant snow storms accompanied by incessant and severe electrical disturbances, necessitating the carrying about of a portable lightning conductor for the observatory tent. Unusual difficulty was experienced on the snow peaks in building the masonry station pillars. The highest part of the snow was not always over the highest part of the rock. Several shafts had to be sunk in the snow before the true summits could be found. Building material had to be dug out, and the snow had to be melted to slake the lime used for mortar.

The first season's triangulation having been laid out, arrangements were made to form a Topographical party to fill in the details of the triangles. Owing to the small establishments of the Survey, the difficulty of obtaining uncovenanted assistants on account of the competition of other departments of the state created by the recent commencement of Railways and Telegraphs, the sudden increase of public works, and other causes, combined with the length of time consumed in training young hands, and the difficulty of retaining them when trained, application was made to Government for the services of three or four Officers of the Quarter Master General's Department to survey Kashmir during the summer months, returning to their regular duties in the cold season, when field operations in Kashmir are not practicable. Three Officers were accordingly appointed to the Survey, and they rendered most valuable assistance during the field season of 1856.

The next year the exigencies of the service did not admit of their return to the Survey. One of them Captain Lumsden, was deputed to join the mission to Kandahar, under his brother the well known commandant of the gallant Guide Corps. The others were actively employed with the troops engaged in subduing the mutiny. Their places were supplied by Officers who were permanently attached to the Department, and have ever since remained with it.

Although the splendid climate of Kashmir and Ladak, added to the special interest attaching to those countries and the adjoining unexplored tracts, make the Survey deservedly a great attraction, still the exposure of surveying in such tracts is very trying to the constitution, and many persons suffer from it. The solar radiation at high altitudes is very great, as was shown and to some extent measured by Professor Piazzi Smyth in his astronomical experiments on the Island of Teneriffe. At the height of 9,000 feet the mercury in his radiation thermometer rose above 178°, the graduated length of the scale, and accumulated to an unknown extent in the bulb at the end of the tube, the Professor estimating that on one occasion it would have reached 212° had the tube been long enough. The radiation increases as the altitude increases and the temperature diminishes.

Under such circumstances, the labor of climbing great elevations is much increased, as has often been noticed by explorers. The surveyor arrives heated with his exertions and has to stand on ridges or peaks exposed to strong cold winds, while he is observing angles or sketching the ground. The alternations of heat and cold, and the laborious exertion, limits success to those persons who to the requisite professional qualifications can add the physical constitution to stand the hardships which the work imposes. It is very doubtful whether the ability to undergo the fatigue and exposure can be reckoned on for a long continuance; and it is believed that, excepting in rare instances, a frequent succession of assistants will be necessary for these extensive mountain Surveys.

But neither the physical character of the country, nor the constant task of training new hands, formed the chief difficulty of a survey conducted in a foreign territory, and which at no time could be expected to be agreeable to the ruler, his officials, and people. To them the influx of a body of surveyors spread all over the country, however orderly and well conducted, must bear the aspect of an intrusion. That amicable relations should have been uniformly maintained with the Court of Kashmir is sufficient testimony to the cordiality and good will of the successive Maharajahs, Goolab Sing and his son Rumbeer Sing, and of the tact and ability with which Captain Montgomerie transacted business with the native authorities. His difficulties were much enchanced by the Military Rebellion of 1857, during the whole of which excited period the party continued its peaceful labors without cessation.

Ample testimony to Captain Montgomerie's services is borne in a letter from, alas that we should have to say, the late Lord Canning to Sir Roderick Murchison, President of the Royal Geographical Society, which we quote from the Proceedings of the Society for 1860.

CALCUTTA, *August 29th* 1859.

'DEAR SIR RODERICK,

'Last month I sent to the Secretary of State for India the 'first sheet of the Great Trigonometical Survey of Kashmir, the 'work of Captain Montgomerie, of the Bengal Engineers, done 'under the Superintendence of Colonel Waugh, the Surveyor 'General of India. To my unlearned eye it is as fine an example 'of topographical drawing as I have ever seen, though the subject 'is one upon which I do not pretend to be an expert judge.

'But I can speak to the difficulties under which Captain Mont-'gomerie's task has been accomplished: not the physical difficul-'ties of the ground only, but the awful discouragement and 'anxiety of finding himself almost alone in those wild mountains, 'the people of which had, to say the least, no sympathy with the 'English rule in India, and surrounded by Hindostanee Sepoys, 'whose comrades and relatives were amongst the most active 'movers in the chaos of murder and rebellion which was boiling 'in the plains below. You perhaps have heard that at Roorkee, 'the Head-Quarters of the Sappers, and at the foot of the Hi-'malayas, the men of that corps early in the mutiny, shot their 'Commanding-Officer at the head of his column, and joined the 'ranks of the rebels.

'Captain Montgomerie, however, by his own courage and tact, 'not only kept his men (soldiers of that same regiment) under 'discipline and got good work out of them, but brought them 'back loyal and attached to the service. They have now good 'cause to thank him.

'I know that these incidents add nothing to Captain Montgomerie's claims to notice on scientific grounds; but if as I hope may be the case, the Royal Geographical Society should consider that his labors deserve to be noticed for their result, the circumstances under which they were carried out may perhaps be taken into account. If the Society think this young officer worthy of any honor, I shall greatly rejoice, both for his own sake and for that of the distinguished corps to which be belongs.

'I believe that there does not exist under any Government in the world a body of officers surpassing that of the Engineers of the Indian Army in the combination of high intellectual ability and acquirements with the most daring and persevering courage, if indeed there be any equal to it.

'I wish I had been able to push forward the Geological Survey more rapidly in accordance with your exhortations of four years ago. But the last two years and a half have given me other things to think of, and which is worse other things whereupon to spend our money; even you yourself had you been here, would have had to turn your hammer once more into a sword. I hope however, to get some practical benefit out of the Kumaon iron district very shortly in the shape of castings (wrought iron will be a longer job); and the recent discovery of the extent much greater than was known, of useful coal fields, not far from the line of the East India Railway in Lower Bengal, is a very welcome incident. On the other hand, I am sorry to say that I have just received a most discouraging report from Mr. Oldham of the hopelessness of finding coal Northwestward of Allahabad.

'Believe me, dear Sir Roderick,

'Your's very faithfully,

'(Sd.) Canning.

'Sir Roderick J. Murchison, &c. &c.

'Belgrave Square.'

Lord Canning appears to have been misled by the circumstance that the Trigonometrical Survey of Great Britain and Ireland is for the most part executed by soldiers of the Royal Sappers and Miners, to believe that in India Native Sappers are similarly employed on the Survey. This has never been the case, and Captain Montgomerie had no Sappers to keep under discipline, nor any Hindostani soldiers but a Havildar's guard from a Native Infantry Regiment. But he had to endure 'the awful discouragement and anxiety of finding himself almost alone in those wild mountains,' and his position won the sympathy and respect of the great man who knew what it was to have been almost alone in those wild times, and who had borne himself bravely in the boiling chaos of murder and rebellion, always unsympathized with, often vilified. Alas that his wisdom, and his bitterly gained experience should be lost to his country and India for ever!

The filling in of the triangles in the Topographical operations in the Himalayas is effected by Plane Tabling. Numerous points previously fixed by the Trigonometrical operations are projected on the Plane Table chart for the assistance of the Surveyor, to serve as points of origin and verification, and to enable him to interpolate his position on the chart whenever necessary. This method of filling in details is particularly well adapted for rugged and difficult ground, and for Native states. It is independent of measuring chains and all such instruments, which could not possibly be employed in the Himalayas, and would be viewed with considerable mistrust and suspicion in Native states where they might raise the belief that an inventory of lands and property was being taken, with a view to future annexation.

Two scales have been used for the Topography of Kashmir, one of two miles to the inch for the valley and the hills immediately around, the other of four miles to the inch for Ladak and the higher and wilder ranges. A map of the former portion has been lithographed in London, and is now for sale in the office of the Surveyor General, Calcutta. It embraces the country between the parallels of 33°20', and 34°40', and the meridians of 74°, and 75°30', including the Kamraj and Miraj divisions of the great valley, and the numerous small vallies leading into them from all sides, the Woolar and other lakes, the cities of Sirinuggar and Islamabad, the Pir Punjal and Rutton Pir ranges, with their passes of the same name, the Murbut and Banihal passes, and the vallies of the Banihal, Rajaori and Kohi districts, near the British frontier.

Several copies of this map have been handsomely bound in velvet and silk, in mindful deference to a Sikh's prejudice against common leather binding, for presentation to the present Maharajah of Kashmir, who was greatly pleased to receive them and gave directions that the English names, should be translated, into Persian for his own use and that of his Court.

By the end of last season the districts of Dras, Sooroo, Kurtse, Kargil, Baltistan and the plains of Deosai, had also been completed, with portions of Ronyul, Ladak, Zanskar, Rupshee, Nubra and Astor or Hasora;—these last have to be finished, as well as the districts of Hanle, Yanktse, and Pangong which have still to be surveyed, together with as much of the adjacent frontier of Chinese Tibet and Tartary as can be approached. Already the operations extend from lat. 32° 20′ to 36° 12′, and from long. 72° 48′ to 79° 31′.

Captain Montgomerie reports that 'year by year as the Sur- 'vey has advanced, the physical difficulties have increased; the 'average height of the stations has latterly been from 17,000 to '20,000 feet above the sea, though fortunately the quantity of 'snow has not increased in the same proportion as the height. 'Indeed beyond the Himalayas the snow has been less than on 'lower peaks of the outer ranges, but, on the other hand, there 'has been a great increase of hardship from the sparseness of 'population. and from the difficulty of procuring food and fuel, 'the latter being particularly felt in such inclement regions. 'For a time the surveyors have been entirely dependent on argols 'of Yak and other dung for fuel, occasionally aided by the thin 'roots of the Tibetan furze which can be grubbed up here and 'there.

'At first the population dealt with could all understand Hin- 'dustani, but latterly hardly any of the inhabitants have had 'the least idea of that language, and communication in Little 'Tibet and Ladak has been necessarily carried on by means of 'interpreters.

'Notwithstanding the great elevation of the country surveyed 'and the consequent severity of the climate, the rigorous rules 'of the G. T. Survey have been adhered to throughout.

'Luminous signals, either heliotropes* or reverberatory lamps, 'were used even on stations from 15,000 to 19,000 feet above 'the sea.

'The Hindustani clashees of the Survey seemed to have a real 'pride in serving the instruments entrusted to their charge. No 'matter what the weather might have been, and though the snow- 'falls on the stations were occasionally so heavy that rays had to

---

* A heliotrope is a circular mirror fitted with mechanism for vertical and horizontal motion, that it may be turned by hand so as to follow the motion of the sun and reflect rays in any required direction. It is usually 10 to 12 inches diameter to be capable of sending flashes powerful enough to attract notice at a distance. As, however, so large a blaze of light would dazzle the eye of any one observing it through a powerful telescope, the heliotrope is supplied with diaphragms, like the stops of a photographic camera, to regulate the diameter of the transmitted pencil of rays, which is usually made about a tenth of an inch per mile of distance from the observer.

'be cleared through the snow, yet the signal men were always 'ready to show their heliotropes and lamps.

'As a general rule they responded at once to the observer's 'signals.

'A heliotrope shining out from the top of a snowy cone was 'by no means an uncommon sight, and its effect can be better 'imagined than described.

'The difference of elevation between the stations being usually 'very large, orders were transmitted to great distances by means 'of the heliotropes.

'Altogether great credit is due to the natives of the plains 'who served the signals at such elevations in such a rigorous 'and to them uncongenial climate.

'The commissariat and financial arrangements for a large Sur-'vey party were in themselves very difficult. Food had some-'times to be carried fifteen to thirty marches. Ready money pay-'ments had to be made to the Tartars. The transmission of letters 'was not easy. Besides which numerous other difficulties naturally 'occur in carrying on survey operations over a vast tract of the 'most rugged and elevated country in the world. Altogether 'this Survey formed a very complicated task as will be readily 'admitted when the extent of the country under Survey is known 'to nearly equal the area of Great Britain, and to be in many 'places destitute for seven to fifteen marches of all the necessaries 'of life except water, which even occasionally failed, nothing but 'salt water being procurable.

'The junction which has been made between the Kashmir 'series and the North West Himalaya series in the neighbour-'hood of the Barra Lacha Pass gives every confidence in the 'accuracy of the results, which indeed is remarkable, bearing in 'mind that the junction made is between secondary stations.

'In a total circuit of about 890 miles, of which nearly 500 'appertain to the Kashmir series, there is only a discrepancy 'of eight-tenths of a second in latitude, and one-tenth of a 'second in longitude, and a difference of $4\frac{9}{10}$ feet in the height 'of peaks over 18,000 feet, after levelling across mountains of 'every altitude, from the plains up to 20,000 feet,—a result which 'must be considered decidedly satisfactory.'

In the seven years 1855-61 the triangulation executed by the Kashmir party has covered an area of 93,500 square miles, executed at a cost of Rs. 2-9 per mile, while 47,000 miles have been topographically filled in at an additional cost of Rs. 1-12. For some years nearly one third of the whole strength of the

Trigonometrical Survey has been concentrated on these interesting operations.

The numerous notices which have been published from time to time in the Journals of the Asiatic Society regarding the progress of the Kashmir Survey, and which have usually been reprinted in the columns of the local newspapers, render it unnecessary for us to dwell much longer on this the most interesting and popular section of the Trigonometrical Survey. The latest accounts mention the discovery and survey of great glaciers by Captain Austen in the Braldo and Baska branches of the Shigar Valley,—the Baltora glacier no less than 36 miles long, the Biafogause, nearly as long and forming with the glacier on the Nuggair side, from which the watershed is not sufficiently marked to part it, a continuous mass of ice nearly 64 miles in length, unequalled in dimensions by any known glacier out of the Arctic regions. Capt. Melville has recently added photography to his topographical operations, and has commenced a series of very admirable photographs, which we hope soon to see published, in illustration of the inhabitants and the scenery of the districts under survey.

Each succeeding season some surveyor ascends higher than he or either of his comrades had ever done before. The latest and greatest exploit of this kind was achieved by Mr. Johnson, who took observations at a station more than 20,600 feet above the sea or upwards of 600 feet higher than any on which a theodolite had been previously up, though a mark has been erected as high as 21,480 feet. The height of Mr. Johnson's station, be it remembered, has been rigorously deduced from reciprocal trigonometrical operations, and not obtained by boiling point thermometers, which scientific explorers have been known to employ, and flatter themselves they had reached altitudes never before attained, while in reality their fancied exaltation was caused by their not having enough fuel to make water boil. In the Survey, thermometers are only used when it is required to fix the height of a pass, or other position which cannot be seen from any of the Trigonometrical stations. But the thermometers are invariably boiled in the first instance at the nearest convenient stations above and below the places where they are to be employed. Thus their boiling points become known for certain known altitudes, and it is hence easy to find by interpolation the altitudes corresponding to intermediate boiling points. All the errors to which these instruments are liable are more surely eliminated by this process, than by any other.

It is a singular circumstance that the heights of the mountains around Kashmir have been generally greatly under-estimated by all the scientific travellers who visited the valley previously to the operations of the Trigonometrical Survey. They obtained the mean height of the valley very closely, but the great Nunga Purbut, which reaches a height of 26,630 feet, was supposed by Vigne and Cunningham to be only 19,000 feet high, which is nearly a mile and a half less than its true altitude; while the Huramook mountain was under-estimated by 3560 feet, a mistake the more curious because the mountain is so near Sirinagar that its summit may be seen by reflection in the lakes, and its altitude can therefore be easily measured with a sextant. These mistakes created the erroneous impression that the mountains of the Western Himalayas are much lower than their Eastern sisters, which is far from true ;—on the Karakoram Range a peak has been discovered whose height is 28,290 feet, the highest known mountain in the world after Mount Everest.

We have placed among the publications at the head of this article the first volume of the results of the De Schlagintweits' mission to India and High Asia, as it gives values of the Geographical positions of several places subsequently fixed by the operations of the Trigonometrical Survey in Ladak and Thibet, which therefore serve as a measure of the accuracy of the methods of observation adopted by the members of the mission.

We do not share the annoyance which has been so extensively occasioned by the selection of foreigners instead of our own countrymen for these interesting scientific enquiries. So long as science is advanced it matters little who are the instruments employed in its promotion. Our rulers fall into no very uncommon mistake when they prefer and show most honor to the prophets of science of countries other than their own. Nor is the selection without its advantages, for the work done is likely to be all the more thoroughly analyzed and sifted ; its errors will be more certainly and speedily exposed ; while all in it that is good and valuable will find friends enough to espouse and protect it.

While we readily acknowledge the extent of valuable information collected by the learned pupils of the illustrious Alexandre Von Humboldt, we cannot but wish that they had published the result of their labours with less pretension and elaboration. We believe that the astronomical and magnetic observations contained in their first volume might have been very easily and with great advantage compressed into one small octavo volume rather than expanded over a large quarto. We confess to feeling somewhat appalled on learning that eight more such quartos are still in store for us to hunt through, and patiently attempt to extract the wheat from its husk.

We find no less than seven pages of quarto devoted to the details of a few latitude and longitude observations at Leh, depending on a small Theodolite and Chronometer. Elegant as is the process by which they are reduced, we do not feel much interest in the details of the differential equations, or their treatment by the method of least squares, and we doubt their utility as much as we dislike their ostentatious display, when we find that the resulting longitude is erroneous by about 22 miles, being 77°14′36″ instead of 77°36′42″ as subsequently determined by the Trigonometical Survey. We are not surprised at the amount of the error, as the observations were dependant on a single Chronometer which had been rated at Simla four months previously, and had meanwhile been carried over the highest mountain ranges in the world. But we think the Messrs De Schlagintweit should have been more cautious in adopting their thus obtained value of the longitude of Leh, in preference to that given in map of the Punjab (1854),* which they merely notice with the remark that 'it makes the longitude more than 20′ farther to the East.'

From Leh northwards their map exhibits a series of western proclivities culminating in Tibet and Turkestan, where the chief towns are placed about 2° west of the positions hitherto assigned them, for the most part by the astronomical observations and itineraries of the French Jesuits in China. It is much to be regretted that the Missionaries were unable to extend their triangulation of China to these provinces, but, so long as they remain the only European geographers who have visited these countries, and have been allowed to take observations without molestation or hindrance, we must adopt their positions, however roughly determined, in preference to any other values. Humboldt makes the following remarks on this subject in the second volume of his Asie Centrale:—

'Je pense qu' aussi longtemps que dans les mêmes points on 'n'aura pas fait de nouvelles observations astronomiques, il est 'prudent de conserver les positions adoptées par des personnes 'qui non-seulement avaient l'habitude d'une discussion sévère des 'directions et des distances, mais qui ont pu se livrer à ces 'discussions dans l'interieur même de l'Asie.'

The Survey operations have fixed the positions of the Ka-

---

* Published under the superintendence of Captain Thuillier, at the Office of the Surveyor General, Calcutta.

rakoorum and Mustak passes which are within twenty marches of Yarkand, and we know that the prevailing impression of the officers employed in these operations is that Yarkand is slightly to the East of the position assigned by the Missionaries, whereas the Messrs De Schlagintweit place it 2°, or about 120 miles, further West. They make a similar alteration in the position of Lake Sirikol in the Pamer mountains, most unjustifiably we think, for its longitude was determined in person by Lieutenant Wood of the India Navy, the only European who is known to have visited the lake during the present century, and who moreover was a very skilful observer and geographer.

Bokhara they place, without visiting, 2½° west of the position hitherto assigned, and Toshkend upwards of 4°; on which an eminent geographer has remarked that 'if the Aral were to 'recede in the same proportion, it would fall into the Caspian.'

These hasty and inaccurate alterations are not creditable to their authors, who were evidently in a hurry to furnish the public with the fruits of their labours, of the value of which they do not seem to have had any misgivings. We doubt whether any geographer would adopt their positions instead of those hitherto accepted, and we are not surprised to find that in a map of 'Asia between the parallels of 20° and 60°, recently published in the Office of the Surveyor General, the original values of places in Tibet and Turkestan have been used in preference to those adopted by the mission to 'High Asia.'

We must now bid farewell to these interesting topics, and continue our narration of the progress made by the Survey in other parts of India since we last reviewed its operations. Our limits warn us to be brief, nor do we care to inflict on our readers the dry details of the ordinary operations of the Survey. Few persons have any idea of the labor they often involve. The mere measurement of the angles of a triangle would seem to have nothing so difficult about it, but that a slight training would enable most persons to acquire the necessary skill in manipulating the large Theodolites. But the successful carrying of a connected series of triangles, without a single weak link in the whole chain, along any given direction, without turning to the right hand or to the left, whatever the nature of the country or the obstacles to be crossed, is a matter of no small difficulty, and requires a rare combination of energy, judgment, and physical ability. The number of measures of each angle which have to be taken, and repeated on different parts of the graduated circle, to eliminate accidental and instrumental errors, entail an amount of labor which is little imagined. Often in the morning, always from noon until sunset, and afterwards for at least half the night, the observer is at work, watching his signal heliotropes and lamps through all their mazy wanderings, and patiently trying to make his telescope bisect their paths. Years ago Colonel Everest wrote as follows, of the difficulties of carrying a rigorous triangulation over the plains.

'The smoke from the daily and nightly fires, which, particular- 'ly in the cold season envelopes the villages and clings to the 'groves surrounding them; that arising from brick and lime 'kilns and conflagration of weeds; the clouds of dust raised by 'herdsmen and their cattle, in going out to graze in the morning 'and returning in the evening; by travellers and processions of 'men, carriages and cattle proceeding along the divers roads for 'business or pleasure, and by the force of the wind, the slightest 'action of which suffices in this arid parched-up soil to obscure 'the view, form an assemblage of obstacles which it is only 'possible in very favorable contingencies to surmount.'

These favorable contingencies only occur for short intervals which happen at very varying times of the day and night; and thus the observer has to be constantly on the watch that no opportunity may escape him. Few persons, but those who have tried, know the wearisomeness of ten or twelve successive hours, or even half that time, spent in an observatory tent measuring angles. Great is the amount of strong green tea which has to be imbibed at night on these occasions, to keep the observer from falling down asleep on his instrument. And the results so laboriously obtained are not of a showy nature. The chart of triangulation possesses far less general interest than the topographical map of which it is the basis. It is no slight addition to the ordinary discouragements of the triangulator that his labors are so slightly appreciated, while those of his comrades of the pencil and color box are so highly prized, and he needs considerable hardiness and pertinacity to carry his work steadily forward, heedless of the soft seductions of local authorities, who are ever anxious to catch hold of a Surveyor, and employ him on making maps to illustrate their favorite projects, for the amelioration and development of the districts under their control.

We might enlarge on the other trigonometrical operations which have been carried on simultaneously with those we have already described. But we have promised not to inflict dry details on our readers, so we will merely state that they comprise the following principal series of triangles with their usual accompaniments of secondaries; a double series from Purneea eastwards to Gowhatty, and thence to Sylhet;—another along the East coast from Calcutta to Vizagapatam;—a third, West of the great Arc, along the meridian of Rahoon, from the Himalayas to the Calcutta longitudinal Arc;—a single series, laboring under the cruel appellation of Goorhagur, because it unfortunately has for its meridian the Goorhagur Station of the N. W. Himalaya triangles, though we think it might with greater intelligibility and equal propriety have been termed the Umritsur series, as it follows the meridian of that city,—is the southern extension of the Kashmir triangulation to the longitudinal Arc;—a meridional series, provokingly denominated the Jogi Tila, from Jhelum to Pak Puttun;—an oblique Sutlej series from Mittun Kote to Pak Puttun;—and several small longitudinal and meridional series in the northern portion of the Bombay Presidency, the triangulation of which is now completed.

In the twelve years since 1849, to which year Colonel Waugh's Blue Book gives the details of the progress of the Survey, the following amount of work has been executed :—

Himalayan Triangulation,...	161,011	sq. miles.
All other Triangulation, ...	171,112	,, ,,
Amounting to, ...	332,123	,, ,,
Himalayan Topography, ...	89,895	,, ,,
Spirit leveling (commenced in 1858)	1629	linear miles.

In other words, the triangulation performed in these twelve years covers an area nearly treble that of Great Britain and Ireland, of which a portion almost exactly equal to England, Scotland and Wales* combined, has been topographically delineated in the Himalayas, on the scale of four miles to the inch;—in addition a line of levels has been executed, which is probably the longest ever measured in any part of the world. The average cost of the Triangulation, including superintendence, head quarters offices, special astronomical observations,

* The following areas are taken from Black's Atlas—

England,	50,898	square miles.
Wales,	7,430	,, ,,
Scotland	32,164	,, ,,
Ireland,	31,874	,, ,,
Total	122,366	,, ,,

and all charges other than Military salaries connected with the department, has been less than Rs. 9 or eighteen shillings per square mile, while the Topography has cost less than Rs. 3-8, or seven shillings.

During almost the whole of this period the Trigonometrical Survey was superintended by Andrew Scott Waugh of the Bengal Engineers, who was appointed to its charge, together with the Surveyor Generalship of India, in succession to Colonel Everest, in the year 1844, while he was still a subaltern. After holding the combined appointments for seventeen years, he resigned the service in March 1861 as Major General Sir Andrew Waugh, having been knighted by the Queen in acknowledgement of his services to Geography.

Colonel Everest who for so many years was the iron chief of the Indian Survey, and who enjoys the rare merit of having initiated methods of operation and formulæ of computation of superior rigor and accuracy to any ever before employed, and who never did any thing by halves, wrote thus strongly in favor of Lieutenant Waugh on recommending him to the Hon'ble Court of Directors as a successor to himself.

'He is beloved and respected by all the subordinate members 'of my department and held in honor and esteem by all who 'know him personally; his talents, acquirements and habits, as a 'scholar, a mathematician, a gentleman and a soldier are of high 'order, and as such I feel that in recommending him as a fit 'person to succeed me, I do but perform the last essential service 'which I may ever have it in my power to render to masters from 'whom I have received so many acts of kindness, and to whom 'my gratitude will be for ever due.'

While his labors in the service of Government were unremitting, he at the same time succeeded in winning the regard and affection of his assistants to an extent which few heads of departments are fortunate enough to obtain. More particularly was he beloved by that large and important section of the Survey whose members belong to the Uncovenanted Service, which has furnished the department with many true men and brave, who have worked side by side with their military Officers, and vied with them in readiness to undergo fatigue, exposure and privations of every kind, and one of whom at present holds the palm of having ascended the loftiest Himalayan summit yet reached by any surveyor.

Sir Andrew's kindness and consideration were most displayed where most needed. And he has bequeathed to his successor in the Superintendence of the Trigonometrical Survey the task of retaining the regard and esteem which has thus been created for the Head of the department.

A few words on the future operations of the Trigonometrical Survey may fitly close this Article.

The greater portion of the triangulation of India Proper is now completed, and only three meridional series, East of the great Arc and South of the Calcutta longitudinal series, remain to be done. One of these will extend from Jubbulpore to Madras, and might afterwards be continued Southwards to Ceylon. West of the axis of Indian Geography four small series have still to be completed, the Southern continuation of the Jogi Tila, two meridional series in Rajpootana between the Sutlej and the Karachi arc of longitude, and one on the meridian of Mangalore between the parallels of Mangalore and Bombay, in southern continuation of the Khanpisura series, which is again a continuation of the Goorhagur and Kashmir series, all being nearly on the same meridian. Mangalore and Madras should be connected by a longitudinal triangulation, crossing the great Arc at Bangalore, where there ought to be a base line. The series of triangles on the meridian of Madras and Mangalore will thus become especially valuable, as additional arcs for the determination of the figure of the earth; their lengths may be made as much as 11½ degrees without bringing their northern extremities into dangerous proximity to the plummet-attracting Himalayas.

Of most immediate importance is the extension of the Calcutta longitudinal Arc to the Eastern Frontier, which is required for the Atlas sheets of the districts East and North of Calcutta. It will probably be taken in hand immediately, and as the triangulation is not of great length, we may hope at no very distant date to receive the long delayed Atlas sheets of these districts, which are so much wanted.

Formidable is the task which awaits the Trigonometrical Surveyors on the Eastern frontier. Their triangles have to be carried through independant Tipperah, Chittagong and Arracan into Pegu, thence into the Tenasserim Provinces and down the Malayan Peninsula to Singapore. The greater portion of this vast distance is covered with dense jungle, through which in many parts roads have not yet been constructed. This sort of ground is the most difficult of any for Survey operations. When the Surveyor who is reconnoitering for stations reaches the summit of a hill, instead of seeing the country around mapped out before him, enabling him almost at a glance to decide on a line of operations, he has often to spend days in cutting down trees to open out the view, perhaps to find all his labor lost, because some other hill, before invisible, is discovered to intervene between him and the objects he wishes to see.

A longitudinal series of triangles has to be carried eastwards from Gowhatty to the extremity of the Assam valley, where a terminal base line should be measured which will be nearly on the same meridian as the base line to be measured in Pegu.

It is hoped that our relations with the Burmese Government may allow of the connexion of the Assam and Pegu base lines by a meridional series passing through Ava, which will be a fitting boundary to the eastern triangulation of British India and its dependencies.

On the completion of the topography of Kashmir and Ladak, which may be expected in one or two more seasons, unless the falls of snow are unusually severe, the surveyors will be transferred to take up the topography of Kumaon and Gurwal. We hope that arrangements may be made with the Nepalese Court for the extension of the Survey into Nepal, which is a very great desideratum, not only for the ordinary practical purposes of a survey, such as affording local information and opening out routes for trade, but for the sake of Geographical science. Higher mountains than Mount Everest may still await discovery in the interior ranges, which the jealous and exclusive policy of the Nepalese has hitherto concealed from the gaze of our surveyors. Surely Jung Bahadoor might with a little exertion be persuaded to imitate the liberal and enlightened policy of the Ruler of Kashmir, for recent events ought to have disabused him of the now puerile idea that the entrance of Europeans into a native state is but the precursor of its annexation to the British dominions.

While the more purely practical operations of the Trigonometrical Survey will be carried on as rapidly as the strength of the Department will permit, opportunities of adding to the stores of Geodesical science will not be lost sight of. It is in contemplation to carry a series of Astronomical observations for the determination of latitude down Colonel Everest's great meridional Arc, and another series along the longitudinal arc between Calcutta and Karachi. These may be expected to throw some light on the question of local attraction, as well as to give a more correct mean figure of the Indian arc than can be deduced so long as the Astronomical observations are limited to its centre and extremities. The Mangalore and Madras arcs will also be valuable contributions to Geodesy.

But an operation of greater interest and importance will be the employment of the Electric Telegraph, which now connects the remotest parts of British India, to determine Astronomical differences of longitude between the most important Stations of the Survey. Thus an Astronomical arc of longitude extending from Rangoon to Karachi, of no less than 30° in length, will be eventually measured, and when compared with the Trigonometrical value of the same Arc, will throw light on the figure of the Earth. The Telegraph lines which are now in process of construction between the Mediterranean Sea and Karachi will be employed as links of a chain of operations which are required to determine the difference of longitude between India and England, and will be further useful in fixing the longitudes of places in Egypt, Arabia, and Persia, which no Trigonometrical Survey is likely to reach during the present century.

Whether Submarine Telegraphs will ever succeed in Indian seas is very questionable, but it is probable enough that sanguine capitalists may expect them to do so, and risk the venture. We entirely approve of a suggestion which has been made to Government to allow Officers of the Trigonometrical Survey to accompany all such enterprises, more particularly those of which the eventual success is most doubtful, in order to take advantage of the primary success which, though often short-lived, has always hitherto attended these operations. Had a few Astronomers accompanied the expedition for laying down the Submarine cable between Suez and Karachi, and been furnished with the requisite instruments, they could easily have taken a sufficient number of observations for determining the arc of longitude, during the time that communication remained perfect. Thus the cable would have been the means of effecting at least one object during its ephemeral existence.

The Survey does not yet possess suitable instruments for these purposes, but we understand that the Secretary of State for India has most promptly and liberally sanctioned a recent application for them, which was supported by the Astronomer Royal. In order that their construction may be efficiently superintended, Sir Charles Wood has secured the services of a retired officer of the Trigonometrical Survey of India, Colonel Strange, whose mechanical skill has contributed in no small degree towards perfecting the instruments of the Indian Survey, and whole successful execution of the Western Longitudinal Triangulation we have already noticed in this article.

Alexander Cunningham

The Stupa of Bharhut.

London: WH Allen, 1879

THE

STÛPA OF BHARHUT:

A BUDDHIST MONUMENT

ORNAMENTED WITH NUMEROUS SCULPTURES

ILLUSTRATIVE OF

BUDDHIST LEGEND AND HISTORY

IN THE

THIRD CENTURY B.C.

BY

ALEXANDER CUNNINGHAM, C.S.I., C.I.E.,

MAJOR GENERAL, ROYAL ENGINEERS (BENGAL, RETIRED).
DIRECTOR GENERAL ARCHÆOLOGICAL SURVEY OF INDIA.

"*In the sculptures and inscriptions of Bharhut we shall have in future a real landmark in the religious and literary history of India, and many theories hitherto held by Sanskrit scholars will have to be modified accordingly.*"— Dr. Max Müller.

Published by Order of the Secretary of State for India in Council.

LONDON:
Wm. H. ALLEN AND CO., 13, WATERLOO PLACE, S.W.;
TRÜBNER AND CO., 57 & 59, LUDGATE HILL; EDWARD STANFORD, CHARING CROSS;
W. S. WHITTINGHAM AND CO., 91, GRACECHURCH STREET;
THACKER AND CO., 87, NEWGATE STREET.
1879.

PREFACE.

The remains of the Great Stûpa of Bharhut were first discovered by me in the end of November 1873; but as the whole of my camp was then on its way to Nâgpur, I was not able then to do more than to ascertain the fact that portions of two gateways, with the included quarter of the circular railing, were still *in situ*, although nearly all thrown down and buried under a mound of rubbish from 5 to 7 feet in height. On my return from the Chânda district in February 1874, I spent 10 days at Bharhut, when I succeeded in uncovering the whole quadrant of the buried railing. The curious sculptures were a source of much wonder to the people who visited the place by hundreds every day. But the inscriptions excited even greater curiosity when it was known that I was able to read them. At every fresh discovery I was importuned to say what was the subject of the writing, and great was the disappointment when I made known the simple records of gifts to the Stûpa, or of the names of the guardian Yakshas, Devatas, and Nâgas. Few natives of India have any belief in disinterested excavations for the discovery of ancient buildings, or of works of art, or of records of ancient times. Their only idea of such excavations is that they are really intended as a search for hidden treasure, and from the incredulous looks of many of the people, I have no doubt that I was regarded as an arch deceiver who was studiously concealing the revelations made by the inscriptions as to the position of the buried treasures.

In the beginning of March the work of excavation was taken up by my zealous assistant Mr. J. D. Beglar, who continued the excavation round the whole circle of the railing. To him we owe the discovery of the valuable Prasenajit Pillar, of the famous Jetavana scene, and of many of the most interesting coping stones. He made photographs of the sculptures as they were found; but as each day's discoveries only showed how much was still left to be explored, the work was closed in the beginning of April. In the middle of that month I forwarded to Government a statement of the discoveries that had been made up to that time. This statement was published in the London papers, and I was much gratified to find that my discovery was everywhere received with much interest. To it I owe the beginning of a correspondence with Professor Childers which ended only with his too premature death. The age which I then assigned to the Stûpa, between 250 and 200 B.C., has not been shaken by any subsequent discoveries, and I have reason to believe that it is now almost universally admitted.

In November 1874 I again returned to Bharhut with Mr. Beglar to make a complete exploration of the mound of ruins, and to photograph all the sculptures systematically on the fixed scale of one-sixth of the original size for all basreliefs, and of one-twelfth for all statues and larger objects. It was during these excavations that all the smaller pieces of the East Gateway were found; from which I was able to make the restoration shown in Plate VI. The exploration was carried on until the end of December, by which time the whole extent of ground covered by the railing to a breadth of 10 and 12 feet, both inside and outside, was completely excavated. At the same time all the neighbouring villages within a circuit of 10 miles were carefully explored for portions of the missing sculptures. This search was rewarded with the discovery of two pillars of a second or outer railing of which portions had already been found *in situ* at Bharhut. The basrelief of the *Indra Sâla-guha*, or " Indra's Cave Hall," was then discovered at Batanmâra, and the missing half of the famous *Chhadanta Jâtaka* at Pataora, 7 miles distant, degraded to the ignoble position of a washerman's plank.

During 1874 I had written an account of the discoveries made during the first season's excavations, but all these important additions necessitated a re-arrangement of the plates and the re-writing of the whole account of the Stûpa. This was in great part done during 1875, at the same time that I was carrying on the arrangement of Asoka's inscriptions to form Vol. I. of the projected " Corpus Inscriptionum Indicarum." The discovery of a new inscription of Asoka at Sahasarâm, in which I believed that there was a figured date, similar to some unknown symbols in another recently discovered record of Asoka at Rûpnâth, made it necessary that I should visit Sahasarâm myself, which I did during November 1875.

During all this time I was in frequent correspondence with Professor Childers in London, and with the learned Buddhist priest Subhûti of Ceylon, regarding the subjects of the Bharhut sculptures, and more especially of the *Jâtakas*, or previous Births of Buddha. In the summer of 1876 I completed the present account of Bharhut, but as I had reason to believe that some further discoveries might still be made, Mr. Beglar and myself visited the place a third time, and once more thoroughly explored the whole neighbourhood. The remains of the corner pillar of one of the missing gateways were then discovered together with several fragments. These are not included in the plates; but I may mention that the story represented on the pillar was almost certainly the celebrated *Wessantara Jâtaka*. About two thirds of each face have been cut away, but in the remaining portion of one of the scenes there is a four-horse chariot with a boy and girl being led by the hand, which leave no doubt in my mind that these are intended for the two children of Prince Wessantara.

This last visit proved of value in another way, which, though not quite unexpected, serves to show how judicious was the course which I took for the acquisition and despatch of these valuable sculptures to Calcutta. When Professor Childers heard of the intention to get these sculptures removed to a place of safety, he wrote, "It is "impossible to read General Cunningham's most interesting account of these sculptures "without a sigh of regret that they should be so far beyond the reach of our inspection. "*I hear of a proposal to remove them from Bharhut.* The scheme carries with it a certain "aroma of Vandalism (fancy carting away Stonehenge!)."[1] I am willing to accept the *aroma* since I have saved all the more important sculptures. Of those that were left behind *every stone that was removable has since been "carted away" by the people* for building purposes. So inveterate is this practice in India that Babu Rajendra Lâl, when he first heard of the Bharhut discoveries, boldly addressed the Government of India, suggesting that the sculptures should be removed to a place of safety to prevent the people from carrying them off. At my request the whole of the sculptures were liberally presented to Government by the Raja of Nâgod, in whose territory Bharhut stands, and I am happy to say that they have arrived safely in Calcutta, where the fine large view of the famous Jetavana monastery, given in Plate LVII., was kindly taken for me by Captain Waterhouse. This view will show that the sculptures have not suffered in their long travels of 600 miles. In his letter already quoted Professor Childers expressed a "hope that the "sculptures may find their way to the India Office [in London] instead of being "consigned to the peaceful oblivion of an Indian Museum." In this hope I should most cordially agree were I not afraid that they might be consigned to the still more oblivious vaults of the British Museum, where some 10 years ago I discovered no less than seven Indian inscriptions in the full enjoyment of undisturbed repose, unseen, uncared for, and unknown. At present there is no Indian Museum in London, while there is one in Calcutta where the sculptures are now deposited. And there I may hope that they will fare better than did my Srâvasti statue of Buddha in the Museum of the Bengal Asiatic Society. This ancient statue of Buddha, which certainly dates as early as the beginning of the Christian era, was placed in the midst of a herd of stuffed deer and antelopes, which completely hid its inscribed pedestal from view. The result was unfortunate, as the chief value of the statue was its ancient inscription. But perhaps the Naturalists, who then monopolised the direction of the Museum, may have considered this arrangement a highly appropriate compliment to Buddha, who in several previous births had been a "King of the Deer."

---

1 "Academy," 28th November 1874.

W.W. Hunter

'Chilka Lake'. *The Imperial Gazetteer of India.*
London: Trübner and Co., 1885.
Vol. III. 415–417.

Chilká Lake.—A shallow inland sea, situated in the south-east corner of Purí District, Orissa, and in the extreme south extending into the Madras District of Ganjám. Lat. 19° 28′ to 19° 56′ 15″ N., long. 85° 9′ to 85° 38′ 15″ E. A long sandy ridge, in places little more than 200 yards wide, separates it from the Bay of Bengal. On the west and south it is walled in by lofty hills; while to the northward it loses itself in endless shallows, sedgy banks, and islands just peeping above the surface, formed year by year from the silt which the rivers bring down. A single narrow mouth, cut through the sandy ridge, connects it with the sea. The lake spreads out into a pear-shaped expanse of water 44 miles long, of which the northern half has a mean breadth of about 20 miles, while the southern half tapers into an irregularly-curved point, barely averaging 5 miles wide. Smallest area, 344 square miles in the dry weather, increasing to about 450 during the rainy season. Average depth, from 3 to 5 feet, scarcely anywhere exceeding 6 feet. The bed of the lake is a very few feet below the high-water level of the sea, although in some parts it is slightly below low-water mark. The distant inner portion of the lake keeps about 2 feet higher than the exterior ocean at all stages of the tide. The narrow tidal stream, which rushes through the neck connecting the lake with the sea, suffices to keep the water distinctly salt during the dry months from December to June. But once the rains have set in, and the rivers come pouring down upon its northern extremity, the sea-water is gradually driven out, and the Chilká passes through various stages of brackishness until it becomes a fresh-water lake. This changeable inland sea forms one of a series of lacustrine formations down the western shores of the Bay of Bengal, the result of a perpetual war going on between the rivers and the sea—the former struggling to find vent for their water and silt, the latter repelling them with its sand-laden currents. The Chilká may be regarded as a gulf of the original Bay of Bengal. On the south, a bold, barren spur of hills runs down to the coast; on the north, the land-making rivers have pushed out their rounded mouths and flat deltas into the ocean. Nor has the sea been idle; but meeting and overmastering the languid river-discharge that enters the Chilká, it has joined the two promontories with a bar of sand, and thus formed a lake. At this moment the delicate process of land-making from the river silt at the north-east end of the lake is slowly but steadily going on; while the bar-building sea busily plies its trade across its mouth. Old documents show that a century ago the neck of land was only from half a mile to a mile broad in places where it is now two miles. On the other hand, the opening in the bar, which was a mile wide in 1780, and had to be crossed in large boats, was described forty years later as choked up. Shortly before 1825, an artificial mouth had to be cut; and although this also rapidly began to silt up, it remained, as late as 1837, more than three times its present breadth. The villagers allege that it still grows narrower year by year; and the difficulty in maintaining an outlet from the Chilká forms one of the chief obstacles to utilizing the lake as an escapement for the floods that desolate the delta. Engineers report that although it would be easy and cheap to cut a channel, it would be very costly and difficult to keep it open; and that each successive mouth would speedily choke up and share the fate of its predecessors.

The scenery of the Chilká is very varied, and in parts exceedingly picturesque. In the south and west, hill ranges bound its shores; and in this part it is dotted with a number of small rocky islands. Proceeding northwards, the lake expands into a majestic sheet of water. Halfway across is Nalbana, literally 'the reed forest,' an island about 5 miles in circumference, scarcely anywhere rising more than a few inches above water-level. This island is altogether uninhabited, but is regularly visited by parties of thatchers from the mainland, who cut the reeds and high grasses with which it is completely covered. On the eastern side of the lake lie the islands of Párikúd, with new silt formations behind, and now partially joined to the narrow ridge of land which separates the Chilká from the sea. At some places they emerge almost imperceptibly from the water; at others, they spread out into well-raised rice-fields. Their northern extremity slopes gracefully down to the lake like an English park, dotted with fine trees, and backed by noble masses of foliage. Water-fowl of all kinds are very abundant in every part of the lake. Salt-making is largely carried on in PARIKUD. Beyond the northern end of Párikúd, the lake gradually shallows until it becomes solid ground. At this point, the Purí rivers empty themselves into the lake, and the process of land-making is going on steadily. The northern shores of the Chilká comprise the *parganás* of Sirái and Chaubískud, and it is these tracts which have to bear the greatest suffering in times of general inundation in Purí. Until Ganjám was abandoned, on account of its unhealthiness, the Chilká lake was during the hot months a frequent resort of Europeans from the Madras Presidency. At the southern extremity of the lake stands the populous and important village of RAMBHA, having an extensive trade in grain with Orissa, for which it gives salt in exchange. A steam launch plies between Rambhá and

Burukudi on the Purí side, a distance of about 34 miles. The Chilka Canal, connecting the southern extremity of the lake with the Rushikulya river, is 7 miles in length, and navigable throughout the year. Large quantities of grain and salt are carried to and fro along it.

C.S. Middlemiss

"Preliminary Account of the Kangra Earthquake of 4 April 1905".

Records of the Geological Survey of India.
London: Kegan Paul, Trench, Trübner & Co., 1905. Vol. XXXII. 258–271.

PRELIMINARY ACCOUNT OF THE KANGRA EARTHQUAKE OF 4TH APRIL 1905. BY C. S. MIDDLEMISS, B.A., F.G.S., *Superintendent, Geological Survey of India.* (With Plates 14 and 15.)

CONTENTS.

1.—INTRODUCTION.

Brief outline of the shock: its great range and importance.

AFTER a lapse of only eight years since the great earthquake of 1897, India has again suffered a similar, though somewhat less intense calamity, in the disastrous shocks of the 4th of April last. Whilst that of 1897 originated in Assam and Northern Bengal, the starting-point of the present earthquake was the Kángra district of the N. W. Himālaya. Beginning at an early hour of the morning, when many people were still asleep, the more violent phases of the shock dealt summary destruction to life and property in the neighbourhood of the Kángra valley and Dharmsála; accomplished very great damage and caused considerable loss of life in the hilly tracts of Mandi State and Kulu; did serious damage to Dehra Dun, Mussoorie, Chakráta, and other towns in the vicinity; and slight damage to the large towns of Lahore, Amritsar, Jullundur, Sahåranpur, and others similarly placed with reference to the centre. Outside these points, again, in ever-widening closed curves, the earthquake was felt with continually diminishing intensity, until the limits of its appreciation by the unaided senses coincided roughly with part of an ellipse passing through the following localities:—Quetta, Surát, Ellichpur, False Point, and Lakhimpur. This curve, if continued, passes into the little-known and unreported-on regions of the higher Himālaya and Tibet; but it may be trusted to represent approximately the limit of sensible appreciability in that direction also, and to include a total area of about 1,625,000 square miles. Finally, outside these points (save for a few doubtful observations from isolated places) the record of the now greatly reduced vibrations is instrumental alone, but at the same time very complete. Not only did the seismological stations of India and the Far East—including those of Bombay, Kodaikanal, Calcutta, Batavia, New Zealand, and Japan—automatically register the earthquake, but so also did those of Europe and America, the records being unmistakably those of a very powerful shock. The earthquake must therefore be regarded as a notable one in the seismological history of the present and just concluded centuries, and, inasmuch as 20,000 human beings are estimated to have perished by it, it must also be ranked as one of the most disastrous of modern times.

Organization of its investigation.

Owing to the interruption of communications, it was not until the 6th of April that the full significance and magnitude of the shock became generally known in India, and steps could be taken by this Department for the proper scientific investigation of it. By that date, however, telegraphic warnings were issued by the Director of the Geological Survey to all District Engineers, Meteorological Observers, Telegraph Masters, Railway officials, and others, through their respective Departments, to record in writing the exact time and other details of the shock. These were followed by letters sent to the principal newspapers inviting volunteers all over India to answer a formulated set of questions, and to help in other ways by furnishing exact data. Question-forms were also printed, and in due course despatched, to all the provinces through the above channels, as well as to Political Officers and Residents of Native States. For the personal gathering of detailed observations of the effects of the earthquake in the more seriously disturbed tracts, the following officers of the Geological Survey were deputed: Mr. R. R. Simpson (followed later by Mr. K. A. K. Hallowes) to Dehra Dun, Mussoorie, and the neighbourhood lying S.-E. of Simla:

Mr. E. H. Pascoe to Lahore, Jullundur, and other large cities of the plains, and myself to the epicentral tracts of Kángra, Mandi, and Kulu, lying north-west of Simla. Mr. R. D. Oldham (late of the Geological Survey, and the compiler of the account of the Assam earthquake of 1897) has been asked to collect all information available from the extra-Indian instrumental records.

Basis of the present account.

The present account—which must only be considered as a preliminary one—has been compiled as quickly as possible on my return to head-quarters from the field. It, therefore, makes no pretensions to finality, except as regards the general features and effects of the shock. Besides expressing the results of my own field-work, it is based (1) on special reports sent in by my colleagues, Messrs. Simpson, Pascoe, and Hallowes; and (2) on the results of a necessarily brief examination of over a thousand earthquake-forms returned filled-in by official observers all over India, as well as by a considerable number of private individuals, to whom, collectively at present, the best thanks of the Department are here expressed for their generous response, which will be recorded in full detail in the final memoir. In addition to the above as sources of information, mention may be made of the principal newspapers of northern India, which spared no pains in reporting the earthquake in great detail, and whose early telegraphic accounts I found an excellent guide for prosecuting my own particular enquiries.

2.—GENERAL ACCOUNT OF THE SHOCK: ITS SUPERFICIAL ASPECTS.

Its suddenness.

All reports gathered from places near the earthquake centre agree as to the suddenness with which the great shock came, and the absence of anything of the nature of a crescendo. In this respect it presents a feature common to most earthquakes of the destructive class. To obtain a very connected account of its inception and progress from eye-witnesses in the more violently affected areas, has, however, been impossible—partly from the fact that many of those who would have been best fitted to speak were overwhelmed and lost their lives; partly because, on account of the early hour, many were still asleep, or only just preparing to rise; and partly because, out of those who escaped with their lives, so many were incapacitated by wounds, injuries or fright, that only a small minority remained who might have made useful observations had not they at once been fully occupied in aiding the wounded and rescuing those buried alive. The silent testimony of the long death-roll is, however, sufficiently convincing as to the rapid development of the shock, and the absence of any reasonably prolonged warnings conveyed by the preliminary tremors. In Kángra and the civil station of Dharmsála the proportion of killed to living is exceedingly high, and indicates a proportionately sudden attainment of the maximum vibrations. In Dharmsála cantonment the single-storied barracks and bazars were mostly evacuated just in time by the able-bodied, whereas double-storied buildings became either death-traps or scenes of extraordinary escapes. If one allows 3 seconds for the severity of the shock to awake and impress itself on any one situated in an upstairs room, 2 more seconds to prepare for flight, and 5 more to traverse rooms and passages and to descend a staircase to the means of exit, we might, I think from the evidence before us, limit the time for escape to, in all, about 10 seconds after the commencement of the earthquake. Many who were fortunately situated, or alone, probably accomplished this; but in a crowded double-storied barracks the outlets would become congested, and confusion cause further delay; whilst (as was certainly the case with households) the search for the various members, especially children, must have delayed the escape too long, and so the occupants were caught and overwhelmed by the falling débris. Of reliable witnesses whom I interviewed, no one of those living in upstairs rooms who must have extended the moments of grace beyond about 10 seconds were able to get clear of the house before the crash came; and their ultimate escape was due to their protection by the fortuitous falling of wood-work, beams, etc.

In other localities along the epicentral tract there is also a consensus of opinion as to the suddenness of the shock, whilst even at Lahore and the neighbouring cities of the alluvial plains it is described as jerky and abrupt, following on preliminary tremors to be reckoned in seconds only.

Preliminary tremors.

That there were preliminary tremors of very brief duration is, however, clear from the accounts of survivors in the Kángra valley and neighbourhood, as well as at more distant points. In some cases in Dharmsála these preliminary warnings are stated to have enabled persons to leave their dwellings just in time. Although 135 perished in the big Gurkha barracks, such tremors are nevertheless implied by the fact that scarcely any of them were found killed in their beds. One account from McLeodganj bazar states that these first effects were of the "nature of tremulous vibrations" and were likened to the "rustling of leaves in the wind." In Dehra Dun, also, minor preliminary vibrations are recorded which enabled those who were awake to reach the door. In Mussoorie, according to an eye-witness, preliminary tremors lasted from 15 to 20 seconds; and the same were noticed in Landour by several people. In Lahore preliminary shocks with intervals appear to have lasted for about 11 seconds before the arrival of the main shock.

The main shock. Regarding the nature, duration, and direction of the main shock or shocks, there is considerable diversity of opinion expressed in the narratives of observers within the epicentral tract. This is probably due, not so much to personal bias, as to actually subsisting differences in the character of the shocks, especially so in widely-separated areas differently aligned with reference to the actual centre. A common description of the main destructive oscillatory movement applicable to the Kángra valley and Dharmsála, and based on such scanty information as is available, is that it consisted of a violent horizontal shock from north to south followed by an equally violent counter-shock from the opposite direction. A few observers noticed a third shock like a "downward sinking." There is preponderance of evidence in favour of the second shock being slightly the more violent, or at least the more destructive of the two, inasmuch as it was during it that "everything collapsed." The evidence is not clear as to the time intervening between the two shocks, but it seems to have been from one to four seconds. Sometimes the evidence appears to be distinctly contradictory, but it is highly probable, as already stated, that there were actual differences in often closely related localities. That these shocks really were brief and of powerful intensity, rather than long-continued and moderate, seems a generally correct deduction from the havoc wrought to many strongly and solidly-built structures, as well as from the testimony of survivors. The evidence from the former source will be considered later under a separate heading. As regards testimony, it seems certain that not only was it a physical impossibility at Dharmsála to keep one's feet whilst standing or walking, but also that people were "thrown to the ground." A similar violent effect is related at Pálampur, at least in double-storied buildings, whilst even as far away as Bajaura in Kulu, where the shock was considerably less intense, men clung to trees to steady themselves and some were sent "sprawling on all fours."

Kangra. At Kángra the mortality was so terrible, especially among Europeans and officials, that no accounts have come to us through the usual channels—a sad fact which must be left to speak for itself as to the devastation wrought.

Dharmsala. At Dharmsála cantonments Captain Muscroft first felt a tremor, called out to his companions, and escaped outside where he was "thrown to the ground as the house crashed down amidst the roar of the two shocks."[1] The Kotwáli bazar, Dharmsála civil hill, was shaken to pieces in a few seconds, tilted upwards, it is said, by the first shock, which ran down from the hills above, and then sent crashing to the ground by a second shock which came from the opposite direction almost instantaneously.[2] Mr. Naurojee Khujoorina (of Messrs. Framjee & Co.) was an eye-witness at McLeodganj bazar, Dharmsála civil hill, and he says that he rushed out at the first shock. He looked into the valley and saw native houses falling one after the other, and as the second shock came his house collapsed into a heap of ruins.[3] In his report to the Geological Survey the same observer describes three shocks, first a tremulous vibration with a minute's interval between it and the second shock. No sound was heard before, but a "rattling noise with a shrill high note" preceded the second shock. Captain C. Stansfeld, 7th Gurkha Rifles, in his report, describes two distinct shocks with 3 or 4 seconds' interval. The houses fell flat and not to any one direction, and he thinks without any oscillation. The first shock woke him, then a roar came from the north or north-east. He ran out of the house and was thrown to the ground south-east or east.

Palampur. Mr. A. H. Machean, of Clachnacuddin Tea Estate, reports three shocks, the second longer and more violent than the first and from the north-east or east. The third seemed a sudden circular shock in which all the buildings collapsed, followed by a sudden jerk from north-east and back again.

Baijnath. Mr. F. A. FitzGerald, of the Baijnáth Tea Estate, was standing before a window open towards the south, when, preceded by a terrific roar, the house began to shake.

[1] *Pioneer* of 17th April 1905.
[2] *Civil and Miltary Gazette* of 16th April 1905.
[3] *Pioneer* of 19th April 1905.

He rushed outside with difficulty. The shock appeared to come from south to north beginning with a tremulous vibration, which increased in intensity until he was nearly thrown off his feet. His houses partially collapsed, trees swayed to within a few feet of the ground, birds rose from the trees with deafening shrieks and a cat and dog ran away terrified.

Summing up the meagre narrative evidence for the main shock in the Kángra valley and Dharmsála neighbourhood, the following characteristics are plainly established :—

(1) The sound was a roar or crash.

(2) There were two or three violent shocks.

(3) People were thrown to the ground.

(4) Buildings fell almost instantaneously into utter ruin.

(5) There was very great mortality.

Mandi and Kulu.

In the less violently affected parts of Mandi State and in Kulu, where everything points to a greater depth of the focus, the evidence is still scanty, owing largely to the fewer inhabitants and the absence of large towns and military stations. Fortunately, we have been supplied with detailed accounts by Colonel R. H. F. Rennick (Indian Army, retired), and General Osborn, both residents of the Kulu valley, and present at Bajaura on the morning of the earthquake. Neither of these observers record a distinct breaking up of the main movement into separate shocks. General Osborn states that the brief preliminary tremor increased with a regular accelerating motion till it reached its climax of greatest violence, remained at that for a few seconds, and then diminished and died away as it had begun. Colonel Rennick was awakened by the approach of an underground sound of the nature of a dull rolling noise, which became a roar like a bombardment when the main shock was established. Both observers place the direction of the vibration as approximately north and south, but whereas General Osborn puts the duration at 1½ minutes, Colonel Rennick estimates it at fully 5 minutes. The former also thought the vibration a fairly regular to-and-fro motion, whereas the latter observed a vertical component in the shock, which made the house and other things dance like "peas on a drum." Considerable damage was done to buildings, the upper stories of even well-built houses being partially wrecked. The loss of life was also great. Landslips and earth-fissures were a prominent feature as is natural in a country of steeply-carved mountain-slopes and precipices. These will be referred to again later. Captain A. T. Banon's account of the effects in the Upper Kulu Valley agrees substantially with the above. In a second letter, dated 6th May, he gives some further interesting details of the earthquake effects in the higher valleys north of the Dhauladhar range.

Summing up, we have for Kulu:—

(1) A dull, rolling noise which became a roar.

(2) The shock was a single, continuous vibration, increasing and diminishing regularly.

(3) People had to cling to trees for support, or were sent sprawling.

(4) Buildings show considerable damage, amounting to ruin in some cases.

(5) There was considerable mortality.

Dehra Dun-Mussoorie area.

In Dehra Dun, Mussoorie, and the neighbourhood the chief vibrations appear to have been horizontal, and to be once more divisible into two or three main shocks, or maxima of oscillation, accompanied by a rocking motion causing trees to sway, and sufficient to disturb the balance of people standing or walking. Estimates of duration vary from 15 seconds to 2 minutes. A positive bit of exact information is afforded by Colonel S. B. Burrard, R.E., F.R.S., Superintendent, Trigonometrical Survey, at Dehra Dun, who considered that the horizontal vibrations had a frequency of 3 per second, as also by Lieutenant H. W. Kettlewell of Landour, who estimated them at 4 horizontal vibrations per second. Some observers at Mussoorie noted 3 distinct shocks with intervals of 2 or 3 seconds. The earthquake sound was a moaning, rushing, rumbling or rattling noise, just before and accompanying the shocks. The direction was north and south or N. E.—S. W. There can be no doubt from the recorded sensations of observers, as well as from the evidence of damage to buildings, that the intensity of the earthquake was generally less at these places than in the greater part of Kulu or in the Kángra valley.

Summing up for the Dehra Dun-Mussoorie area we have:—

(1) Moaning, rushing and rattling sounds.

(2) There were two or three discontinuous shocks.

(3) People standing or walking lost their balance.

(4) Buildings show serious damage, chiefly fissures and cracks.

(5) Loss of life insignificant.

At Lahore, Amritsar, Jullundur, Sahâranpur, Rurki, and other cities on the alluvial plains, where the energy of the earthquake had already been so greatly reduced by diffusion, that the fall of even parts of high and unstable buildings was a rare occurrence, the shocks are still often described as jerky and abrupt, and as causing considerable alarm. There were two or three distinct shocks, the second (where two are mentioned) being the stronger. Rumbling sounds were generally heard, but they are not recorded from Lahore. There was no difficulty in standing with feet wide apart. Trees rustled as in a strong breeze, and books and light articles as well as cupolas from towers were projected from their supports. The direction of the shocks was either very complex or else there was more than one distant source of them.

Lahore and other cities of the plains.

Outside the limits just indicated, the progress of the shock must for the present be followed in very brief outline. The sound phenomena gradually die away; damage to buildings and even cracks in walls cease; the effects become limited to shaking of bedsteads, rattling of doors and roofs, with the swinging of light articles, especially clothes suspended from pegs.

More distant effects of the shock.

Next come very great areas where the shock, although felt distinctly, was a mere vibration; beyond that, again, others where it was scarcely felt at all, and where the evidence for the shock is very largely made up of observations of the movements of water in reservoirs.

3.—THE ISOSEISMALS.

The accompanying two maps will show the disposition of the few isoseismals, or curves of approximately equal surface intensity, which it is considered prudent to insert in this preliminary account. In the full report, when all the earthquake forms and other sources of information have been estimated, it is hoped that the intervening lines may be added. Notwithstanding their present deficiencies, the curves express much of a very interesting nature, which it is the object of this section to roughly outline.

Maps.

In drawing these curves the Rossi-Forel scale of intensity has been used, with the exception that isoseismals 1 and 2 must necessarily be differently interpreted at the present day, when great earthquakes are recorded

Scale of intensity used.

by seismographs all over the world. Prof. Omori's intensity scale for destructive earthquakes, on the other hand, though very complete in the higher grades, allows place for two more isoseismals of still greater degrees of intensity than the Rossi-Forel No. 10. These latter were framed by their author to include surface intensities sufficient to destroy large iron bridges and railway lines, to shatter and convulse low cultivated lands, causing trees and vegetables to die, and to produce fault scarps at the surface—a degree of surface intensity not reached by the present earthquake. On this account, and because the lower isoseismals are less complete in Omori's than in the Rossi-Forel scale, the latter has been found more useful in the present instance. Only the outermost curve, No. 1, representing the limits of human sensibility, and the innermost four isoseismals, Nos. 7, 8, 9, and 10, representing the highest intensities, are here given, that of greatest intensity, No. 10, appearing to fit the position assigned to it fairly accurately.

Isoseismal No. 10.

The area of maximum intensity included within isoseismal 10 is roughly bounded by Dharmsála, Rehlu, Daulatpur, Bawarna, and Pálampur; and it includes of course the important town of Kángra, besides some smaller towns and hamlets. The size of the area is about 200 square miles; but on the east-south-east it fades away very gradually into the area of next intensity. With few exceptions, all or practically all buildings were found to be destroyed within this area; only the very strong, *e.g.*, the Dharmsála magazine and treasury, and a few pliable wooden structures and low huts escaping. Bazars such as those at Kángra and the Kotwáli bazar at Dharmsála, built mostly of sun-dried bricks and with slate or thatch roofs, were literally levelled to the ground. Many of the smaller scattered bazars of Dharmsála, Bawarna, Pálampur, etc., were nearly so levelled, and the same is true for the hamlets dotted about at intervening points. During my tour through area 10 of the epicentral tract, nothing impressed me so much in the valley area as the contrast between the expanse of ripening wheat fields, the trim tea-gardens, the well-kept roads, the avenues of trees and occasional wooded patches—all untouched by the earthquake—and the utter desolation presented by the mounds and rubbish heaps that alone marked the sites of former villages and towns. This contrast clearly indicates:—

(*a*) That the shock was of very great violence at the surface.

(*b*) That it was not, however, cataclysmic,

thus giving a fairly precise upper limit for the surface energy over the area of greatest destruction.

Besides the usual roughly-built bazars and villages, the following were also ruined and mostly wrecked :—

(1) The stronger and massively-built temples of considerable antiquity, *e.g.*, the Golden Temple and others at Kángra, besides many small overturned temples and shrines.
(2) The ancient massive fort at Rehlu.
(3) Solidly-built court houses, police stations, jails, and barracks.
(4) Tea factories with their heavy machinery.
(5) Mission houses, and the English churches at Dharmsála and Pálampur.
(6) Many bungalows of various designs and strength.

Of all these, the roofs, towers, and generally all the walls were demolished, or with here and there mere remnants left. The degree of destruction to such solid masonry buildings was perhaps not so extreme as at Shillong during the 1897 quake—where scarcely a stone was left in position ; but still it represents complete ruin with no alternative but entire rebuilding. There were, however, one or two notable exceptions in the hilly parts of Dharmsála : a particularly well-built bungalow, a few of the Gurkha lines, a portion of a bazar—all sheltered in hollows or bays along the hill-side—having marvellously escaped, sometimes without even a pane of glass being broken.

The damage to hill-sides by fissuring and slips is reserved for description to a section to follow, as such damage depends far more on the rock-structure and angle of slope, than on the actual intensity of the shock.

Isoseismal No. 9.

The next isoseismal, No. 9 of the scale, embraces the much larger area of about 1,600 square miles, surrounding No. 10 in a rough ellipse. The greater part of this area lies to the east-south-east of the 10 area with only a comparatively narrow band continuing round the north-west part of that area. On the west and south this isoseismal can be located with considerable accuracy as it cuts Sháhpur, Ránital, and Sujánpur ; but further east-south-east by Mandi and Manglaur it is less well defined, the destructive effects within it dying away very gradually in that direction just as was the case within isoseismal 10. Its northern course also is somewhat vague where it cuts the uninhabited and little-trodden snowy ridge of the

Dhauladhár, passing thence to the Beas valley between Sultánpur and Naggar.

The destructive intensity within this area was found to vary considerably, but as regards the number of houses destroyed it averages about one-half. The western part of the area is geographically continuous with the area within No. 10, and it possesses a similar style of village architecture. To the east-south-east, however, the Kángra valley proper comes to an end, and a few parallel and lofty hill-ranges sweep round from the north, through which two chief passes, the Bubu and Dulchi, over 8,000 and 6,000 feet respectively, give entrance to the Kulu valley with its imposing and varied mountain scenery, its bazars built in many styles, and the quaint timber-bonded houses of the hill-people. Throughout this area the only approach to a constant type of building able to be used as a rough intensity measure, is to be found in the road-inspection and travellers' bungalows, which occur at regular stages along the various routes. These buildings were in most cases badly rent and broken, but not often entirely ruined, as were all buildings in area 10. They were, however, completely uninhabitable, and demanded reconstruction amounting nearly to entire rebuilding.

From the large portions still standing, the towns of Baijnáth, Guma, Mandi, Sultánpur, Bajaura, etc., were seen to compare favourably with the devastation wrought within isoseismal 10; but individually these towns show so many and such various stages of destruction according to purely local conditions, that their further description must be held over until the full report is written. Most of the small solidly stone-built Hindu temples within this area at Mandi, Baijnáth, Bajaura, Kulu, etc., successfully withstood the earthquake, as compared with those of area 10 which have mainly fallen.

The more steeply mountainous country beginning east of the Dhelu-Mandi road, and extending throughout the rest of this area, has given rise to many landslips, which severely damaged road communication and caused the Lárji lakes. They will be mentioned again later.

The next isoseismal, No. 8, may be split into two detached parts.

Isoseismal No. 8.

The greater of these elliptically surrounds the ·9 area, and in its southern curve cuts Telokenáth (Mangla Devi) near Kotluh, a point between Dera Gopipur and Jawálamukhi, Suket, and Rámpur; whilst in its northern curve it cuts less definitely a point between Naggar and Manáli, another a little east of Manikarn and a third at Gaora near Rámpur. Its area is about 2,150 square miles. The lesser part of the isoseismal embraces a small detached area of about 1,200 square miles including Mussoorie, Landour, and Dehra Dun, and takes an elliptical form with long axis parallel to the greater ellipse. The evidence for this separation and parallelism is considerably strong, being based on the reports of Messrs. Simpson and Hallowes in the Dehra-Mussoorie area, combined with local reports from other outside places along the same axis, namely, the Chor mountain, Náhan, Tiri, Srinagar (in Garhwál), Ránikhet, and Almora. It is only fair, however, to say that one strip of intervening ground between it and the Rámpur end of the greater area has not been examined and no local reports have been received from it. At the same time any connection that way seems to me highly improbable, and could it be proved by surface indications would even then be difficult of explanation.

The damage to buildings within these two ellipses was found to be still sufficiently pronounced to be apparent at a glance. In the northern area it took the form of a roof gone here, the end house of a row there, a hill-tower bulged or partially shattered, and so on. But there is no doubt that the intensity has become greatly weakened, especially near the boundary line. The road bungalows were found to be partially habitable, and obviously repairable without entire reconstruction. The accounts of Messrs. Simpson and Hallowes with regard to the area within the southern ellipse, indicate about the same grade of intensity, and are well illustrated by the record of damage to buildings at Dehra Dun, Mussoorie, Landour, etc. There, badly built and unstable structures have been seriously shattered, verandahs and house corners are out of plumb or partially shot away, cracks, amounting sometimes to rents and fissures, pervade most brick and stone buildings, and have sometimes necessitated extensive repairs and partial rebuilding.

From Chakráta accounts implying a similar or slightly inferior degree of damage have been received.

Isoseismal No. 7.

As just mentioned, the 8th isoseismal is coincident with a great, and universally marked, rapid decline in the visible intensity as expressed in house damage, so that on entering on the very large area circumscribed by isoseismal No. 7, we are manifestly getting away from the epicentral regions altogether, and into a tract where the power of the earthquake to carry destruction with it had very nearly ceased. Up to isoseismal

No. 8, the effects of the earthquake were found to be everywhere sufficiently dominant to command general attention. Beyond it the villages and towns presented an ordinary everyday appearance, and it was only on investigating things closely, by overhauling individual houses, that cracks, generally of small account, falls of plaster and of unstable light articles were still to be found subsisting. Nevertheless, the great alluvial plains away from the hills, and especially the larger towns and cities, undoubtedly did evince a slight amount of easily apparent damage that might at first sight be imputed to a slightly increased intensity in this direction. As instances may be cited the serious damage to the Town Hall, Railway Station, and market in Lahore; the practical universality of cracks in bungalows in Jullundur, the twisted and broken clock-tower at Amritsar, and the earth-fissures at Rurki. It seems probable, however, that the natural intensity at these localities has been really augmented in the above instances by the nature of the alluvial bed. It should also be remembered that very large towns such as Lahore, with their numerous and diverse architectural subjects, give a greater range for the law of probabilities to furnish us with some few remarkable effects.

The isoseismal surrounding the above area has been drawn passing slightly to the south of Jamu, cutting Sialkote and Lahore, passing between Jullundur and Ludhiána, and thence curving round by Muzuffarnagar and Bijnor. Its course on the north-east side of the epicentral tract is altogether problematical. It may be said to include an area of about 36,000 square miles where damage to buildings in the form of small cracks is very slight as a rule, sometimes almost entirely absent, and only very occasionally destructive. But in the terms of the Rossi-Forel scale, it nevertheless represents a degree of intensity sufficient to have caused general panic, coupled with overthrow of moveable objects. In using the above expressions it must be understood that percentages of damage and not actuals are meant. Now that our isoseismals are so large, and the affected area so immense, a very small percentage of destruction aggregates a great deal.

The remaining isoseismals.

The systematic description of the lower isoseismals will not be continued further in this short paper, because their delineation no longer depends on personal observation, but on the comparative estimation of a large number of individually recorded impressions furnished by the earthquake forms.

ABOUT THE EDITOR

Pramod K. Nayar teaches at the Department of English, University of Hyderabad. His works on British India include, *English Writing and India, 1600-1920* (2008), *The Great Uprising* (2007), *Colonial Voices* (2012), *The British Raj: Keywords* (2017) and *Indian Travel Writing in the Age of Empire* (Bloomsbury 2020). He has edited *The Trial of Bahadur Shah Zafar* (2007), *The Penguin 1857 Reader* (2007), *Days of the Raj* (2009), *Women in Colonial India* (5 volumes, 2013), *English Siege and Prison Writings* (2016), *Indian Travel Writing, 1830-1947* (5 volumes, 2016) and *Colonial Education in India* (5 volumes, 2019). Besides these, he has also published extensively on Human Rights and Literature, the graphic novel and celebrity culture.